stains noted
1/18

LAGRANGE ASSOCIATION LIBRARY
W9-AZQ-241

PLAY AT WORK

PLAY AT WORK

HOW GAMES INSPIRE BREAKTHROUGH THINKING

ADAM L. PENENBERG

PORTFOLIO / PENGUIN

PORTFOLIO / PENGUIN
Published by the Penguin Group
Penguin Group (USA), 375 Hudson Street,
New York, New York 10014, USA

USA | Canada | UK | Ireland | Australia | New Zealand | India | South Africa | China

Penguin Books Ltd, Registered Offices: 80 Strand, London WC2R 0RL, England
For more information about the Penguin Group visit penguin.com

ISBN 978-1-59184-479-2

Printed in the United States of America
1 3 5 7 9 10 8 6 4 2

Book design by Pauline Neuwirth

FOR THE PENENGIRLS:

Charlotte, Lila, and Sophie

CONTENTS

PLAY AT WORK

INTRODUCTION

Over the years, Ian Bogost has developed a colorful palette of interactive games, although probably not the kind you're accustomed to playing. As a game designer and professor of digital media and interactive computing at the Georgia Institute of Technology, Bogost is the antithesis to profit-hungry entertainment behemoths such as Electronic Arts, creating games as a mode of expression for social, political, and artistic commentary, and not so much for commercial gain.

For instance, in *Jetset,* which Bogost released through his company, Persuasive Games, a player assumes the role of TSA screeners at an airport and deals with angry passengers and ever-more-complicated rules (shirts are banned, then cell phones) until the line grinds to a halt and he's fired. *Simony,* rendered predominately in Latin, is a combination art installation and iPhone/iPad game that addresses "the role of belief and religion in a technological, secular world." Bogost has released games that feature snippy Kinko's employees serving irate customers, tomato growers confronting *E. coli* outbreaks, and dieters forced to manage their menus on ever-leaner budgets. The ingenious *Oil God* seeks to explore the ties that bind geopolitics, gas prices, and oil profits. "Wreak havoc on the world's oil supplies by unleashing war and disaster," reads the promotional copy that Bogost penned. "Bend governments and economies to your will to alter trade practices. Your goal? Double consumer gasoline prices in five years using whatever means necessary: start wars, overthrow leaders, spawn natural disasters—even beckon the assistance of extraterrestrial overlords."

Given his approach to game design, you shouldn't be surprised to learn that Bogost despises "gamification": the integration of gamelike elements into nongame activities. The way he sees it, over the past few years gamification has become the "it girl" of business, spawning conferences and a hefty dose of me-too-ism as some companies, eager to embrace it, tack on points or badges to just about any mundane activity to trick employees into thinking it's actually fun. That way they'll complete it more quickly and efficiently. Meanwhile, marketers use it in an attempt to get us to buy more stuff. Think Tropicana, which tried rewarding frequent orange juice drinkers with redeemable points. You might call that lame-ification.

Bogost dismisses gamification as "exploitationware," a "grifter's game, pursued to capitalize on a cultural moment," and "to bring about results meant to last only long enough to pad [gamification proponents'] bank accounts" before the next trend comes along. It "gives Vice Presidents and Brand Managers comfort: they're doing everything right, and they can do even better by adding 'a games strategy' to their existing products, slathering on 'gaminess' like aioli on ciabatta at the consultant's indulgent sales lunch."

The mellifluously acerbic Bogost also aims his ire at social game makers such as Zynga, which he dubbed "the Wall Street hedge-fund guys of games" for its purveyance of uncreative, unchallenging experiences. Bogost's own games also have players engage in uncreative, unchallenging work and game play, too, but that's precisely his point. He views them as tools to educate, to show players how the other half lives, to embrace the mundane and "disrupt and change fundamental attitudes and beliefs about the world, leading to potentially-significant long-term social change." His videographic work, like *Jetset* and *Oil God,* are more performance art than commercial product, and few outside a cadre of gamesian academics have actually played them. But that changed when Bogost shined his critical klieg lights on Zynga's *Farmville,* which requires players to return over and over to water plants that would otherwise die. Bogost "feared" this "behaviorist experiment with rats," as he told CNET, arguing that Zynga's designers were exploiting people's compulsions. If there were a deeper, more critical artistic or social aspect to Zynga's games, that would be one thing. Bogost found it maddening that the company was simply in it for the money.

On his blog he railed against the whole idea of social games, where "friends aren't really friends; they are mere resources," and "not just resources for the player, but also for the game developer, who relies on insipid, 'viral' aspects of a design to make a system replicate." The makers of these games "build compulsion into their design" and "the play acts themselves are rote." If a player gets stuck, he can buy his way to the next level. What's worse, "Social games so covet our time that they abuse us while we are away from them, through obligation, worry, and dread over missed opportunities." They not only waste our time when we play them, "they also destroy the time we spend away from them."

Instead of merely talking about it, though, Bogost decided to make a statement with a satire that would deploy the same inane, albeit addictive, hooks as *Farmville.* The result: *Cow Clicker,* a Facebook game he unveiled at a "Social Games on Trial" seminar held at NYU in 2010.

I'll let Bogost describe it:

> It's a Facebook game about Facebook games. It's partly a satire, and partly a playable theory of today's social games, and partly an earnest example of that genre. You get a cow. You can click on it. In six hours, you can click it again. Clicking earns you clicks. You can buy custom "premium" cows through micropayments (the *Cow Clicker* currency is called "mooney"), and you can buy your way out of the time delay by spending it. You can publish feed stories about clicking your cow, and you can click friends' cow clicks in their feed stories. *Cow Clicker* is Facebook games distilled to their essence.

Bogost made *Cow Clicker* extra social by allowing each player to invite eight others to join his pasture, and whenever someone clicked on a cow, everybody would receive a point (adding incentive, savvy that?). A leaderboard tracked the clickiest cow clickers.

Then something remarkable happened. His parody of a game became a hit. It started with those in on the joke playing for the love of irony, but quickly spread well beyond. Soon tens of thousands of players were feverishly clicking on Bogost's bovines, and most weren't in on the joke. Perhaps he shouldn't have been surprised. He had intended *Cow Clicker* to ape *Farmville*—inane, insipid, insultingly easy—except his was a practical joke made at the expense of its players, while Zynga's designers produced theirs for commercial gain. Their ends might have diverged, but their means didn't.

While disturbed by the success of *Cow Clicker*, Bogost, like any good designer, added features to keep players hooked. He introduced "mooney," a virtual game currency that users could purchase with Facebook credits, which they in turn bought with real money. (The micropayment exchange rate: 125 mooney = 10 Facebook credits = $1.) This allowed them to purchase *Steel Cow* (a bargain at 10 mooney); *Oil Cow* (200 mooney), which was slathered in petroleum and sported a BP-like emblem; *Bacon Cow* (200 mooney), exactly as it sounds; *Mao Cow* (500 mooney); and a herd of others. Then, to really mess with his users, he created special-issue cows at obscene prices. There was *Bling Cow*, which ran 10,000 mooney, or a cool $80. Many paid, though some became alienated. The introduction of *Stargazer Cow*, which was identical to the standard-issue cow except it was turned the other direction and priced cynically at 2,500 mooneys (or $20), drove 8,000 irate players (16 percent of his playing base) to quit the game in one day. Bogost couldn't have cared less.

To poke fun at the idea of "clicktivism," the term coined to describe what Bogost views as an inherently lazy expression of online political activism when a user chooses to like or follow a cause or person, he partnered with Oxfam America. On a special page called "Cow Clicktivism" ("Click your cow. Change the World."), players could transform virtual cows into real cows by taking part in click-ins every six hours, with Bogost promising to donate a real cow to Oxfam if enough people clicked. He also offered for sale a special-edition Cowclicktivist Cow (sad-faced, skinny, ribs showing, ears sagging) for $110. In the end, he raised more than $1,125, or enough to donate fifteen real-life, mooing cows.

In Bogost's view, *Cow Clicker* "distilled social games to their essence, offering players incentive to instrumentalize their friendships, obsess over arbitrary timed events, buy their way out of challenge and effort, and incrementally blight their offline lives through worry and dread." Nevertheless, he layered in more features. Some were conceived to juice the game's virality by awarding mooneys to those who clicked on clicks announced by players in Facebook's news feed. Others played on the idea of badges, like his awarding the Golden Cowbell to players who hit 100,000 clicks. Still others added an element of chance by letting players randomly win or lose money on each click. He sold *Cow Clicker* T-shirts, hoodies, commemorative mugs, and car decals. Still, people bought and Bogost made money.

His friend and Gamasutra columnist Leigh Alexander noticed a change had come over *Cow Clicker*'s creator, as his joke, which took him a grand total of three days to create, surpassed in popularity all the other projects on which he had lavished attention. Bogost had entered a "no-win spiral," she wrote, "taking on the aura of a mad scientist, making triumphant declarations over equations that were comprehensible only to him and to his inexplicably entrenched players, now indistinguishable from his fellow satirists." He was hooked on administering the game he had created as a satire on the inanity and addictiveness of social games. Bogost also recognized these dangers. "Just like playing one, running a game as a service is a prison one may never escape."

Six months after *Cow Clicker*'s release, Bogost launched, with some fanfare, *cowclickification,* his not-so-veiled swipe at gamification, which he defined as "the application of cow-clicking mechanics to non-cow-clicking applications." Businesses, he boasted, could "employ new cow-clicking mechanics such as clicking a cow to distract customers from the vapid pointlessness of their products and services." Then there was *Cow Clicker Connect,* which allowed Web sites to embed cow-click buttons. "Think about it," Bogost wrote: "would you rather order a pizza, submit a comment, or rate an escort service by clicking a boring button . . . or by clicking your cow?" He churned out a sister game (*Cow Clicker Blitz*), a search engine (Moogle), and a mobile app ("Cow Clicker Moobile") that you could buy in "The Stockyard"—the *Cow Clicker* app store.

When he was finally ready to wind down the game, Bogost introduced a clock counting down to its end but with an ingenious Zynga-like twist: each time a player clicked a cow time ran off the clock, but Bogost also let players pay $1 for an additional hour (or $400 for a month). Some eleventh-hour remittances delayed but could not postpone the inevitable "rapture." When the clock struck zero, Bogost unleashed the Cowpocalypse, and all the cows "were raptured to their heavenly pastures," even the ones players spent money on. The game continued to live on with eerily empty pastures. Players could still click where cows used to be and possibly earn a Diamond Cowbell award if they achieved one million clicks. "In so doing," Bogost signed off, "the game has perhaps reached its maximum level of minimalism, although it's clear that nobody is clicking empty space, but rather they are clicking the memory of where a cow once nobly stood."

For his part, Bogost told *Wired* he wasn't sure whether *Cow Clickers* represented his greatest success or a colossal failure. All these people clicking on cows. What did it mean? He wasn't sure.

What it does show is that games and game mechanics can be, if designed intelligently, a powerful way to drive engagement, something that even gamification's most ardent critics would have to agree with.

The Game Layer

Look around. Games are everywhere. Start with that carton of orange juice in your fridge, which might advertise it's worth three points, redeemable for discounts and prizes. It's a game. What about frequent-flier miles, which are games that reward loyalty? Mega Millions, Powerball, Take Five, and other state lotteries? Games. Nissan has an in-car gaming system that encourages drivers to compete for best efficiency levels (Bronze, Silver, Gold, and Platinum). Talk about a mobile game. You could look at Twitter as a game, the payoff being more and more followers and greater numbers of retweets the more you use it. Peer at the gamelike iconography of your iPhone and you might recognize it as reminiscent of old video games like *Pac-Man* and *Space Invaders*. The next time you go to Target notice the checkout screen. On it you'll see a game that rates the cashier's speed. According to one report, Target maintains a running average of an employee's scores, requiring that more than 88 percent of transactions make the speed cut, with a cashier's score affecting salary and promotions. Target has turned cashiers into players of a corporate game. In some urinals men may see a fly stuck on the bottom, a game mechanic put there to steady their aim (and keep restrooms cleaner).

The term "Baader-Meinhof" describes that feeling you get when you hear or read a word you've never encountered before then subsequently notice it all around you. It's born of our brains' tendency to filter out uninteresting information until it isn't uninteresting anymore. (If you think about it, the first time you read "Baader-Meinhof" may be to experience Baader-Meinhof.) This is what may happen when you begin to notice all the games—and their corresponding gamelike elements—that surround you. That's because games (or at least the characteristics of games) have been creeping into almost every facet of our lives. Some refer to it as the "game layer."

Because games are about players achieving goals while having fun—a very powerful, very human drive—an array of companies such as Google, Microsoft, Cisco, Deloitte, Sun Microsystems, IBM, L'Oreal, Canon, Lexus, FedEx, UPS, Wells Fargo, and countless others have embraced them to make workers more satisfied, better trained, and more focused on their jobs, as well as to improve products and services. Google and Microsoft have created games to increase worker morale, quality control, and productivity. At Google, engineers have been able to spend an in-house currency called "Goobles" on server time—often a scarce resource at Google—or use it to bet on certain outcomes as part of a company-wide predictions market. The Brobdingnagian search engine has also gamified its expense system. If an employee spends less on an airline ticket than he has been allotted, the savings can be donated to a charity of the worker's choice. Microsoft released a game, *Ribbon Hero,* to teach users how to make better use of its Microsoft Office software and has experimented with games in its workplace.

Canon's repair techies learn their trade by dragging and dropping parts into place on a virtual copier. Cisco has developed a "sim" called myPlanNet, in which players become CEOs of service providers, and adopted gaming strategies to enhance its virtual global sales meeting and call center, lessening call time by 15 percent and improving sales between 8 percent and 12 percent. IBM created a game that has players run whole cities. L'Oréal created games for recruitment, for gauging the skills of potential employees and helping them discover where in the corporation they would most like to work. Sun Microsystems has games for employee training. Meanwhile, Japanese automaker Lexus safety tests vehicles in what it brags is the world's most sophisticated driving simulator at its Toyota research campus in Japan. FedEx and airlines deploy game simulations to train pilots, and UPS has its own version for new drivers—one even mimics the experience of walking on ice.

We can trace the term "gamification" to 2002, when Nick Pelling, a young British video game designer, started Conundra, a consulting firm that combined game mechanics with business strategy. Alas, he was too early, and his consultancy didn't last. Over the past few years an entire industry has sprouted up around gamification—the very thing that Ian Bogost detests. The Entertainment Software Association estimates that 70 percent of major employers use interactive software and games for training. Research firm Gartner projects that by 2014, 70 percent of two thousand global organizations will depend on gamified applications for employee performance, health care, marketing, and training, and 50 percent of corporate innovation will be gamified, with American corporations spending several billion dollars on it.

Companies like Badgeville, based in Redwood City and backed by forty million dollars in venture capital, boasts hundreds of Global 2000 businesses as customers. Wells Fargo uses Badgeville for customer and employee engagement, Chevron depends on it for juicing worker collaboration, GE deploys it on its sales team, while Deloitte reports that training programs that have been gamified take workers half the time to complete than traditional ones while concurrently improving attention span. With Badgeville, Coursera, the online education company, reports more activities per student per week, higher grade point averages, far fewer failures, and a significantly higher retention rate. After Samsung layered Badgeville over its Samsung Nation online community with its hundreds of thousands of members, the number of product reviews quintupled and four times as many people leveled up to being "advocates"—those identified as spending ten times as much on Samsung products as regular consumers.

"I think of gamification as music that you listen to when you run," Kris Duggan, Badgeville's founder and chief strategy officer, says. "It's more fun with music."

Games are proving good for business. Popchips' sales increased 40 percent to more than a hundred million dollars after the company created mobile games designed to overcome users' resistance to mobile ads, and Bell Media increased customer retention by 33 percent after introducing "social loyalty" rewards on its Web site. Games are contributing to a healthier workforce: NextJump tasks games with helping to induce employees to hit the gym more often, while AETNA uses Mindbloom's *Life Game* to encourage customers and employees to adopt healthier habits. Gamification may even be good for the environment. SAP created a game to encourage workers to carpool to cut down the company's carbon footprint, while RecycleBank and OpowerL increased recycling 20 percent.

Naturally, business isn't alone in embracing games. The military has been leading the charge into 3-D virtual worlds and experimenting with video games since 1997, when the marines adopted *Doom*, the game that popularized the first-person shooter, which it purchased for $49.95, then modified by changing demons into Nazi soldiers firing M-16s. The army budgeted fifty million dollars to develop gaming systems, applying simulations to everything from recruitment to training soldiers in fixing tanks, using satellite feeds, piloting drones and aircraft, and full-out combat missions. Now "militainment" is a state-of-the-training methodology—perfect for young men and women who have already mastered the art of simulated war.

And why not? Army life often imitates art. Operating the gunnery on a tank or firing missiles from a naval destroyer resembles a first-person shooter game, while piloting a predator drone over Pakistan from the comfort of a computer nine thousand miles away is a skill that brings to mind *Missile Command*, a star of the 1980s arcade. Lockheed Martin manufactured *Virtual Combat Convoy Trainer*, a system in which soldiers who shipped out to Afghanistan simulated battles over the same terrain and even the same streets as the ones they would patrol, grappling with everything from improvised explosive devices to snipers to suicide bombers, and was awarded a $146 million government contract to develop a war-game training system for U.S. and allied commanders.

It's perhaps telling that the army's most successful recruitment tool is a first-person-shooter game called *America's Army*, in which players get points for blowing up enemy combatants. One study concluded that the game has done more to influence recruits "than all other forms of army advertising combined," with "30 percent of all Americans aged 16 to 24 having a more positive impression of the Army because of the game." Extremely popular—more than seven million people, including 40 percent of new enlistees, have played the game since its 2002 release—it's also cost effective: *America's Army* cost six million dollars to create and the Web site is a mere four thousand dollars a year to maintain.

Three-lettered agencies like the CIA, FBI, NSA, and DoD use games to train agents in antiterrorism. The Defense Intelligence Agency (DIA) trains spies with PC-based games such as *Sudden Thrust*, written by David Freed, a B-list television writer. *Sudden Thrust* players take on the role of a DIA analyst confronting terrorists who have hijacked a tanker brimming with natural gas and steer it into New York Harbor. The CIA has commissioned the creation of video games to help train agents in counterterror techniques. Meanwhile the FBI uses Microsoft's Xbox in the classroom to show trainees how to plan and execute an arrest and secure crime scenes.

Games have been popping up at rehab facilities and encouraging people to adopt healthier lifestyles. Doctors practice cutting open avatars instead of cadavers before turning to living, breathing humans and perform surgeries in completely simulated environments. Game design has even been changing how we educate our kids, with the mechanics that make games so irresistible retrofitted into curricula and layered into students' classroom experiences. While the last decade witnessed the rise of the social Web, establishing the online framework for how we connect with one another, the next ten years will usher in the era of game design and carry with it a pervasive net of behavior-altering mechanisms.

On some levels this shouldn't be surprising. A large percentage of Americans have been reared on games and it's only fitting that something that has profoundly shaped our connections to the world would be transposed to other aspects of our lives. Today, about 97 percent of twelve-to-seventeen-year-olds play computer games, and so do almost 70 percent of the heads of American households, says the Entertainment Software Association. One survey found that 35 percent of C-suite executives play video games. Before turning twenty-one, the average American has spent two thousand to three thousand hours reading books—and more than three times that playing computer and video games. You could argue that this much game play makes them experts, if you buy the theories of Dr. Anders Ericsson (popularized by Malcolm Gladwell in his book *Outliers*) on the value of ten thousand hours of deliberate practice. Globally, 350 million people spend a combined three billion hours per week playing these games. PricewaterhouseCoopers estimates that global sales of video games will grow from 2007's $41.9 billion to $68.4 billion in 2012, when they will exceed the combined global revenues of film box office and DVDs.

The massive multiplayer online game *World of Warcraft* boasted at its peak twelve million registered users paying fifteen dollars a month to spend an average of eighty hours per month inside the game. Since the game's release in 2004, users have racked up more than fifty billion hours of playing time—the equivalent of 5.93 million years. Game designer Jane McGonigal, author of *Reality Is Broken*, points out that 5.93 million years ago is when early primates began to walk upright. "We've spent as much time playing *World of Warcraft* as we've spent evolving as a species," she notes.

Play at Work is not about games per se. It is about harnessing the characteristics that make them so engaging and applying them to other aspects of our lives. These game mechanics can be applied to the workplace to make employees happier, more productive and motivated, to increase company profits and improve worker safety, to market new products, and to help with customer service. They can help people learn and better retain information, to create new products and solve big problems. And they can foster healthier lives. Because they are predicated on providing a system of principles, mechanisms, and rules that govern a system of rewards that lead to a set of predictable outcomes, they can ratchet up a person's engagement, and increase happiness and productivity, which in turn can pay big dividends.

There's a real need for this. Unhappiness in the workplace is endemic across all generations, even though, as Shawn Anchor, a Harvard professor and author of *The Happiness Advantage*, points out, "Nearly every company in the world gives lip service to the idea that 'our people are our greatest asset.'" The Conference Board, a private economic think tank in New York, found in a 2010 survey that only 45 percent of American workers were satisfied with their jobs, down from 49 percent two years earlier. Contrast that with the Conference Board's first survey, conducted in 1987, when 61 percent of workers reported being happy with their work. One reason: only half found their jobs interesting, another low in the survey's twenty-two-year history, and the same percentage were satisfied with their bosses, while in 1987 almost 70 percent found their work interesting. The youngest workers—those twenty-five and under—claimed the highest levels of dissatisfaction, with 64 percent unhappy with their duties.

Mercer's What's Working survey in 2011 reported that 32 percent of workers were seriously considering leaving their jobs, with several factors contributing to the malaise. Workers cited a lack of fair treatment as the most important reason, followed by "work/life balance, type of work, quality of co-workers and quality of leadership." Base pay ranked only sixth. A Gallup poll that same year found that 71 percent of American workers are "not engaged" or "actively disengaged" in their work, and highly educated workers are the least engaged. This is all the more disturbing because, as Gallup notes, engaged employees are more productive, more profitable, more customer-focused, safer, and more likely to remain with their employer. They are also healthier, with workers who are emotionally disconnected from their work about as likely as the unemployed to report suffering from chronic illnesses, obesity, diabetes, and high blood pressure and cholesterol. Further, "actively disengaged employees erode an organization's bottom line while breaking the spirits of colleagues in the process," according to Gallup, which estimates that this costs the American economy more than three hundred billion dollars in lost productivity alone.

Play at Work shows how to combat this abject negativity, which companies, educators, heath care practitioners, and individuals ignore at their own peril. It illustrates how businesses from the smallest start-ups to nonprofit organizations to schools to government agencies and the biggest multinational corporations are unleashing gameful design—the characteristics that make games fun and addictive—to increase worker productivity and job satisfaction, train employees, get them to communicate better and interact more, incent them to be more environmentally conscious, and contribute to the creative process. It addresses how individuals can adopt games to rehabilitate serious injuries, to gin up motivation and help them conquer necessary tasks, to get fitter and stronger, lose weight, get smarter. It peers into the brain and sheds a light on our biochemistry at the instant total engagement is achieved, and considers strategies to mimic this state of mind in the workplace and beyond. It addresses simulations as training tools for surgeons, and looks at ways game design is transforming education.

While games are a powerful mechanism in triggering rapt engagement, they aren't the only way. Communities often coalesce around shared interests, and the book looks at several instances where passion for a hobby has been redirected to help solve big problems in science by tapping the combined force of thousands of people or cocreating products from their initial inspiration through the design process to manufacturing and beyond. With the right approach, it's even possible to harness short bursts of drudgery—such as the security protocol that hundreds of thousands of Web sites have adopted that has you retype fuzzy letters into a box so the computer knows you're not a spambot—and transform it into something that benefits mankind.

Play at Work is divided into three parts. "Gameful Design" focuses on the process of tapping game mechanics and fostering our natural inclination to play to organize massive numbers of people to solve big problems. It introduces a MacArthur "genius" grant recipient who specializes in combining vast computing power with human intelligence, retrofitting a security precaution used by millions of people to stamp out fraud in online purchases to clean up thousands of articles in the *New York Times* digital archive going back to 1850, as well as millions of pages of old books and maps, and his audacious plan to translate the entire Internet. It takes you into DARPA's headquarters to learn about experiments the agency has instituted to organize large groups of people to locate hard-to-spot clues and come up with better combat tactics. It offers a bird's-eye view of a factory in Phoenix, Arizona, where designs for cars and trucks are "cocreated" by a community of fifteen thousand gearheads. It recounts how one company taps the power of game mechanics to foster competition and lead regular people to post ideas for simple inventions that are collectively designed by thousands of contributors, as well as professional designers, before being brought to market and sold at major retailers such as Target.

"Serious Play" looks at using games to solve big problems. It searches for a workable definition of what a game is, analyzes the mechanic that make them engaging, and shows how our brains react when we play them. It looks at ways that "pleasure technologies" (movies, music, and video games) hack our brains by triggering innate reward systems. It explores how educators are increasingly using games to engage hard-to-reach students and the Wii as a staple in rehabilitation (so much so it's been dubbed "Wii-hab"). It profiles a game designer who works with nonprofits to code serious games to promote exercise, help diabetics make healthy food choices, and remind preteen and teenage HIV carriers to take their medications. It relates how games are being used in scientific discovery, helping researchers in ways that few could have imagined. It examines the use of simulations and lifelike mannequins in medical training, leading you on a guided tour of a six-million-dollar simulation center used for preparing surgeons and health-care professionals for surgery and medical emergencies.

"Games at Work" describes the integration of gamelike mechanics and dynamics to improve business processes, customer experience, and the workplace. It traces the explosion of social media coupled with the expansion of mobile technology and how it is altering the relationship between consumers and products, and what this means for tomorrow's companies. It checks into the use of game mechanics in restaurants to improve service and the gamification of virtual call centers, predicting the call center of the future, where operators may operate inside video games. It takes you to Microsoft's main campus in Bellevue, Washington, to see how one man has been introducing games into the workplace to confront a generational divide that every business faces, improve bug testing and quality control, and in the process increase worker satisfaction and lessen attrition.

While *Play at Work* looks at some of the wonderful ways that games can help us, it is not a paean. Games are not a panacea to everything that ails us. After all, someone has to pick up trash off the streets and unclog sewage pipes, and it's doubtful that games could make these pleasurable activities. Nor are they likely, despite what some game-design boosters claim, to offer the path to a solution to problems like nuclear proliferation. To quote Gabe Zichermann, author of *Gamification by Design* and Chair of the Gamification Summit: "Game mechanics cannot solve fundamental business problems. It will not rebuild poor infrastructure, nor will it heal disastrous customer service."

But intelligent use of game mechanics can help us achieve great things, and that is what this book is about.

GAMEFUL DESIGN

In a memorable scene in Mark Twain's *Adventures of Tom Sawyer,* Tom's aunt orders him to whitewash a fence as punishment for playing hooky. He doesn't relish this, so, ingenious boy that he is, he tricks several children to do the job for him by convincing them the task is so enjoyable that he doesn't want their help. The boys beg him to let them take over—they even pay him with twelve marbles, a chunk of blue bottle glass to look through, a kite, a key that wouldn't unlock anything, and a dead rat he could swing from a string.

Tom, Twain wrote:

> had discovered a great law of human action, without knowing it—namely, that in order to make a man or a boy covet a thing, it is only necessary to make the thing difficult to attain. If he had been a great and wise philosopher, like the writer of this book, he would now have comprehended that Work consists of whatever a body is *obliged* to do, and that Play consists of whatever a body is not obliged to do. And this would help him to understand why constructing artificial flowers or performing on a treadmill is work, while rolling ten-pins or climbing Mont Blanc is only amusement. There are wealthy gentlemen in

England who drive four-horse passenger-coaches twenty or thirty miles on a daily line, in the summer, because the privilege costs them considerable money; but if they were offered wages for the service, that would turn it into work and then they would resign.

If Tom had money, he might have tried to buy his way out of his plight. In other words, he could have proffered what are known as "extrinsic rewards," that is, tangible benefits. In the workplace these are usually manifested as bonuses or a raise in pay. Although Tom Sawyer's friends would likely have been pleased to receive some extra cash, their hearts wouldn't have been in the task at hand. Instead, Tom served up "intrinsic rewards" by convincing the children that whitewashing a fence was fun. Suddenly something they viewed as drudgery was transformed into a raucous party. Not only were they willing to take over painting the fence, they insisted, and the fence got whitewashed faster than if Tom had worked alone.

Tom was deploying a secret weapon: gameful design. On her blog, Chelsea Howe, an independent game designer who once worked at Zynga, believes that gameful design "helps you do what you want to do." As with Tom Sawyer's friends, "No one is telling you to play, no one is giving you money to play, no one is holding a gun to your head making you play," she told me. "You're intrinsically motivated." Even failing is a virtue—and that happens between 70 percent to 90 percent of the time. Yet they don't put the game down, they try harder. "But we love failing and love knowing that all that's holding us back is learning the system better," she says. "Learn what not to do, learn how to do the good things better, learn how to master the environments so you can get through it quicker, learn more about the people that you are up against so that you can do better against them. It's just a matter of effort and time and skill and harnessing your mental energy and attention."

Tapping into our innate desire to learn can aid all sorts of big-picture enterprises—harnessing the drive and determination of massive numbers of people through judicious use of gamelike characteristics, which, with the aid of gameful design, can help solve big problems. In some instances, the by-product of playing a game or engaging in an action yields something beneficial. In others it's merely taking an activity that people already engage in and incenting their behavior with gamelike properties. The key, Howe says, is recognizing that "play is learning." When we play a game, "we learn its system, and the fun of the game is actually learning," she says. "Once we've learned the system, once we've mastered it, once we've finished the game, it becomes 'unfun.'"

In this section on gameful design we'll look at our brains and why they respond so well to play, as well as learn about ways that marketers, movie directors, and game designers hack our brains to induce us to do their bidding. We'll search for a workable definition of games, try to figure out what makes a game good, and differentiate between games and game mechanics. We'll visit with a man who combines the best of what humans and computers do well to organize millions of people to achieve great things, check out an automobile factory outside of Phoenix, Arizona, that cocreates its flagship product by combining the collective wisdom of thousands of car buffs with professional car designers, and look at an entrepreneur who has designed an intriguing crowd-based work flow to make invention accessible to all.

All of these rely on the organization of massive numbers of people, made possible by the same game mechanics that enabled Tom Sawyer to persuade his friends not only to whitewash the fence—for free—but to *want* to.

CHAPTER 1

THIS IS YOUR BRAIN ON GAMES

I first became interested in games and their use in nongaming environments after stumbling across a video of a speech by game designer Jesse Schell, which he presented to a crowd of four hundred or so attendees at the 2010 DICE (design, innovate, communicate, entertain) Summit, the video-game industry's answer to TED. Organizers had invited the forty-year-old game designer and Carnegie Mellon professor dressed in a crinkly button-down shirt and chinos to share insights about his work at Disney Imagineering, where he had helped design large-scale theme-park rides such as Pirates of the Caribbean. But "the Mouse" would have his head if he violated any nondisclosure agreements, so the day before his speech, on the flight from Pittsburgh to Las Vegas, he sketched out something radically different, which he titled "Beyond Facebook." Later he changed it to "Design Outside the Box."

"There are all these ways that games are creeping into places we didn't think about," he said. This was already happening, and the games were altering human behavior. What were American Express points and frequent-flier miles but games that reward loyalty? Weight Watchers? A game with points. Fantasy football? A game stacked on top of a game that "leeches off a game." In the Ford Fusion, there's a game installed in the dashboard to incentivize fuel economy. The more gas you save, the more the plant grows. "They put a virtual pet in your car," Schell said in his speech, "and it changes the way people drive."

Sensors have gotten so cheap they are being embedded in all sorts of products. Pretty soon, every soda can and cereal box could have a built-in CPU, screen, and camera, along with Wi-Fi connectivity. And at that point, the gaming of life takes off. "You'll get up in the morning to brush your teeth and the toothbrush can sense that you're brushing," Schell said. "So, 'Hey, good job for you! Ten points'" from the toothpaste maker. You sit down to breakfast and get ten points from Kellogg's for eating your Corn Flakes, then grab the bus because you get enviro-points from the government, which can be used as a tax deduction. Get to work on time, your employer gives you points. Drink Dr Pepper at lunch, points from the soda maker. Walk to a meeting instead of grabbing the shuttle, points from your health-insurance provider. Who knows how far this might go? Schell said.

He offered some pretty psychedelic scenarios, like one in which you recall a dream from the previous night where your mother was dancing with a giant Pepsi can: "You remember the REM-tertainment system, which is this thing you put in your ear that can sense when you enter REM sleep, and then [it] starts putting little advertisements out there to try and influence your dreams." If the ads take hold, you win big points for discounts at your local grocery store. "Then there's your office mate," Schell continued, "and he's like, 'Check out this new digital tattoo'" that he got from Tatoogle AdSense, and when you show him yours, you realize you're both wearing Pop-Tart ads. You get paid for the ads, plus thirty additional points just for noticing.

After work, you go shopping. Points. Your daughter gets good grades in school and practices the piano? More points. You plop down on your sofa for some television, and "it's just points, points, points, points," because eye sensors ensure that you actually watch the ads. In the meantime, you chat with other viewers, play games designed around the ads, and tally more points. It's crass commercialization run amok, Schell conceded, but "this stuff is coming. Man, it's gotta come. What's going to stop it?"

The applause was nothing compared to the reception his speech received online. The video went viral, downloaded millions of times. Om Malik, founder of the blog GigaOM and an astute observer of all things tech, called it "the most mind-blowing thing I've seen in a long, long time." Others viewed Schell's prediction that in the near future we might collectively exist in a giant Skinner box as abjectly sinister: "the most disturbing presentation of the year" and a "tech nightmare" that would doom us to lead our lives inside the massive multiplayer game of life. My interest gets piqued when something engenders such polarizing reactions.

I meet Schell six months after his DICE speech. He greets me with a grimace and complains of cluster headaches as he takes me to his office at the Entertainment Technology Center (ETC) at Carnegie Mellon University in Pittsburgh. He looks taller in person and guides me through the ETC geekorama, showing me full-size R2-D2 and C-3PO *Star Wars* robots, a Commodore 64 console, walls covered with photos of movie stars and video game characters, and a student lounge that seems to have been designed by the folks who created the original control deck of *Star Trek*'s USS *Enterprise.*

ETC is a feeder farm to the top companies in gaming—Disney, Zynga, Electronic Arts, and many others, including Schell Games. One alum was a lead designer on Zynga's *Mafia Wars*; Schell refers to another as "the Alan Greenspan of *Farmville*" because she sets prices for everything from the seeds to tractors and land. Asi Burak, class of 2006 and now copresident of Games for Change, led the project for *PeaceMaker*, an award-winning game inspired by real events in the Middle East conflict. Jessica Trybus founded Etcetera Edutainment, which was spun out of Schell's program in 2005 and provides game-based learning software for businesses and organizations, and her first employee was another ETC grad, Eben Myers.

Schell, whose official title is assistant professor of the practice of entertainment technology ("My business card is six inches long," he says), is a juggler and a magician who has been designing games all his life. Ultimately, it all boils down to this: "A good game," he says, "gives us meaningful accomplishment, clear achievement that we don't necessarily get from real life. In a game, you've beaten level four, the boss monster is dead, you have a badge, and now you have a super laser sword. Real life isn't like that, right?"

No, it's not. A game is, at its root, a structured experience with clear goals, rules that force a player to overcome challenges, and instant feedback. Everyday life is usually anything but. Because games offer clearly articulated rewards for each point players score and new level they achieve, they trigger the release of dopamine, a hormone in the brain that encourages us to explore and try new things. Since we like the feeling we get when our brains are awash in it, we'll do whatever it takes to get it, over and over. We also miss it in the event we run low. That's when our cravings are dashed and we experience disappointment. You find out you didn't make the swim team, your boss didn't approve your raise, or your local bakery ran out of your favorite chocolate chip muffin. Video and computer games, as well as slot machines, are particularly good dopamine generators. In fact, video games uncork almost double the levels experienced by humans at rest. They provide "threshold effects," in which prizes or level changes are dribbled out to keep us hooked. It's the same system that drives compulsive gamblers and cocaine addicts.

As a kid in New Jersey, Schell and his younger brother would play Monopoly with two boards or three dice just to see what would happen. He would change the rules of tag, so that neighborhood kids would have to hide and seek people. When his parents' marriage hit a rough patch the two boys would wander a local mall unsupervised, Schell gravitating to the Atari 400s and Commodore 64s on display at JC Penney, dedicating hours to testing programs he cut out of computer magazines. "That was where I learned to type," he says. At thirteen he designed his first computer game, *Fish on a Lake*. "You put your hook in the water and measure success by how many fish you caught," he says. After his mother whisked him and his brother to Springfield, Massachusetts, after the divorce, Schell fell into hacking. He also continued to create more games: one helped his brother with math homework, while another was based on *Doctor Who*.

He was learning what makes a game a game. What he couldn't have known then is that he was really after "flow," a mental state that game players enter when they're completely immersed in what they are doing and lose track of time. In sports, it's referred to as the "zone," when a basketball player feels like he can't miss a shot or Tiger Woods smokes the field in the first round at Augusta then hits double bogeys the next day. It's a powerful state of mind that overrides all manner of other feelings. In 2003, two researchers at the University of Southern California studied the impact of violent video games on brain activity. Test subjects climbed into an MRI machine and played a popular shoot-'em-up. These machines are cramped, uncomfortable, and noisy. Most people having an fMRI want to get out of the machine as soon as possible. But the test subjects were content to remain crammed inside for an hour or more as long as they could keep playing.

The originator of the term "flow," Mihaly Csikszentmihalyi (pronounced *CHEEK-sent-me-HIGH-ee*), a professor at Claremont Graduate University, has made it his life's work to explore what drives human creativity and happiness. He believes it stems from "enjoyment," and has isolated eight components he says contribute to it. They include the chance to complete the task, concentrate on what we do, seek clear goals and receive immediate feedback, achieve "deep, effortless involvement, so engaged worries slip away," and have a sense of control over our actions. Through all of this, "concern for the self disappears, yet sense of self emerges stronger." He also found that most "optimal experiences are reported to occur within sequences of activities that are goal-directed and bound by rules—activities that require the investment of psychic energy, and that could not be done without the appropriate skills." That means it has to offer challenge.

Flow is a state that anyone who has ever played a game knows all too well. Such is the power of games to influence behavior. Games and their mechanics are, Schell says, "a powerful psychological magnet that can connect into anything that we do." Really, though, humans' reward circuitry is a product of evolution. Our brains are tuned for survival, and our ancestors living in the wild learned to identify dangerous predators passed on their genes to future generations, while those that couldn't, didn't. As a result, our brains evolved so that we earn a dash of biochemical pleasure through a hormone called dopamine and experience a sense of accomplishment each time we predict the next sequence in a series of events—such as the number of minutes between sightings of a prowling lion. Sounds a bit like a game, doesn't it?

As Gary Marcus, a research psychologist at New York University and director of the NYU Infant Language Center, wrote in *Kluge: The Haphazard Evolution of the Human Mind*, "Our pleasure center consists not of some set of mechanisms perfectly tuned to promote the survival of the species, but a grab bag of crude mechanisms that are easily (and pleasurably) outwitted." He cites "pleasure technologies" (a term coined by Steven Pinker) such as movies, music, and video games as forms of entertainment that effectively trigger our reward systems, "culturally selected," he argues, "to tap into loopholes in our preexisting pleasure-seeking machinery."

In other words our brains can be hacked, something that directors of romantic comedies and marketers take full advantage of. It's amazing how much influence our environment can have without our being aware. I have photos of me when I lived in Japan and traveled around Asia for a couple of years in my early twenties, and recall my parents wondering if I'd turned Japanese, since my eyes had taken on a somewhat almond shape. Once, in my third-grade music class, we were subjected to Edvard Grieg's "Peer Gynt Suite" when one of my classmates tossed a wadded-up note at another kid. The teacher stopped playing the record—not to yell at him but to point out that he had thrown the note, and his friend caught it, in perfect time to the rhythm of the music.

Several studies show that background music in a store or restaurant can affect what and how much you buy, and how quickly you move through. One study had researchers from the University of Leicester, England, construct flag-draped displays of French and German wines and play French and German music. Customers purchased forty bottles of French wine and only eight German bottles on days when French music played, versus only twelve bottles of French and twenty-two bottles of German wine when German music blared over the supermarket's speakers. Another, dating from 1982, found that slow music resulted in a 38.2 percent increase in sales compared to faster-tempo songs, because customers moved more slowly through the store. Muzak, a company synonymous with sickly sweet elevator music, reported that customers in a supermarket walked 30 percent more slowly and spent 12 percent more than when there was no music. Other studies chimed in with findings that found that slow music causes restaurant patrons to stay longer and order more food, while fast music lessens the length of time it takes to drink a can of soda.

All around us are similar commercial influences. If you look closely, you'll be amazed at how we are being constantly manipulated by our surroundings: the playful label of that expensive facial cleanser, the choice of materials for that new phone, the inscrutable smile of a fashion model in a photo—all are subtle catalysts intended to trigger responses in our brain. They are not games, of course, but they share similar characteristics to the elements that make a game enjoyable.

It's a sun-drenched afternoon in Berkeley, California, in 2010, and to learn more about the subtle power that products have over us I am touring the shops at a local mall with A. K. Pradeep, founder and CEO of a neuromarketing firm, which claims to possess the ability to tap into your brain (or, as Woody Allen called it, "my second favorite organ").

Swizzle-stick thin and topped with unruly jet-black hair, the forty-eight-year-old Pradeep is nattily dressed, from his spectacles to his black jacket and red-and-black silk shirt—he favors Gucci—all the way down to his shiny boots. I first met him a few months earlier at a neuromarketing conference in New York City, where he had come to unveil Mynd, the latest version of the company's portable, wireless electroencephalogram (EEG) scanner. It sported twenty prongs that rest on your head like a crown of thorns, capturing, amplifying, and transmitting brainwaves via Bluetooth to an iPhone, iPad, or other smart device.

Pradeep urges me to try one, then points to my brain waves, represented by colorful bars jouncing on the iPad screen. "Good news," he cracks. "You're alive." Then Pradeep reels off volumes of info in a single breath, covering the human brain's hundred-thousand-year history and the business and scientific rationale for neuromarketing, while simultaneously plugging his book, *The Buying Brain*. It is a mesmerizing and exhausting performance, Pradeep speaking with the speed and percussive enunciation of an auctioneer. That morning I had awoken at 5:30 a.m. to get work done before making cinnamon toast for my daughters' breakfast, tuna sandwiches for lunch, and hustling them out the door so my wife could take them to school. I am tired. Eventually my mind wanders, thinking about how nice a cup of coffee would be.

Pradeep admonishes me. "Are you falling asleep?" he asks, peering at my brain waves on the iPad screen.

"No, no," I say.

But he knows I'm lying.

At the mall in Berkeley, Pradeep stops in front of a Victoria's Secret plate-glass window and points out the ambiguous expression of a lingerie model on a poster. He explains that the brain is constantly looking out for our survival and is therefore always ready to measure another person's intent. Is that stranger happy? Angry? Sad? When an expression is not easy to decipher, we do a database search through our collection of faces—curious, worried, nervous, threatening—to choose which is closest to the one we see, and match it. "If the expression is easy to decipher, I hardly glance," he says. "But if the expression is relatively hard to decipher, she makes me open the cupboard of memory." Contrast this with the nearby Bebe store, where Pradeep shakes his head at the headless mannequins in the window. "Now that's what I call a crime against humanity. Money down the drain."

Inside the Apple store, we pause at a desktop computer and he explains why it's better to put images on the left side of the screen and text on the right: "That's how the brain likes to see it," he says. "If you flip it around, the right frontal looks at the words and has to flip it over the corpus callosum to the left frontal lobe. You make the brain do one extra step, and the brain hates you for that." It's also why you see stores touting prices that end in .99. Our eyes see the lower number first, which tells us it's a bargain even when it's not.

Pradeep loves Apple because he believes the company has elevated basic design to high art. He shows me an iPad. Pradeep claims the brain loves curves but detests sharp edges, which sets off an avoidance response in our subconscious. In the same way our ancestors stood clear of sticks or jagged stones fashioned into weapons, we avoid sharp angles, viewing them as potential threats. NeuroFocus has performed several studies for retailers and food manufacturers and found that test subjects prefer in-store displays with rounded edges over those with sharper edges. In one instance, when these new rounded displays were rolled out to replace traditional store shelving, sales rose 15 percent.

But curved edges are only one reason for the iPad's success. We also like how the tablet feels, how sleek and well balanced it is. Signals generated by our palms and fingers, along with lips and genitals, take up the most surface area within our brain's sensory zone. The way a product feels in our hands can be a major selling point. It's why we prefer glass bottles to cans, which NeuroFocus product-consumption studies bear out, although it's not just the material, it's also the slender curve of the bottle and the ridges in it. The touch screen, too, is a mental magnet and can induce those hormonal secretions Pradeep likes describing. Why we like these curves no one knows for sure. Perhaps our brains correlate curves with nourishment—that is to say, Mommy. (Calling Dr. Freud.) In men, it could be sexual. One study asked men to view before-and-after pictures of naked women who underwent cosmetic surgery to shrink their waists and add to their derrieres. The men's brains responded as if they had been rewarded with drugs and alcohol. But this response to curves may be even more primal than sex or beer. Another study suggested that men seek women with curves because women's hips and thighs contain higher doses of omega-3 fatty acids, which nurture babies' brains and lead to healthier offspring.

All of these—the music, Apple's curved edges, the mannequin's expression—subtly affect us without us realizing it. Their purpose is, of course, not altruistic. These marketing mechanics are there to induce us to either buy more or help us forge a closer connection to a product. Now imagine the power of games, which require our active participation, and they have an even greater ability to influence behavior.

"Video games change your brain," University of Wisconsin psychologist C. Shawn Green told Robert Lee Hotz, a colleague of mine at NYU who penned a piece for the *Wall Street Journal.* So does playing the piano, learning to read, and wandering London's streets, which work our neural circuits in the way that exercising helps build muscle. Several studies indicate that playing video games, even extremely violent shoot-'em-ups, can influence our behavior in positive ways. Combat veterans who play violent games sleep better and suffer fewer nightmares than soldiers who don't play, lessening symptoms from post-traumatic stress. Researchers at the University of Toronto found that playing video games, even for just a short time, improves a player's visual attention so he can better locate a target secreted among a bevy of distractions in complex landscapes—an important skill for radiologists who read MRIs and X-rays, airport baggage screeners who identify potential dangers in thousands of suitcases and carry-on bags, scientists who interpret satellite imagery, and soldiers: they may have a split second to separate enemy targets from innocent bystanders. Another study found that players of action-packed games make decisions 25 percent faster than those who don't, without sacrificing accuracy. University of Rochester researchers concluded that regular game players could pay attention to more than six things at once, while most people track four. In a study from Michigan State University's Children and Technology Project and involving almost five hundred children over a three-year period, researchers found that the more the kids played video games, the higher they scored on a test designed to measure creativity. It should be noted, Holtz reported, that cell phones, computers, and the Internet had no effect on these kids' creativity.

There is ample research to support the idea that doctors who play games are better at certain tasks than those who don't. They improve decision making, vision, hand-eye coordination and reflexes, and provide a more effective and efficient way to learn. One study found that surgeons who play games three hours a week commit 37 percent fewer errors and work 27 percent faster in laparoscopic surgery, which requires deft use of a joystick, instruments, and a tiny camera, than doctors who don't. And the more surgeons played video games in the past, the better they performed at surgery, with the top gamer docs committing 47 percent fewer errors and working as much as 39 percent faster than others. A group of surgical residents at Yale who practiced in a virtual-reality simulator known as a MIST VR trainer performed gallbladder surgery 29 percent faster than those who did not, while the group that didn't train in the simulator was five times more likely to injure the gallbladder or burn nontarget tissue. In another study, a researcher at Arizona State University reshaped a Wii golf club into a laparoscopic probe and had doctors play games that depended on fine motor coordination. The game players exhibited 48 percent more improvement in performing a simulated laparoscopy compared with a group that didn't play.

A. K. Pradeep's insight into psychological marketing techniques shows that we can harness our knowledge of human behavior in productive ways. The same is true for games: under the right circumstances, channeling their influence can help make us better people.

What Is a Game?

Before we go further, I want to define what I mean by "game," and that's no easy task. Perhaps the broadest definition is an "activity engaged in for diversion or amusement." (Thank you, Merriam-Webster.) But I like to read, listen to jazz, and watch stand-up comedy—all are diversions I engage in for amusement and entertainment, but none are games. Another, from the same source, is "a physical or mental competition conducted according to rules with the participants in direct opposition to each other." But crossword puzzles and solitaire are games, and they don't involve "participants in direct opposition." A third definition is: "A game is a system in which players engage in an artificial conflict, defined by rules, that results in a quantifiable outcome." Closer, but still not all encompassing. I play tennis, often hitting with friends. Is tennis a game only when we play sets or points but not when we rally? Within rallies, though, I try my hardest to whack the ball and win the point, even if we're not keeping score. Is it a game only when I'm trying to hit a winner or an ace but not a game when I'm just trying to keep the ball on the court? It's all pretty squishy.

Fortunately, game designer Jesse Schell can help: "A game is a closed, formal system that engages players in structured conflict, and resolves in an unequal outcome." That's a pretty unfun definition for something that's supposed to be fun. Let's parse it. On one hand, his definition is limited to good games, since a bad game probably doesn't engage players. If it's a bad game, does that mean it's not a game anymore? This reminds me of college dorm room debates over how you define art. Can you have bad art? At any rate, let's assume we're talking about a well-designed game. By "closed," Schell means, "there are boundaries to the system." A crossword has a grid and so does a chessboard, while a baseball diamond and football field provide the playing surfaces.

In a video game there's a whole simulated environment where the action takes place. Same goes for social games on Facebook, app games on the iPad and Android tablets, and on mobile devices. The "formal system" means there are rules. Sometimes you know them in advance (chess), and other times part of the experience is learning them as you play (as in a video game). Structured conflict? That also works for the crossword puzzle aficionado or Sudoku fiend, as well as the fantasy baseball player. With puzzles you want to fill in all the clues. With fantasy baseball you want to win. Finally it "resolves in an unequal outcome." Yep. When I'm hitting a shot down the line in tennis, even when we're not tracking points, I really want an unequal outcome. This is equally true when I do crossword puzzles. And like a card player, I'm playing against the house, so to speak.

What's more, Schell provides a ten-point list in his book, *The Art of Game Design:*

- Games are voluntary: Players play because they want to, not because they have to.
- Games have goals: Short-term goals may include shooting down attacking planes or winning a point, a game, or a set in tennis; long-term goals could be racking up the highest score.
- Games have conflict: Players confront challenges and try to outdo other players.
- Games have clear rules: But they don't need to be understood in advance of playing, and maximizing understanding of the rules leads to maximal scoring.
- Games can be won or lost: Each results in "winners" and "losers."

- Games are interactive: Players catalyze a reaction by clicking, moving a joystick, typing a key, and so on, and receive immediate feedback.
- Games are challenging: They have to be hard enough to keep users interested in playing.
- Games espouse their own internal values: Points are worth something within the confines of the game by ranking a player's actions.
- Games engage players: It has to be fun to play so that players enjoy doing it.
- Games are closed, formal systems: They are their own universe, which defines the rules.

Games also transport a player or participant to another place other than the one they physically occupy. I may be sitting on a plane, but if I'm playing an iPad game, I'm not all that aware of my surroundings. Same goes for reading or watching a movie. All provide instantaneous learning. With reading, it is hoped you're getting something out of the experience (like now!), increasing your knowledge or getting caught up in how a novel's heroine escapes the clutches of the villain. Likewise with a movie. You watch to find out what happens minute to minute. Not knowing what will happen is a strong motivator. With reading and film you know how to achieve this enlightenment. With a book, keep reading; a movie, keep watching. But many games—I'm referring specifically to video games—don't even give a newbie that much. There is no need for manuals. Through trial and error players learn the rules that govern their environment. It's part of the game and their success is tied to how well they learn.

It's a three-dimensional approach to knowledge acquisition even if that knowledge is solely put to use knocking down invading aliens.

What Makes a Game Addictive: A Cognitive Teardown of Angry Birds

Pinpointing how a game is able to attract such fiendish devotion among its players is like trying to explain why "Gangnam Style" (and two decades before that the "Macarena") became a worldwide phenomenon, while other, one could argue more deserving, songs disappear with nary a trace. It's far easier to deconstruct after the fact why something becomes popular than to predict that it will be.

If we define "great" in this context as being synonymous with popularity, than perhaps no game has been greater over the past few years than *Angry Birds*, with its many versions (including an *Angry Birds Star Wars* edition) having been downloaded almost two billion times across multiple platforms. Launched on the Apple iOS in December 2009, it was created by Rovio Entertainment, a modest-sized game developer in Espoo, Finland, about ten miles west of Helsinki. In 2011, at the height of the *Angry Birds* craze, the game was being played two hundred million minutes a day, or 1.2 billion hours a year around the world, and it has spawned books, advertising tie-ins, a TV series, and a soft drink. Rovio has sold more than ten million *Angry Birds*–themed toys, including a Matchbox car and a board game. A wide array of celebrities such as Angelina Jolie, Justin Bieber, *Mad Men*'s Jon Hamm, *Satanic Verses* author Salman Rushdie, and British prime minister David Cameron have all confessed to an *Angry Birds* addiction. *Angry Birds* is premised on a silly idea. Players fire irate birds from a slingshot. Flying through the air, tucked into cannonballs, they strike their prey: pigs protected by flimsy wood and glass structures. The object is to blow up all the sitting-duck pigs that seem to have no idea what is about to befall them. If a player doesn't destroy them all, he can't advance to the next level, each of which gets progressively harder. The only thing sillier than this game is the feeling you get by failing to level up.

But underneath all of this cartoonish glitz is ingenious cognitive science at work. Simply put, playing *Angry Birds* can be good for your mental health. Researchers from East Carolina University found in two separate studies (both funded by PopCap, a game maker) that playing casual games can boost a player's mood, induce a sunnier outlook, and reduce anger, stress, depression, and fatigue. Dr. Carmen Russoniello, director of the ECU Psychophysiology Lab and Biofeedback Clinic, who ran the study, claims "the findings support the possibility of using prescribed casual video games for treating depression and anxiety as an adjunct to, or perhaps even a replacement for, standard therapies including medication."

I don't know about that, but it's clear the game is ingeniously designed to ensnare us. Charles L. Mauro, a usability engineering consultant and certified human factors engineering professional in New York, provided a cognitive breakdown of the game's user experience on his company Web site, attempting to answer why players find the interface so engrossing. First, the game is so simple that a person playing for the first time knows exactly what to do without a single direction. This is vital because first impressions matter. When someone opens up a game for the first time, this brief period of experience embeds in his mind a mental model of how the interface behaves. There's a term for this: "schema formation." During this "first user experience," the player sifts through a lot of impressions quickly and the simpler the interface, the less likely the player will walk away in frustration, unable to grok what he's supposed to do.

Simple on its own is not, of course, enough to drive engagement. *Angry Birds* accomplishes this by offering colorful detail "to the user's mental model at just the right time." A player looks at the blinking, dumbfounded pigs in their flimsy barricades on the right, the squawking bird that's being preloaded into the slingshot on the left, and knows precisely what to do. Naturally a slingshot is a universally understood weapon. He puts his finger on the bird, pulls it back, and lets it fly. The first shot is most likely way off, but that doesn't matter. The experience gives the player a chance to improve. More important, he has already "developed a mental model of the game's interaction methodology, core strategy and scoring processes." Then the game makers, through what Mauro labels "carefully scripted expansion of the user's mental model of the strategy component and incremental increases in problem/solution methodology" completely suck in the player. "These little birds are packed with clever behaviors that expand the user's mental model at just the point when game-level complexity is increased."

One behavior, besides their quirky personalities and the way they've been animated, has to do with response time. When a bird is shot through the air it doesn't fly with the speed of a missile or even a real-life sparrow. It arcs ever so slowly, drawing out the player's anticipation, and this, as we know, taps our dopamine response system. Bird flies where player expects. Boom! Houses shatter. Pigs die. Points are amassed. Dopamine squirts. We like that, let's do it again!

Then, Mauro points out, the designers cleverly incorporated error correction into the game play with a dotted line representing the previous bird's flight path. If it landed too low, it's easy to adjust the angle of the next shot. It cuts down on the frustration a user might experience if, for the first time, he can't get the hang of things. What's more, the pigs don't die quickly. Their houses crumble ever so slowly, large slabs of wood and glass slipping and sliding downward. The pigs themselves roll, teeter, and totter until they are either crushed or fall a sufficient distance, their bodies exploding into fiery plumes of smoke as their respective point tallies are flashed where they used to stand then quickly fade. It's done faster than slow motion, but slower than what we might expect would happen in real life—provided we could actually fire birds with a slingshot at helpless porcine targets.

Rovio's designers did a masterful job of controlling players' short-term memory management. This is what allows us to react quickly to something without taking the time to think about it, which involves long-term memory that takes much longer for us to access. It's really a temporary condition that enables us to retain patterns and behaviors for short bursts. Some might think of it as intuition or even reflexes. You're playing Ping-Pong and can't believe you returned that guy's slam. But short-term memory is also extremely limited. Have you ever tried to enter a ten-digit-phone number into your contact list after glancing at it just once? If you're like most people, you can't do it. What's more, even if you remember it, you probably won't recall it very long. That's because short-term memory is volatile. "It can be erased instantly, or more importantly, it can be overwritten by other information coming into the human perceptual system," Maurer says.

Angry Birds bakes short-term memory manipulation into the interface, bending it so a player feels a sense of challenge but not busting it by throwing too much at him. It starts with screen flow. At the onset of each sequence, a player is shown the pigs in their glass and wood houses on the right. Then the camera pans left to those blinking, bouncing, tweeting, clucking birds. This distraction resets a player's short-term memory and frees him to come up with a strategy for the next shot. Most will either scroll back to the right to look at the pigs in their protective structures or pinch the screen for a full-screen view before firing again.

Another piece in Maurer's cognitive teardown of the game involves mystery. As Pradeep pointed out with his analysis of the Victoria's Secret model on the poster, we humans have an innate need to interpret what we see or hear and derive some meaning. We often like wordplay, puzzles, puns, and anagrams. They get us to stop just long enough to think, and overcoming that tiny challenge means we are in on the joke, which gives us a brief moment of satisfaction. The need for mystery is why we tell a joke with the punch line last, not first. Most don't want to know what will happen in advance on *Downton Abbey*, which is why so much media coverage of the show involves "spoiler alerts" to protect unsuspecting readers from finding out what they are not ready to learn.

Maurer identifies several mysteries in the game. First of all, why are these birds so angry? Why do they have it in for these passive pigs that live in weird wooden houses with no back or front walls? Why do some birds somersault when they're loaded into the slingshot? Why are others shaped like irons? Why do bananas sometimes appear in some segments but not in others? Why don't these pigs fight back? Why can some birds be manipulated in flight, magnifying their explosive megatonnage, speeding up or dividing into three with a brush of the finger, while others can't?

The final component involves sound. In the way that music is used in horror flicks to raise tension before a character is about to get sliced and diced with a machete or used to sweeten romantic scenes, *Angry Birds* also has a soundtrack. In movies it's called "action syncing." Not music, in this case, but the utterances of its combatants. Before each shot a player hears the birds chattering encouragement and as one of them soars it screams "Wheee!" When it hits, it's accompanied by a satisfying crunching noise and sound of structures crashing down. Then there's either the oinkifying trash talk of any surviving pigs or, if successful, celebrating birds that leads to the game's music and a prompt for the next level.

This probably tells you far more than you ever wanted to know about *Angry Birds*. But no wonder the game is addictive. It was designed to be.

Game Mechanics

At their most fundamental level, games provide feedback loops. Daniel Cook, chief creative officer at Spry Fox, a Seattle-based game design firm, divides them into four parts:

1. A player performs an action. In *Angry Birds* it involves pulling back the rubbery band of a slingshot, aiming, and letting the fowl fly. For a crossword puzzle it means filling in blank spaces in a grid with a word, words, or phrase based on a clue. In a first-person shooter it's piloting an avatar through a simulated world, avoiding obstacles and firing weapons.

2. The action results in an effect. The *Angry Birds* player watches the bird soar through the air and strike makeshift structures housing oinking, blinking pigs. The crossword puzzle solver sees how his answer fits in a given space and whether it runs afoul of other answers he has given. For the first-person shooter player, the avatar reacts to his control of the joystick, mouse, or touch screen, and there are lots of explosions.

3. The player receives feedback. After an irate, chattering bird hits its targets the structures protecting the pigs shatter like a house of cards tumbling down, pigs are vaporized, and points accrue. Each crossword answer affects other answers—for example, a word running horizontally fills in vertical spaces on the grid, and a quick glance at the corresponding clues confirms or debunks the validity of the original answer. The shooter observes how every movement affects the avatar's actions, which are buttressed by visual and sound effects and growing point tallies for each successful shot or action.

4. Armed with additional knowledge, the player performs more actions. A new bird is loaded into the slingshot and the player adjusts his trajectory based on what happened on the previous shot. (How many pigs are left? Where are they located and how are they protected?) Five down has three of six letters filled in courtesy of other answers the player has already inputted into the grid. The player in the first-person shooter aimed too high on the previous shot so he adjusts the angle of his weapon or he knows to avoid that floating jellyfish-like alien skittering into his avatar's path.

At the heart of any good game are mechanisms to help deliver enjoyment, the stuff that makes a game a game. They need to have what Chelsea Howe describes as a "fractal elegance," which means "self-similar," that the pattern at the beginning of a game is the same at the end. That makes it eminently graspable to virtually anyone. Because we humans are, in Cook's words, "infovores" who "are wired to solve black boxes," a "fundamental aspect of our neurological learning wetware," these game mechanics play on our innate need to learn. They are "rule-based systems" that encourage a user to explore and learn through feedback mechanisms how to navigate a simulated environment. At its essence, a game is simply "a set of interlinked puzzles where solutions to one puzzle lead to clues that help on additional puzzles." Maybe Albert Einstein was right when he said, "Play is the highest form of research."

A cheat sheet of game mechanics from a mobile app game maker in Boston called SCVNGR leaked to the media in 2010. And while SCVNGR is no longer around (it became a mobile payments company), its list of forty-seven game mechanics that it mixed and matched to create its games is particularly revealing. Using SCVNGR's nomenclature, the first game mechanic a player encounters in a particular game is something it called "cascading information theory," which holds that a minimum amount of information be doled out so a user gains an appropriate level of understanding at each level. A child can look at *Angry Birds* for the first time and see how the game works. A crossword puzzle is obvious. So is a first-person shooter. Then the player takes action and experiences another game mechanic: "achievement." A bird strikes a pig that blows up and the players rack up points. A word fills in all the spaces horizontally in a crossword puzzle and works with answers to clues that come on the vertical. An attacking alien is obliterated by a player's avatar; that leads to points and perhaps another more challenging level.

An additional mechanic might be "contingency," the immediate challenge or challenges facing a player. Those porcine pests are just sitting there, begging to be expunged from their simulated world. The crossword puzzle fanatic experiences a driving need to fill in those blank word spaces. Amid the cacophony of a first-person shooter, a player spots a target and fires. Then there's "behavioral momentum," because the game is designed to induce a player to keep playing. You can't stop after shooting just one bird when another is preloaded into the slingshot, ready for action. It's hard to leave a partially filled-in crossword puzzle. With so much action a player would be hard-pressed to pull himself away from a first-person shooter. "Chain schedules" link rewards to accomplishments. Wipe out all the pigs and advance to the next level. Fill in a clue and help yourself with solving other clues. Kill all the enemy combatants and amass more firepower to use on higher levels.

Games have mechanics of all sorts. A leaderboard can induce a greater sense of competition and drive players in search of bragging rights to try even harder. An "appointment dynamic," also known as an "open loop mechanic," popularized by Zynga's *Farmville*, requires a player to return at a predetermined time to take an action that will benefit his performance in the game. That is, you have to come back in six hours to water your crops or they'll wither away. A "countdown" adds a time element to play, which, as the seconds tick away, leads to more frenetic activity (you have thirty seconds to shoot down as many invading spaceships as you can). Incentives can add to a player's point tally, while disincentives (losing points for certain actions) can also alter a player's behavior. A "progression dynamic" is confirmation of a player's success—a progress bar, for example, or a visual showing the levels he has passed and the ones he is yet to unlock. A "viral game mechanic" requires a player to spread the game to, say, six other people before she can proceed.

Often game mechanics are used in nongaming situations, too. For example, the title of this book, *Play at Work*, is a paradox. My editors and I chose it because we hope a potential reader will see the title and be intrigued by the puzzle it promises. Have you noticed when you update your résumé on LinkedIn there's a status bar that informs you your profile is only 90 percent complete? It's there to nudge you to add more information. That's a game mechanic, too. Starbucks has a rewards program that relies on game mechanics to induce greater customer loyalty. In one, the company offers a free drink after a customer receives fifteen stars. With thirty stars, he levels up to "green" and is eligible for free syrup, coffee and tea refills on the house, and a free tall drink with purchase of a pound of coffee beans. On the Starbucks mobile app a customer keeps track with a visual tally board.

You'll find in later chapters examples of game mechanics used to organize massive numbers of people to accomplish great things—from helping to digitize books dating from the nineteenth century to engaging in scientific discovery to translating the Internet. They're part and parcel of platforms that motivate people to create designs for cars and submit inventions for sale at department stores. Game mechanics help make the workplace a more enjoyable experience and assist surgeons in training and operations. These gameful design elements aid in education and improve customer service.

They're everywhere. You just have to look.

Social Games and the Human Brain

Why do people play massive online multiplayer games like *World of Warcraft* or social games like Words with Friends, Texas hold'em, and their ilk? Perhaps because humans have an innate need to socialize, and these games, layered over existing social networks, allow us to do that. Research shows that engaging with friends helps us live longer and better lives, with those with strong friendship bonds having fewer incidents of heart disease. They even get fewer colds and flus. A decade-long Australian study found that subjects with a sizable network of friends lived longer than those who had a small circle of friends. Here's the really surprising part: it didn't matter if the friends were in the same room, lived on the same block or town, or were even in the same country. The distance separating two friends and the amount of contact was irrelevant. It appears it doesn't matter if friends stay in contact via phone, by letter, or by e-mail. Just having friends acts as a protective barrier.

There is, I think, a good reason for this. We humans are hardwired to commingle with one another offline and on, and the Web and its platforms like Facebook and Twitter, as well as multiplayer games and crowdsourcing projects involving large numbers of people, make it more efficient than ever. That's because virtual relationships can be as real as, or even more real than, actual relationships. The truth is we're all one step removed from reality, living life through the prism of our own minds. Let me toss another study into the mix. Researchers at Washington University in St. Louis found when they scanned the brains of fiction readers they reacted to what they read as if they were actually living the events in the story.

In addition to the vividness that on- and offline relationships bring to our lives, they also provide another key ingredient. In 2011 the Pew Foundation released a report that found the Internet, in particular social networks, engender trust, and the more time you spend on them the more trusting you become. According to the report, "The typical

Internet user is more than twice as likely as others to feel that people can be trusted," with regular Facebook users the most trusting of all. "A Facebook user who uses the site multiple times per day is 43 percent more likely than other Internet users and more than three times as likely as non-Internet users to feel that most people can be trusted." What's more, while the average American has two "discussion confidants"—those they discuss important matters with—Facebookers who log in several times a day average 9 percent more close ties.

Trust is something of an obsession for Paul J. Zak, a neuroeconomist at Claremont College in California. In a series of studies spanning more than a decade, Zak has altered our understanding of trust as it relates to human beings as economic animals and social beings. He's tracked it to oxytocin, a drug created in our brains that he has dubbed the "moral molecule." More famous as the hormone that forges the unshakable bond between mothers and newborn babies, oxytocin (not to be confused with OxyContin, the much abused painkiller) is now, thanks largely to Zak, also recognized as the human stimulant of empathy, generosity, trust, and more. Although women have it in higher doses, men have it, too, and it is, Zak postulates, the "social glue" that adheres families, communities, and societies, and as such, acts as an "economic lubricant" that enables us to engage in all sorts of transactions.

And that is why, one spring day in 2010, I find myself on my back, trying to remain perfectly still, cocooned in a functional magnetic resonance imaging machine secreted in the basement of a cheerless building at the California Institute of Technology. Even with earplugs and noise-cancellation headphones, it's freakishly loud, sounding like a combination of a jackhammer and the whoosh of air you'd hear driving a hundred miles per hour with the windows down. In other words, it's your typical fMRI experience, save for the Apple laptop bolted a couple of feet above my head, and the mouse with a trackball on my chest. As a test subject, I'm helping researchers gauge the relationship between empathy and generosity, although for obvious reasons my findings would be segregated from the official results. While bestselling behavioral economists such as Dan Ariely (*Predictably Irrational*), and Steven D. Levitt (the "rogue economist" half of the *Freakonomics* duo) ponder how we make economic decisions, Zak wants to figure out why we do what we do.

Around the Claremont campus Zak is known as "Dr. Love," as much for his interest in "the cuddle hormone"—his vanity license plate reads

OXYTOSIN—as his habit of hugging practically everyone he meets. It releases (you guessed it) oxytocin. But I didn't come to L.A. for a hug. I came bearing my own questions, wondering if Zak's research could be applied to social media, an area I'd been exploring in my own work: What explains our BlackBerry-bearing, Twitter-tweeting, Facebook friends with the need for constant connectivity? Are we biologically hardwired to do it? I theorized that social networking is, at its essence, a kind of social transaction, so when we're tweeting or Facebooking, do our brains exhibit the same kind of chemical reactions that enhance trust and generosity? And how does trust play into the maelstrom of human emotion and action? To find out, I badgered Zak to let me participate as a test subject in two of his experiments, as well as one we designed together.

For this initial test I am stuffed inside an MRI machine and shown an unbearably sad video produced by St. Jude Children's Hospital in Memphis, Tennessee, featuring a young boy named Ben with a rare, very aggressive form of cancer and his parents' struggle to cope. It's the kind of video that could make a battle-hardened marine cry. Immediately afterward I play the Trust Game, a staple of behavioral economics. There are many variations, but they all involve a test subject who is instructed to send or receive a portion of money from or to an unknown person. Player one might propose to divide ten dollars by offering three dollars to player two and keeping the remaining seven dollars. If player two accepts the three bucks, the other guy gets seven dollars. If he rejects the offer, neither player gets anything.

The researchers use real money, promising to pay participants whatever they earn in the game. If I simply want to maximize my earnings, I should simply take whatever money is offered, whether it's eight dollars or one dollar, but, like most people, I am miffed when the other player grabs more than half. It just seems so unfair. So I turn down free money. It turns out we humans are not rational economic animals after all, although I suppose you already know that. A research assistant informs me that I made seventy-three dollars, about average, which I donate back to the lab.

This wasn't the first time Zak had based an experiment on the Trust Game. Zak had designed his inaugural study to incentivize generosity to see if there would be a corresponding increase in oxytocin levels. Player one was told that if he gave up a portion of the ten dollars he was awarded to participate in the study to player two, the amount of money in his account would triple. "My hypothesis was that you needed a social signal to release oxytocin," he says. What he discovered was that the more money test subjects received, "the higher their oxytocin levels, and the higher their oxytocin levels, the more they reciprocated."

In fact, subjects who had been shown generosity had 41 percent higher oxytocin levels than those who hadn't. His findings contradicted standard economic theory, largely based on the Nash Equilibrium, postulated by Nobel Prize–winning economist John Forbes Nash, Jr. Nash had predicted that player one would anticipate that player two would return zero and keep all the money for himself. Zak's experiment showed that not only would a player who was shown generosity become more generous, his brain would undergo a profound change.

The particular test I engaged in at Caltech, however, looked at the relationship among empathy, generosity, oxytocin, and trust. A couple of months later Zak walks me through the findings. He shows me photos taken of my brain during the fMRI. At the point in the video where the child's mother, her eyes welling with tears and her voice cracking, says, "They gave us about a 20 percent survival rate. We don't know if our little boy is going to make it," parts of my brain exhibited profound shifts.

"You were both empathic and saddened by his story," Zak tells me. Empathy was associated with an activation of "theory of mind" or putting myself in another's shoes—I am, after all, a parent, too—which was expressed in changes to my "temporal parietal junction." He could also see that I was a bit sad or uncomfortable via activation in my "anterior insula," an area that makes your belly feel uncomfortable and even nauseous. There was additional activation in the ventral tegmental area (VTA), which is associated with learning and reward. Because Zak has used this video in other experiments, he knows it "causes oxytocin release by the bucket full"—a rise of more than 40 percent in most people—which led to "midbrain dopamine release," keeping me "empathically engaged."

Then he shares the results of the Trust Game, customized to measure generosity, which I had played right after viewing the video. "You're 33 percent more generous than baseline folks," meaning those who didn't see the video, Zak tells me. "Congratulations, you have a heart!"

For as long as he can remember, Zak has been fascinated with how things work. While some men might describe their wives as extremely organized, Zak says his has "a highly developed hypothalamus." He describes his own personality by citing the Myers-Briggs test. (He's an NP—Intuitive Perceiver—"all into creativity and making weird connections.") As a child growing up in Santa Barbara, California, he and his dad built a calculator from scratch, an Altair 8800 computer from a kit, and took apart the family car. Now he's all about taking apart the mind to see how it ticks.

Over the years he's reeled off a flurry of related experiments designed to build on the role of oxytocin. One showed that men personalize negotiations over money and a second indicated they react hormonally when they are not trusted. Another trust study found that when an investor in an experimental game was given a dose of oxytocin, he was more likely to allow someone else to control his money, no questions asked. More research showed that touch triggers release of oxytocin—hence Dr. Love's penchant for hugs—and so does massage. Once Zak attended a wedding in England and took blood samples from the wedding party before and after the ceremony. Predictably the bride had the highest levels of oxytocin, followed by her mother. But the groom also experienced a rise. Immediate family measured higher levels of oxytocin than friends. In contrast, the best man saw his testosterone levels kick up, which, Zak hypothesizes, might have been due to the sight of so many pretty bridesmaids.

Not everyone is enamored with the field of neuroeconomics. Dan Ariely, author of *Predictably Irrational*, MIT economics professor, and a friendly rival of Zak's, believes it has been "overhyped" because "if you look at the amount of money invested into it, there has not been a very good return." He's particularly critical of studies that rely on MRIs, which he says are not definitive. Of Zak's work in oxytocin, however, Ariely says he's "a big fan," since it "allows you to see quite clearly what the mechanism is" that drives human behavior.

Others are more dismissive. Ed Yong, a British science writer and author of *Not Exactly Rocket Science*, stops just short of calling Zak a charlatan. After viewing Zak's talk on the "Moral Molecule" at Technology, Entertainment, Design (TED), Yong lambasted him in a lengthy and often humorous Twitter rant with the hashtag #schmoxytocin. While oxytocin may be linked to trust, empathy, cooperation, and a whole lot more, Yong pointed out that other studies have shown that oxytocin boosts schadenfreude and envy, that it actually reduces trust and cooperation in people with borderline personality disorders, and it can promote in-group bias (hugs, but only for people you like). Science, Yong reminds us, is not usually cut-and-dried, and he strenuously objects to Zak's characterization of oxytocin as a "cuddle chemical," "hug hormone," and "moral molecule."

It's true that oxytocin may not be a panacea for what ails us, but it does appear to play an important role in social connections, and that's how I find myself in a room with a dozen undergraduate students participating in a second Zak experiment in a nearby classroom. While some subjects receive oxytocin, others ingest a placebo, administered in an identical manner. Zak makes sure I get the oxytocin, and through a nasal inhaler spritzes forty drops up my nose in five-drop increments in each nostril. There's so much oxytocin (our bodies absorb only 10 percent of it) it drips down my chin and soaks my shirt. We wait an hour to let the hormone seep into our systems. I kill time surfing the Web and note a fuzzy feeling, which could be either psychosomatic or due to lack of sleep.

Then I view a series of public service announcement commercials. The videos—real PSAs that ran in the United States and Europe—dramatize the dangers of taking drugs and drunk driving, or the devastation that global warming could present (courtesy of Greenpeace). Some are gory; others are meant to provoke fear. I watch almost a dozen videos, and after each one am prompted to answer a question to test whether I paid attention. If I answer correctly, I get paid (real) money. In a subsequent question, I'm asked to donate a portion of proceeds to the organization that sponsored the ad. Would oxytocin lead me to be more charitable?

The experiment is ongoing, and the data far from complete, but Zak tells me the initial findings indicate that those of us infused with oxytocin donated 48 percent more to charity—as did I—than those administered the placebo. This, he notes, is the first study showing that oxytocin increases generosity to charitable organizations, and not simply to a particular individual. But it's the final experiment that Zak and I designed, involving a control group of one—me—that reports the most surprising results of all.

Zak greets me at his lab near the Claremont College campus, situated among a block of other Southern California schools such as Pomona, Scripps, and Harvey Mudd. Hammering, yammering workers are converting the three-bedroom house into a spacious new lab. To escape the din, Zak, donning a white lab coat over blue jeans, escorts me upstairs to a study, where a nurse, organizing a set of needles, awaits. "I could take your blood," Zak says (add registered phlebotomist to his list of titles), "but it would probably hurt."

The nurse compliments me on my veins, pokes a hole, draws blood, then she and Zak leave me alone. I pull up TweetDeck on my laptop and get to work. I alert followers that I'm engaging in a Twitter experiment with a neuroeconomist then add to a previous remark I made about the GPS in my rental car and how the automated voice gets snooty whenever I miss a turn. Responding to a woman I've never met who works in book publishing, I type in the language of 140-character Twitterese: "I want Mr. T GPS voice! How abt James Earl Jones? He says turn left you *turn* left. Or Norah Jones? Plaintive directions." Somebody else asks about the notorious Stephen Glass; did he plagiarize and fabricate, or only make up stuff? I tell her (someone else I have never met) that as far as I know Glass was strictly a fabulist, although other icons of journalistic malfeasance—Jayson Blair of the *New York Times*, *USA Today*'s Jack Kelley—were guilty of both. With a former editor with whom I once butted heads, I joke about overweight tourists in Speedo bathing suits grabbing plum spots on Greek beaches.

Meanwhile, some of my "tweeps" respond to my post about the experiment. I field a few questions from a couple of NYU students I've taught until the nurse returns for more blood. Zak labels each vial then takes me downstairs to a centrifuge, where my blood spins for fifteen minutes. He takes out the first vial to show me. The lighter plasma floats on top of the heavier, maroon-colored corpuscles. Zak packs my blood in dry ice and an assistant hauls it off to a lab.

While tweeting, I wondered if the experiment would yield anything of value. I wasn't engaging with close friends. It was a typical short dip into my tweetstream. Yet six weeks later, when Zak shared the results with me, my blood told a far more dramatic story. In just those ten minutes between when the first batch of blood was taken and the second, my oxytocin levels spiked 13.2 percent—as much as a groom at a wedding. ("That's pathetic," my wife says.) At the same time, stress hormones cortisol and ACTH went down 10.8 percent and 14.9 percent, respectively. Zak theorized that as I connected to others by tweeting, the release of oxytocin reduced my stress hormones, which lessened stress. “Your brain interpreted tweeting as if you were directly interacting with people you cared about or had empathy for,” Zak says. “E-connection is processed in the brain like an in-person connection.”

Some months later Zak traveled to Korea and redid our tweeting experiment, this time with three journalists using Facebook. The result: they each demonstrated increased levels of oxytocin. In fact, the oxytocin levels of one of the journalists writing his girlfriend shot up nearly 150 percent. Perhaps, Zak theorizes, the brain's release of oxytocin corresponds with the depth of connection between two people online.

If oxytocin is released when we engage in relationships online—and according to Hitwise, Americans spend one-third of their time online on social networks—I think it's likely, although there have been no studies to support this, that it could play a role in multiplayer gaming, or whenever teams of players work together for a common goal—crowd sourcing, for instance. Game designers are well aware of the role that dopamine plays, but few know that oxytocin release, which comes from social relationships, also promotes the brain's secretion of dopamine.

If true, it could be a particularly potent combination.

CHAPTER 2

MASS ORGANIZER

Luis von Ahn, a PhD candidate in computer science at Carnegie Mellon, was on an airplane in late 2001 when he noticed each passenger in his row, all six of them, pen in hand, scribbling answers to a crossword puzzle. Von Ahn, an avid gamer and TV addict (he loves reality shows) mulled all the effort and intellectual intensity his fellow travelers were pouring into a simple game. Computers can't do that, he thought. (Later he would find out they could.) Here he was twenty thousand feet in the air and six passengers, by their own volition, were tackling word problems. Why couldn't he get people to solve every problem, willingly, and for free? What if, he wondered, he could harness all this energy for practical purposes?

His ruminations led to his PhD dissertation, in which he coined the term "human computation," aka "a way to combine human brainpower with computers to solve large-scale problems that neither can solve alone." While computers are good at many things, they are also bad at many things. Want a machine to crunch an algorithm? A PC does a fine job. Command it to identify Brad Pitt and Angelina Jolie in a photo as they pose on the red carpet at the Oscars, and it'll choke on its processors. A human, however, can do this fairly easily.

What's more, under the right circumstances, humans could teach computers to handle the types of tasks they're normally unable to decode, such as classifying objects, comprehending spoken words, deciphering handwriting, recognizing faces—tasks a child can master. As any parent knows, you need almost Gandhi-like patience to teach young children even though we're biologically hardwired to do it. Few have the patience to answer almost illimitable niggling questions with the aim of helping some bloodless machine get smarter.

Von Ahn knew to accomplish all this would require vast numbers of people. The grandest project of antiquity, the pyramids of Egypt, took tens of thousands of men and more than twenty years to build. In the last century, laborers digging the Panama Canal clocked twenty million hours, while those raising the Empire State Building tallied seven million hours. The tallest building in the world, Burj Khalifa in Dubai, which was completed in 2010, racked up twenty-two million worker-hours over six years of construction. Nevertheless, with the advent of the Internet, von Ahn recognized the potential to harness the collective skills of half a billion people or more. After all, online collective behavior on such a mass scale already exists, made possible by the Internet. Computer solitaire, for instance, eats up billions of worker hours a year. But other than kill time and entertain its players, what tangible good does this activity do? Tens of millions play the massively popular multiplayer online role-playing game *World of Warcraft*, while millions more have joined online social networks. Every month Americans collectively spend the equivalent of one hundred thousand *years* on Facebook. Von Ahn figured if he could conjure a system to harness this engagement in a way that could make boring chores fun, he would be on his way to his ultimate goal: to make all of humanity more efficient by exploiting the time that gets wasted.

I traveled to Pittsburgh to meet von Ahn in 2011 in his office on the seventh floor of Carnegie Mellon's Gates Center, a visually alluring, zinc-coated building that evokes dominos and Lego pieces (it received an award from the American Institute of Architects). Von Ahn, a former MacArthur "genius" grant winner born in Guatemala, talks in quick mumbles, as if his words can't keep pace with his thoughts. His parents are doctors and his extended family owns a candy factory. When he was eight he asked for a Nintendo for Christmas, but his parents got him a Commodore 64, which he used to play games. He first taught himself programming by cracking the copyright protection of games he wanted to pirate.

Von Ahn has a novel approach to work. He'll sit down at his computer for a few minutes then jump up, pace, fidget, settle down again to type a word or phrase, get up, stroll around, then repeat the process. Somehow he gets a lot done. It occurs to me if floor panels could capture the kinetic energy von Ahn creates on his meanderings and use it to power the lights and electronics in his office, that would be the ultimate efficiency.

The idea of transforming what has been typically viewed as unproductive time and creating something productive out of it is an extension of a trend that has long been unfolding. We constantly wring productivity from traditionally unproductive times. We text while traipsing down the street, update our blogs while careening in a taxi through urban jungles, post a photo to Facebook at a diner, check in on Foursquare at the pharmacy, read e-mail at the mall, tweet before the start of a movie. This helps us squeeze a minute or two of work and social interaction into an already crammed day. Naturally this ADD culture that technology enables is not always beneficial to the human condition. There was, for instance, the walking and texting Staten Island teen who fell into an open manhole and despite being covered in raw sewage and losing a shoe, never let go of her phone. The desire for stimulation is an integral part of our technoevolution.

But von Ahn knew that there are very few activities that capture our attention. So to convince people to accomplish a task you give them, you have to make it fun. With this in mind, von Ahn designed the *ESP Game*. Its purpose: to label images so they could be searchable online. For this to happen, you need metadata, words tagged to photos that describe what's in them. Think of metadata as a Dewey decimal system for categorizing images instead of books. Google's search engine can't sift through photos and tell you what's in them; it gloms on to whatever tags of text are associated with them, and returns results based on what it finds. His inspiration was HotorNot, a site that allowed users to rate the relative hotness of people who submitted photos on a scale of one to ten. Almost immediately after it went live in October 2000 the site went viral. Within a week it had logged two million page views and in the span of a few months was one of the most popular destinations on the Internet.

Here's how von Ahn designed his game: two randomly selected players logged on to a Web site and were flashed the same photograph. They had two and a half minutes to label fifteen images by typing words each believed best described what was in the picture. Players tallied points only when their words matched their partner's, then they were rewarded with another picture. Because the only way to tally points was for both parties to agree on a word, they had to enter reasonable and accurate labels to have any chance of scoring. The same images were used repeatedly to ensure the accuracy of the labels different sets of players suggested. Over time the game became more challenging as images garnered "taboo" words—descriptions that couldn't be used again once they were associated with a specific picture. These were typically the most obvious descriptors, the low-hanging fruit, so participants were forced to be more creative and specific.

For example the first time the image popped up in the game it would have a clean slate. Player one might type "Brad Pitt, tuxedo, red carpet, Oscars," while player two could opt for "Angelina Jolie, Versace dress, Academy Awards, Ferragamo shoes, Brad Pitt." As soon as the players settle on "Brad Pitt" they receive points and move on to the next picture. When that photo of Brad and Angie comes up again to new people, the players could not use "Brad Pitt." Others might earn points for agreeing on "Angelina Jolie" and then her name would also become taboo. The third set of players might settle on "Oscars," and it, too, turns taboo; the fourth, "red carpet," and so forth. Von Ahn designed the system to fact-check, so images that generated a list of descriptors would be stripped of all of its taboo words and start a fresh round with new sets of players. And each set of players was shown the photograph only once.

As games go, the *ESP Game* wasn't as much fun as, say, *Angry Birds*, *Myst*, or *Doom*. Nevertheless, the game was designed to make it engaging, even provocative. In his initial prototype, von Ahn didn't even include a points system. Players simply tried to agree on a word that best described an image. It was so bare-bones he couldn't imagine anyone finding it enjoyable, yet each time he played it he'd race through thirty or forty images. Still, to make it "super-duper fun," he decided it needed to be more gamelike, so he added points. That made it more enjoyable, but he knew that wasn't enough, so he added a timer and gave players two and a half minutes to agree on as many photos as possible. That revved up the action. But he noticed the game became noticeably less engaging when player after player chose humdrum words such as "man" or "woman" to describe a person in a photo. So his final innovation involved adding obstacles in the form of those taboo words. When von Ahn decided to disallow such basic characterizations, not only did the game get more fun, users' descriptions became more sophisticated.

Starting with fifty thousand photos he downloaded off the Internet, von Ahn posted the game to his Web site. His only marketing consisted of telling friends, who told their friends, and so on, until half a million people had played it within the first six weeks and the *ESP Game* was featured on CNN. It proved surprisingly addictive. Some players stuck to it for hours, labeling image after image and e-mailing von Ahn to complain if a glitch interrupted their marathon sessions. Based on user habits, he continually tweaked it. A leaderboard motivated the top players, von Ahn found, but those with little chance of cracking the top twenty—usually the most recent devotees—were discouraged, so he added a second leaderboard to track the day's high scores, which helped.

After word of the *ESP Game* spread, von Ahn was invited to give a talk at Google. Afterward company founders Sergey Brin and Larry Page approached him about licensing the game, which they did, renaming it *Google Image Labeler.* Until von Ahn's game came along, Google had been forced to depend on the person uploading the photo to its image database to provide metatags. With von Ahn's game engine, however, Google could confirm the validity of these metatags and add other terms, which made photos more searchable and created more pathways to each photo. That in turn generated more page views and revenue. From 2006 to 2011 the game helped expand and improve Google's image search database to the tune of millions upon millions of photos. (A Google press representative said the company couldn't share specific numbers for *Image Labeler.*)

Now a tenured Carnegie Mellon computer science professor who drives a Porsche, von Ahn is but one of legions of computer scientists, educators, entrepreneurs, game designers, marketers, media organizations, start-ups, corporations, and city governments that have been pushing game mechanics beyond simple entertainment and layering them into all aspects of our lives. And von Ahn is on to perhaps his most grandiose project, which started with a simple question he posed to one of his graduate students: "How can we get 100 million people to translate the Internet into every major language for free?"

He traces the germ of this idea to another invention he came up with as a graduate student called CAPTCHA, which stands for Completely Automated Public Turing Test to Tell Computers and Humans Apart. (Alan Turing was a computer scientist who in 1950 invented a test to analyze whether a machine could pass for a human.) Yahoo! had come to Carnegie Mellon and asked von Ahn's adviser if there was any way to stamp out online fraud. Fraudsters were deploying armies of spambots to automatically register e-mail accounts on a massive scale, and the company needed to do something about it. Von Ahn's solution was ingeniously simple. He came up with a system to create numbers and letters that would be fuzzy enough so that a machine couldn't read them but a human could. Ever since, people have cursed him for it. Nevertheless CAPTCHA works and is used on millions of sites.

One day, von Ahn learned that roughly two hundred million CAPTCHAs were being typed every day. If it took the average person ten seconds to complete one, then he calculated that humanity as a whole was wasting half a million hours every day typing these annoying numbers and letters. This prompted him to come up with reCAPTCHA, which was the same premise as CAPTCHA only the material came from old books. It was a way to take an act that was unproductive and derive something from it on a mass scale.

To scan an old book and digitize the contents is a laborious process, akin to snapping a photograph of every page. Then it's up to a computer, using optical character recognition (OCR), to decipher each word. The process often results in plenty of mangled text. For older books, those published more than fifty years ago, pages have often yellowed and the ink has faded, which leads to an error rate as high as 30 percent. Von Ahn is taking words the computer can't recognize and getting people typing reCAPTCHAs to recognize them for him. He offers two words because one comes from a book, which the computer doesn't recognize, and the other is a word the computer already knows. The system doesn't tell the user which is which. If she types the correct word that the computer knows the answer to, it will assume she is human and have some confidence she typed the other word properly, too. If ten people agree, then the system has successfully edited another word.

For his new project, von Ahn decided he would borrow concepts from reCAPTCHA and harness an army of helpers to help translate the entire Internet. They would be paid—if that's what you call it—with free language lessons.

On its face, it might sound preposterous. The indexed Web has 15 billion pages. But von Ahn is serious. ReCAPTCHA shows that it's possible to organize truly massive numbers of users. Facebook, Ticketmaster, and 350,000 other sites deploy reCAPTCHA, which works out to about 100 million words a day from 2.5 million books that are, one word at a time, being cleaned up. About 750 million people have typed at least one reCAPTCHA. That means that about 10 percent of the world's population has helped to digitize the world's knowledge.

By capturing a million users for his new project, which is a fraction of the number of people who solve reCAPTCHAS, von Ahn calculated it would take just eighty hours to translate the entirety of Wikipedia from English to Spanish, which, if he had to pay for translators, would run a cool $50 million. Assisting is a National Science Foundation grant for $460,000 and $3.3 million in venture backing from celebrity Ashton Kutcher and Union Square Ventures for a private company called Duolingo, named after the language game cum Web translation tool developed with one of his PhD students, Severin Hacker (yes, his real name. He's Swiss.)

In 2009, Hacker and von Ahn were discussing ways to repurpose user activities for translating material. You couldn't just gather every person who spoke a second language and try to get them to work for you or identify every translator. It wasn't economically viable, first of all. You certainly couldn't pay them. And you couldn't ask them to work for free, plus how would you organize them? The obvious solution was to mimic reCAPTCHA's model of repurposing work in such a way that while a person did something, she was actually doing something else—and not only that, also enjoying herself.

But how? Translation is not exciting for most people, and only a tiny minority would claim to be passionate about it. But if their goal was to translate the entire Web, they would need to enlist millions of people. It was logical to look at education, and they knew they had something when they found out there was tremendous demand for language learning. In fact, they learned that 1.2 billion people worldwide are learning a foreign language. And one proven method of learning a language is through translation.

What they came up with was a language-learning game available free over the Web that doubles as a crowdsourced text translation service called *Duolingo*. From the perspective of the user, it's simple. Sign up and choose a language. For English speakers it's available in French, German, Italian, Portuguese, and Spanish; for Italian, Portuguese, and Spanish speakers, there's only English (so far). It doesn't matter if you have never spoken a particular language before. You click on a lesson and receive a quick tutorial, a series of tips, and frequently asked questions. For each lesson you receive three hearts. Make a mistake and you lose one. Four mistakes and you must repeat the lesson.

Each "skill" contains several exercises. On the left side of the screen you see a phrase in Spanish that you can read (or listen to). Your task is to translate it and type the correct words into a box on the right. For example, you might see *"No quiero una bicicleta porque quiero un carro."* The word *"porque"* might be translated for you. (It means "because.") Then you would type, "I don't want a bicycle because I have a car." If you're right, move on to the next answer. If you're wrong, lose a heart. When you complete one skill it unlocks other skills, which gives you the keys to progress from basic vocabulary to verb tenses and all the way through the language. *Duolingo* is intuitive—it's easy to figure out how to play. It's also motivational, since you get points and can level up. In addition, there's a social component, so you can compete against friends.

Later, each phrase that users attempt to translate is voted on by other users, which helps improve the content of the game. If they need a clue, users can scroll over a word for the translated equivalent, and the program is smart enough to detect obvious mistakes. As they progress through the material, players amass "skill points." A skill is considered "learned" when a player concludes all of the lessons contained within, and "mastered" after completing the assigned number of translations. He earns up to thirteen points per lesson, and loses a point for every mistake. There is also a timed practice feature. Players are given thirty seconds to answer twenty questions. For each correct answer they receive a skill point and an additional seven seconds. Because of an artificial intelligence engine, the game learns as it goes, tracking problematic words or concepts and presenting them in future lessons. Each user, just by playing, is helping the system get better.

In hindsight it sounds easy, but it wasn't. One problem they encountered early on had to do with special characters like the German umlaut, French accents, or the Spanish question mark. Americans with standard keyboards would not easily be able to create these special characters, so the developers threw in their own virtual keyboard and streamlined the interface. Another was keeping users motivated. As many of us can attest, starting a second language is easy, but sticking with it isn't.

Early on the game designers had users learn linearly, that is, complete one sentence at a time, but they ran into the problem of short-term memory overload. By the time a player got to the third or fourth sentence, his attention rate dropped. "They were like completely depleted," says Jose Fuentes, one of von Ahn's PhD students who has been working in the company to develop its business applications. "They were just like, 'Uh, I don't want to continue doing this.' And then their attention rate was really plummeting. Because in a sense, if you think about it, this is kind of like a game of attention, right?"

The team looked at various studies that found that the magic number for maximum attention is roughly seven minutes. In *Duolingo*, players' performance deteriorated at or around seven minutes, when they would finish then click away to somewhere else. The problem was they would then stop using the site. "The lesson there was that, yes, this was a very good way to create translations, but it wasn't a good way to maintain users wanting to continue learning," Fuentes says. The solution was to move to a nonlinear approach. A player would be shown a translation, then shown a different activity, like a discussion thread (called "the stream"). This helps players reset their short-term memory, which has resulted in greater engagement and better results.

Von Ahn told me he and his team had to work hard to gamify *Duolingo*, because at its core it's not a game. They looked to Zynga, particularly *Farmville*, which von Ahn loathes. "*Farmville* shouldn't even be fun," he says. "It's just so dumb. But [Zynga] has done an amazing job gamifying really crappy tasks."

As of early 2013, Duolingo had amassed about 1 million users, with 100,000 spending time on the site daily, and an additional 15,000 to 20,000 new users, most hailing from outside the United States, joining per day. At this rate the number of users could quintuple by the end of the year. And people are learning. Von Ahn commissioned a study of its language-training effectiveness, which found that by using *Duolingo*, a person with no knowledge of Spanish could cover the equivalent of an entire college semester language course in just thirty-four hours.

Ultimately, though, the Guatemalan-born von Ahn wants humans to perform these mind-numbingly repetitive tasks—in this case, translating the Web—so that one day we will teach computers to do it and ultimately they'll do it all for us.

"Don't worry," he tells me. "We're a good fifty years away from the machines taking over."

CHAPTER 3

THE RED BALLOON GAME

When Regina Dugan took the job of director at the Defense Advanced Research Projects Agency, the Pentagon's research and development arm more commonly known as DARPA, she knew she had to do something about spiraling, out-of-control costs and inefficiencies. It took a decade or more for new technologies to make it to the battlefield. As someone who had previously worked as a contractor for the Pentagon—RedXDefense, the company she started with her father and uncle that specialized in explosives detection systems used by American troops in Iraq and Afghanistan to locate roadside bombs—she knew firsthand that military technology had long been trapped in a vicious cycle: the more time it took to produce a piece of battle hardware, the more complexity had to be added to keep up with technological advances; the more complexity there was, the more expensive it became and the longer it took to develop.

By the time Dugan assumed control of DARPA in July 2009, the problem had become so serious she believed it was fast becoming a threat to the nation's defense. A decade went by before the average piece of military hardware went from the initial concept to the theater of war, and each delay added significantly to its expense. The Bell-Boeing V-22 Osprey helicopter program cost taxpayers more than $20 billion, with each plane carrying a sticker-shock-inducing price of $67 million, and needed more than two decades from its initial blueprint to passing its final evaluation in 2005. The USS *George H. W. Bush* warship ran $6.2 billion *for one ship*, and still had serious problems with its toilets. It took the air force twenty-five years to launch a space-based infrared system, a satellite first conceived in 1986. Years of congressional bickering and interservice squabbling drove the price tag into the billions. Indeed, the General Accounting Office (GAO) reported almost three hundred billion dollars in cost overruns for weapons systems between 2001 and 2008.

Really, though, if you want to understand why Dugan was so intent on speeding up the pace of innovation and decreasing the cost of technology, you need remember one number: 2054. That's the year DARPA estimates the cost of a single, state-of-the-art aircraft could equal the entire Department of Defense budget.

The Pentagon isn't alone in struggling with out-of-control product development costs, of course. Hollywood has had hundred-million-dollar movies (*Pluto Nash*, which earned only $4.4 million at the box office, and *Cutthroat Island*) that grossed a fraction of what they cost to produce. In the 1980s, R. J. Reynolds poured $325 million into developing smokeless cigarettes, which were so bad they were pulled from store shelves within four months. It took ten thousand employees five years and as much as $10 billion to develop and ship Microsoft Vista, which *Time* named one of the "Ten Biggest Tech Failures of the Last Decade."

In DARPA's case, Dugan blamed what she called a lack of "diversity" as a major culprit, with the same half-dozen or so fat military contractors bidding for contracts. Her solution: use the open-source software movement as a model and push for the inclusion of small companies, even lone do-it-yourselfers with various levels of expertise, to tackle small pieces of huge projects. She called it "the democratization of innovation." Take the design and construction of a space satellite. Instead of a few large military contractors building each piece, it would be subcontracted to several smaller vendors, each doing what it does best. This would result in a leaner, more nimble, less expensive work flow to create new hardware. To accomplish this, she began looking at crowd sourcing as a mechanism for collapsing a decade of research and development into two years.

This is not to say Dugan assumed it would be easy to change the way the Pentagon does business—not that this deterred her. You'll hear a common expression thrown around the agency's hallways. For a project to be worthy it has to be "DARPA hard"—code for the virtually impossible. It describes an agency unafraid to think big and, at times, fail spectacularly. Dugan's expansive vision for the agency was for it to be a "renaissance of wonder." And over the past half century, DARPA has had its share of hits: its research led to GPS, night-vision goggles, predator drones, and even the Internet. It's invested heavily in telesurgery, exoskeletons that function as wearable robots, landmine detection, a flying car, hummingbird-size surveillance craft, handheld speech translation and biosensors, as well the usual deadly array of guns, bombs, stealth planes, and missiles.

DARPA has also throughout its history divined some pretty far-out, comic-book-worthy schemes, many of which never made it out of the laboratory: steam-powered robots designed to fuel themselves by eating everything in their path, ripping up trees, shrubs and other biomass and stuffing them into built-in furnaces; telepathic spies who could use their psychic powers to spy on remote targets; a futures market to predict terrorist attacks, which was largely a victim of timing, coming not long after 9/11 and leading to public outcry; and, during the Vietnam War, a mechanical elephant to cut through dense jungle. Then there was the August 2011 launch of an unmanned hypersonic vehicle designed to fly at twenty times the speed of sound (thirteen thousand miles per hour)—it traveled so fast its skin burned away. The vehicle malfunctioned, disappearing into the Pacific Ocean forty minutes after launch. The Foxnews.com headline: "DARPA Loses Hypersonic Vehicle, Goes from $320M to Zero in 2,700 Seconds." (A DARPA spokesperson took pains to point out that the craft didn't cost taxpayers $320 million; that's how much was budgeted to the program.)

Dugan brushed aside the criticisms. "You can't lose your nerve for the big failure, 'cause the nerve you need for the big success is exactly the same nerve," she told me in an interview in her office in Arlington, Virginia. "To my knowledge, I have never encouraged anyone to fail. What we encourage people to do is succeed really big and that means that we can't fear failure."

Given the agency's cutting-edge oeuvre, you might expect the building that houses its headquarters to possess the flair of a science fiction flick, with robots trundling down hallways and futuristic gadgets galore. But it's pretty much like any other glass and steel office building. Before I could meet the petite, forty-eight-year-old (at the time) self-described geek, the first female to lead the Pentagon's blue sky agency, a security guard ordered me to stash my iPhone in a locker and hand over my laptop so technicians could disable the Wi-Fi, which they accomplished with a single strip of masking tape. Even Amtrak has more refined security protocols. Up a few floors in a standard-issue elevator and I arrived at the usual office building layout. No robots, no Jetsons flying cars, no sci-fi glitz.

Dugan, who earned a master's from Virginia Tech and a PhD from Caltech, first experienced the sclerotic pace of innovation firsthand right out of college, working at NASA and scoring her first patent with her work in refueling satellites in space. By the time testing was complete there was no need for it. What she learned was that "speed is part of the innovation process and ideas that seem good at the time, if not built upon, if not capitalized in time and with a sense of urgency, can pass you by," she says. Which explains the framed *New York Times* front page from July 1969 commemorating the Apollo 11 lunar landing that sits on a shelf above her desk and the plaque on her wall that reads Great Groups Ship.

She wondered if crowd sourcing, which could be accomplished through games, could help achieve this. Instead of putting science into games, though, would it be possible to put games into science?

Massive Treasure Hunt

Seven months after taking the helm at DARPA, Dugan authorized the agency's first crowd-sourcing experiment. The timing coincided with the fortieth anniversary of ARPANet, the precursor to the Internet. On December 5, 1969, DARPA linked the first four nodes of a network that would ultimately connect hundreds of millions of computers, billions of Web pages, and provide the backbone for modern communications. It was a game involving ten eight-foot-wide red weather balloons that had been raised between fifty and a hundred feet in the air and secreted throughout the continental United States. The object was to identify the GPS coordinates of all ten balloons, each of which would be visible from nearby roads and be aloft for just ten hours. The winner would collect a forty-thousand-dollar prize. It was, at its core, a treasure hunt on a grand scale.

"It was a very DARPA-like experiment," Dugan says. "We didn't know if it was going to work." Indeed, it engendered spirited debate within the agency. Would someone find all the balloons in twenty minutes, in a week, or not at all? A senior analyst at the National Geospatial Intelligence Agency claimed the problem would be impossible to solve through conventional intelligence-gathering techniques such as satellite imagery and airplane flyovers. The forty-eight contiguous states and Washington, D.C., that together comprise the continental United States cover 3.1 million square miles, of which 2.9 million square miles is land (the rest is water). The nation has some 4 million miles of paved roads. Assuming the weather cooperated and clouds didn't hamper the search, satellites, even if you somehow gained access to enough of them with sufficient resolution to make out eight-foot weather balloons, wouldn't be the answer because the country offers too large a landmass. Airplanes, even if you could commandeer enough of them, would take weeks to scour the entire United States. Forget about cars—too slow. The only way to succeed would be for large numbers of people to work together and share information. Which is why DARPA, in its announcement, called it "a competition that will explore the roles the Internet and social networking play in the timely communication, wide-area team-building, and urgent mobilization required to solve broad-scope, time-critical problems."

While the cash prize was a pittance for an agency with an almost three-billion-dollar annual budget, it was a key incentive. A project of this scope would require groups of highly motivated players. Now, forty thousand dollars wouldn't go very far if it were used to reimburse members for the time and resources they would need to dedicate to such a challenging task. Rather, Dugan expected that teams would dip into the cash prize to finance incentives to drive participation. Plus the prize money had the added benefit of attracting news coverage, which helped spread the word.

Realistically the only way to find all the balloons would be to figure out a way to organize thousands of pairs of eyes, but a contestant couldn't simply monitor Twitter and Facebook for mentions of red balloons, although he could tap social networks for information. But not everyone was on Twitter and Facebook. In 2009, when this DARPA competition took place, Twitter reported 18 million users who logged in at least once a month, while Facebook had 120 million members living in the United States. A person sighting a balloon might not be on these platforms, or if he was, he might not be active. Then there were the inevitable false positives, teams engaging in gamesmanship, tossing red herrings in competitors' paths to throw them off the scent while pranksters would glom on to such a high-profile competition. Nevertheless, Dugan placed her faith in the power of the crowd, predicting it would take less than a day for the agency to declare a winner.

This wasn't DARPA's first public challenge. Five years earlier the agency held a competition for robotic driverless cars through a 150-mile course that wound through the Mojave Desert. Not a single entry completed the course; the vehicle that traveled the farthest managed only eleven miles, and no one claimed the $1 million purse. In the second year, five got to the finish line over a shorter course. Then in 2007 the agency changed the route to wind through an urban environment. A team from Carnegie Mellon nabbed the $2 million first prize. The agency discontinued the competition until 2012, when it announced a new one that dealt with humanoid robotics (it's ongoing). Then in April 2013 DARPA awarded a pickup team of three engineers from California, Ohio, and Texas $1 million for their design of a military tank that can swim—in DARPA parlance, a "Marine Amphibious Assault Vehicle." They beat out more than a thousand other entries.

For the balloon game, 4,367 entrants signed up in the five weeks between the initial announcement and the day of the contest—teams from private industry, ad hoc groups, individual citizens, and universities—including Georgia Tech, Harvard Business School, and MIT. Mutual Mobile, based in Austin, Texas, created an app called "Army of Eyes" that enabled iPhone users who sighted a red balloon to snap a photo with a time and location stamp. If the information checked out, the user would receive twenty-five hundred dollars. i-Neighbors, which arose from a neighborhood social network and community Web site, didn't recruit members; organizers simply wanted to gauge how effective its existing network of users would be in reporting phenomena in their neighborhoods. "Open Red Balloon Project" requested that volunteers report any sightings and offer guesses, which it expressed on an interactive map and provided to all. The first to figure out where all the balloons were would collect the whole grand prize.

George Hotz, a twenty-year-old hacker from New Jersey who gained notoriety for being the first to jailbreak an iPhone and hack the Sony PlayStation, tweeted to his thirty-five thousand Twitter followers that he was taking part in the competition; he named his team Dude It's a Balloon and would prove to be a formidable competitor. Jon Cannell, a Web designer from Port Charlotte, Florida, announced in a press release that any prize money would be divided equally among those who supplied accurate balloon coordinates, and relied on friends and family to spread the word. Larry Moss, a professional artist who designed balloon sculptures, promised to make a giant floating cupcake if he won.

The universities possessed the greatest resources and technical know-how, and each pursued different strategies. Researchers from the Georgia Institute of Technology opted for an altruism-based incentive mechanism, pledging to donate any money to the American Red Cross. They organized a team of seven, built a network over Facebook and via word-of-mouth messaging that ultimately grew to more than a thousand volunteers, and posted a Web site called I Spy a Red Balloon. The team placed a premium on the site's search ranking, which it enhanced through media coverage (the group was featured on NPR). This, they theorized, would help them reach people who might see a red balloon but not know about the contest. If they searched for red balloon, "I Spy a Red Balloon" would pop up near the top of Google results. Meanwhile, Project Red Balloon, a team of students and professors from Harvard Business School, pursued a quasi altruism-based incentive model, giving anyone who successfully spots a balloon the option of keeping a thousand dollars or donating to AIDS research and awareness. It asked two thousand faculty and students to tap their social networks and reach out to alumni, estimating the team reached almost a hundred thousand people across the continental United States.

Leading a group from MIT, which included three graduate students and two postdoctoral fellows in Professor Alex "Sandy" Pentland's Media Laboratory Human Dynamics research group, was physicist Riley Crane. His own research centered on the ways information spreads throughout computer networks like YouTube. The team treated the project as an experiment, and within four days agreed on a strategy that aligned the interests of the mob with those of their tight-knit membership. Thirty-six hours before the onset of the competition, they launched a Web site and announced a sliding scale of rewards. This "recursive incentive" strategy was similar to multilevel marketing (think Amway).

Here's how the MIT team explained it on its Web site:

> We're giving $2000 per balloon to the first person to send us the correct coordinates, but that's not all—we're also giving $1000 to the person who invited them. Then we're giving $500 to whoever invited the inviter, and $250 to whoever invited them, and so on . . . It might play out like this. Alice joins the team, and we give her an invite link like http://balloon.media.mit.edu/alice. Alice then e-mails her link to Bob, who uses it to join the team as well. We make a http://balloon.media.mit.edu/bob link for Bob, who posts it to Facebook. His friend Carol sees it, signs up, then twitters about http://balloon.media.mit.edu/carol. Dave uses Carol's link to join . . . then spots one of the DARPA balloons! Dave is the first person to report the balloon's location to us, and the MIT Red Balloon Challenge Team is the first to find all 10. Once that happens, we send Dave $2000 for finding the balloon. Carol gets $1000 for inviting Dave, Bob gets $500 for inviting Carol, and Alice gets $250 for inviting Bob. The remaining $250 is donated to charity.

Structuring rewards this way created incentives for each member to involve others, viewing them not as competitors but as collaborators, with the result that volunteers were motivated to seek targets while being given the incentive to recruit others with the skills and wherewithal to locate them. It also helped the team cast a wider net beyond the geographical boundaries of the United States because the system rewarded participants for simply passing along information even though they might not be in any position to find a balloon. From five original members, the team quickly sprouted to five thousand participants.

On the day of the competition, Dr. Peter Lee, head of DARPA's Transformational Convergence Technology Office, which Dugan tasked with organizing and managing the game, joined his agency colleagues at San Francisco's Union Square, and at 7 a.m. watched as a red balloon was hoisted a hundred feet into the morning sky. (Balloons were also raised in Atlanta, Memphis, Miami, and Santa Barbara, as well as Scottsdale, Arizona; Charlottesville, Virginia; Christiana, Delaware; Katy, Texas, near a baseball field outside of Houston; and Portland, Oregon.) Lee was surprised how small the eight-foot balloon appeared from the ground. He was convinced no one would be able to spot them.

The small size of the treasure hunt targets was just one challenge. Teams also confronted the fog of misinformation. Some players infiltrated rival teams to throw a monkey wrench into the proceedings. In Royal Oaks, Michigan, someone positioned a decoy balloon complete with an imposter DARPA official looking on. False leads spread over Twitter like hot rumors and gossip, such as erroneous claims that balloons were sighted in Seattle; Providence, Rhode Island; and near the Brainerd, Minnesota, public library. One team, 10 Red Balloons, announced that it had spotted a balloon even before the contest kicked off. When asked how this might be possible, a DARPA official replied that perhaps some teams were employing psychics. A 10 Red Balloons member later admitted he made it up to drum up interest and induce more people to join his cause.

"The number of false reports to the number of real reports in the system was about four to one," DARPA's Dugan says. "So trying to figure out how to filter the false reports from the true reports became the essence of the challenge." And with forty thousand dollars at stake, DARPA itself was not immune to information attacks. "We had lots of people try and crack the puzzle just by spamming us, e-mail, and creating fake Web sites, all of those things," she adds.

With so much faulty information, some teams had to sift through thousands of false reports, each having to be verified or debunked. Lee, whose office managed the competition, told NPR: "In most cases, the top teams were able to get people on sight to validate balloon sighting in less than two hours," a feat he called "quite amazing."

To determine the legitimacy of balloon sightings, the MIT team first checked whether multiple submissions came in for a given location and noted various characteristics. If, for example, reports arrived in rapid succession and the coordinates were identical down to multiple decimal points, it was likely a false report. In essence, the information was too perfect, and that's not how humans work. If reports came in out of sequence and at various times, however, and the coordinates were close but not identical, this was viewed as natural noise and reflective of truth in the system. Another telltale sign of fakery involved IP addresses. If the submitter's location (from where he sent the information) wasn't in close proximity to the actual coordinates given for a balloon, the information was likely bogus. The final litmus test involved photographs that came with submissions. Not only did a photo have to contain a red balloon, it needed a DARPA banner and an official from the agency, details not shared with the public.

During the day, Twitter lit up, with players tracking the action through the hashtags #redballoon and #redballoons. DARPA's Lee was amazed at how quickly teams were spotting balloons. It was turning into a "real nail-biter" that eventually settled into a four-way race between MIT, Georgia Tech Research Institute, hacker George Hotz, and Red Balloon Race, a team comprised of two 2008 MIT grads. Each team had embraced a different strategy. While MIT had its multilevel marketing scheme and Georgia Tech its charitable donation model coupled with strong Google search juice, Hotz relied on his thirty-five-thousand-strong Twitter army to locate balloons while horse-trading locations with other teams. The other team from MIT, hamstrung by a lack of resources, waded through Twitter to pull out accurate sightings while relying on Google AdWords to drive traffic to their Web site. Like Hotz, they worked the phones to trade information.

Eight hours and fifty-two minutes into the competition, DARPA declared MIT's Red Balloon Challenge team the winner. Falling one balloon shy was the Georgia Tech Research Institute team. Both Hotz and Red Balloon Race spotted eight balloons. i-Neighbor reported five balloons. The team from Harvard Business School found none.

As Luis von Ahn had discovered with games that mobilized massive numbers of users, Dugan validated her hunch that there was indeed great power in the crowd. You just needed to settle on the right mechanisms to organize them. She could see this approach used to seek out terrorists or missing children—whenever it would be necessary to find a proverbial needle in a haystack.

The Submarine Game

Even a veteran DARPA program manager like Rob McHenry, who was working for Dugan in DARPA's tactical technology office when

I visited, couldn't remember all the acronyms the agency inflicts on its staff. A former submarine officer in the navy, he mentioned SURTASS. I had to stop him to ask what it means. "It stands for Surveillance Tracking and . . . actually I'm drawing a blank on the end of the acronym," he told me. He had to Google it. It stands for Surveillance Towed-Array Sensor System, run by civilian "operations personnel" contracted to SPAWAR (Space and Naval Warfare Systems Command), which is an element of IUSS (Integrated Undersea Sensor System) that relies on SOSUS, a chain of underwater eavesdropping posts hidden in the North Atlantic Ocean originally used to track Soviet submarines. You get the picture. DARPA deputy director Kaigham Gabriel also stumbled over acronyms in an interview and griped, "One of the things [we] are constantly struggling with, everybody comes up with their cute acronym. For them, it's very cute because that's the only acronym they have to remember, but we have to try and remember all of them." I imagine Joseph Heller grinning from his grave.

Despite the acronym stew, Dugan, buoyed by the success of the balloon challenge, pressed ahead on another crowd-sourcing experiment, this one to improve naval tactics, and tapped McHenry to lead it. The project featured a new invention—an unmanned pod called the ACTUV (for Anti-Submarine Continuous Trail Unmanned Vessel) that could travel on the surface of the sea to track potentially hostile submarines. A typical diesel-powered sub might cost two hundred million dollars to make, but cost our military ten times that to defend against. That's where the ACTUV, which would cost a fraction of that, comes in. The vehicle was designed to function like a Roomba, except instead of vacuuming dust it gloms on to a submarine to track it. Unlike a predator drone piloted from a remote location, the ACTUV would rely on software to automatically deploy the optimal naval tactics, and by applying artificial intelligence would learn as it goes. But what were the best naval tactics to code into the software? To find out, McHenry put the question to the crowd in the form of an online game.

He adapted an existing commercial game, the popular *Dangerous Waters*, a naval warfare simulation released on Microsoft Windows in 2005, and on a DARPA Web site challenged players to "best an enemy submarine commander so he can't escape into the ocean depths." It was designed to be a "politically correct" diesel-electric submarine not specific to any one country; nonetheless it posed a danger because it toted an ambiguous weapon of mass destruction. "It was sort of a terrorist submarine that was threatening the East Coast of the U.S." McHenry says, "so the user would have to keep tabs on the submarine so that it could be monitored." When it exceeded a certain threat level, the navy would destroy it.

The software simulated actual evasion techniques that submarines deploy. The player's tracking vessel was not the only ship at sea, so he had to navigate through commercial shipping traffic as he tracked the enemy sub, whose crafty captain had several tricks up his sleeve. As a player completed mission objectives, he tallied points and on a leaderboard could see how he ranked against other players. "As you complete each scenario in the simulation, you may submit your tracking tactics to DARPA for analysis," McHenry wrote on the Web site. "DARPA will select the best tactics and build them into the ACTUV prototype."

The game was posted on DARPA's servers on April 1, 2011, and over the course of a month was downloaded more than fifty thousand times, including one day that saw twelve thousand downloads, which crashed the server. It made for a chagrined public affairs officer, but McHenry was pleased. When users completed a game, they were asked if they would like to anonymously submit the data file back to DARPA, which led to about seven thousand submissions. Each file was analyzed, and a player earned points for things like the amount of time he trailed the enemy sub, maximizing propulsion efficiency, and sticking to sonar bands that are not associated with environmental risks. Points were deducted for burning too much gas by throttling up and down too much or coming too close to passing commercial ships. "Behaviors and actions that didn't comply with the rules of the road or posed safety risks to colliding with other traffic were highly penalized," McHenry said.

After crunching the data, McHenry created five leaderboards then invited a navy officer expert in tracking subs to play the game. Using time-honored navy antisubmarine warfare operations tactics, the highest he placed on a leaderboard was third. On most he was fifth or sixth. Conventional submarine warfare operations maximize the range at which you follow the submarine, so McHenry's antisubmarine warfare expert only got as close to the target as he had to.

The top public users, however, didn't put that constraint on themselves. Whether they were operating with long- or short-range sensors, they drove as close as they could to the submarine and sat on top; because it was an unmanned craft, there was no fear for loss of life. "That gives you the most tactical control over the maneuvers of that submarine and ability to respond," McHenry says, which the top game players "correctly demonstrated . . . in hindsight it's kind of obvious, the closer the better."

One player with the handle MolonLabe (*Molon Labe* in ancient Greek roughly translates into "bring it on!") topped the leaderboards in four of five categories, but McHenry doesn't know who he or she is, because game files were forwarded anonymously. For all he knows the world's best player and greatest ACTUV tactics expert could be a ten-year-old girl from Saskatchewan.

DARPA director Dugan then sought an even bigger canvas on which to test her crowd-sourcing theories.

CHAPTER 4

THE WISDOM OF CARS

In the summer of 2011, John B. Rogers (everyone calls him Jay), chief executive officer of Local Motors, a micro car factory in Phoenix, Arizona, received a surprise phone call. Regina Dugan was on the other end of the line. Would he, she asked, be interested in crowd sourcing a marine assault vehicle for DARPA?

Dugan had found the right guy. Rogers, a former marine, is an evangelist for what he calls "cocreation." It's not an alternative theory for evolution; rather it's an offshoot of crowd sourcing, and Rogers has staked his entire business on the concepts of open-source code, Wikipedia, Creative Commons, and the inherent wisdom of crowds—taking designs and suggestions from the thousands of gear heads that frequent his company's discussion boards, working with those who proffer the best ideas, and putting them to work. Local Motors designs and builds cars by committee—except in this case the committee is comprised of tens of thousands of do-it-yourselfers and professional auto designers. Rogers, in his late thirties, was on a mission to upend 150 years of industrial production tradition. After all, the Wright Brothers were the ultimate DIYers and they had invented the airplane.

At first, Rogers had misgivings about working with DARPA. His life in the military had taught him that government agencies were thick with red tape. Not only that, but as Dugan laid out her plans to crowdsource battlefield armaments and vehicles, using language like "flexible, programmable, potentially distributed production capability able to accommodate a wide range of systems and system variants with extremely rapid reconfiguration timescales" he recognized it for what it was: a series of microfactories churning out highly customizable vehicles. It was if she had read his business plan, which, given whom she worked for, he supposed she had.

He pointed out that Local Motors wasn't a defense contractor. It had no experience with strict regulations and didn't have a federal acquisition record. Dugan assured him none of that would be necessary.

"Look," she said, "you know how to do this so do it and show the world we can do it."

Jay Rogers had always loved tinkering. A child of privilege who grew up in Palm Springs, Florida, the youngest of four children of a real estate developer, he took apart his bicycle and modified his skateboard. Once he designed his own model car with a rocket launcher and minicamera, engaging in long-distance reconnaissance. With a remote control he controlled the car, taking it well outside his field of vision, and fired rockets off the roof. When he was fourteen he took an elective course on automotive mechanics at boarding school at Groton in Connecticut, and under the tutelage of a teacher rebuilt a couple of 1950s Porsches and a Volvo station wagon.

He inherited his love of cars, trucks, and things that run—the "Preston Tucker curse," as he calls it—from his grandfather, Ralph Burton Rogers, an automotive innovator who installed the first diesel engine in a car. Toward the end of World War II he bought motorcycle manufacturer Indian Motors from the DuPont family, a company that had been founded in 1909. When he took it over Indian Motors was a preeminent brand, the biggest motorcycle company in America, bigger than Harley. One of his first moves was to purchase a huge factory where Rolls-Royce produced aircraft engines so that Indian could aggressively expand and brought manufacturing down to a single floor to make it easier to move equipment and parts through. At the beginning, Indian was thriving, riding the motorcycle's prewar popularity, which was in part tied to the poor condition of America's roads. Many were dirt trails while others were pocked with potholes. And the best way to get around these rutted roads was on a motorcycle. With the emergence of the American highway system, however, followed by the import of cheaper bikes that were built for leisure from England and then Japan, Indian found its product mix all wrong. By 1953 it was out of business.

Growing up, Rogers listened to his grandfather's stories and absorbed valuable lessons, which helped shape his vision for Local Motors. Don't get whipsawed by changes in customer preference, make your facility and your capability nimble enough to adapt quickly. There was also a more humanistic life lesson wrapped up in all this: failure is good. Until then, everything his grandfather touched had turned to gold. He made a million dollars as an investment banker by the time he was thirty, and with that he bought Rogers Diesel and Aircraft. Then he acquired Indian, which started off so promising, only to crash less than a decade later.

Like his grandfather, Rogers experienced firsthand what it was like to have a fortune, live in splendor, and lose it all. When he was sixteen his parents sat him and his brothers and sister down to tell them that they were no longer rich. His father had invested heavily in Houston—he had developed much of the city's downtown—and the Texas savings-and-loan crisis hit. Suddenly Houston land values were dropping to pennies on the dollar and the family's entire fortune evaporated. "Things may change," he told his children, and they did. Creditors took just about everything—the mansion, the boat, the cars, furniture. His father had set aside rainy day trusts for his older children, enough to pay for graduate school, but there was little else. Until now Rogers had grown up worldly wise but with a silver spoon, and to have it all disappear was the first glimmer that nothing in life was guaranteed. Instead of being set for life his father, at the age of sixty-five, had to return to work.

Rogers dipped into his siblings' trust funds to pay for Princeton, where he pursued a double major, an esoteric mix of engineering and art history, graduating in 1995. After a couple of years in China, helping his father with a new medical testing products business (like most start-ups, it failed), he worked at an investment bank in Dallas. At twenty-eight he joined the marines, graduating first out of nine hundred recruits in basic school, and serving three tours of duty.

It was toward the end of his military service, when he realized the war in Iraq was at its crux about our nation's reliance on foreign oil, that Rogers first thought of starting a car company. He was concerned about not only our collective carbon footprint but our geopolitical footprint. After returning stateside he considered launching a company to build hydrogen-powered cars, but realized it was too risky: he would be dependent on others' scientific advances. What he really wanted was to build cars that people would actually buy, and that meant getting them from concept to design to manufacturing and on the road in a fraction of the time that Detroit could.

He enrolled at Harvard Business School, where he developed his ideas, and once he graduated set out to raise money for his fledgling car business. It wasn't easy. One of his first calls was to Lew Lehrman, who once ran for New York State governor against Mario Cuomo. But he wanted 90 percent of the company in exchange for a one-million-dollar investment. Rogers asked if there were circumstances that could convince him to invest the money in exchange for a much lower equity stake, and Lehrman replied only if Rogers found another investor whom he trusted. Then he would take a similar deal. Rogers called the owners of Factory Five, a Wareham, Massachusetts–based company that designs and manufactures assembly kits for cars, who had been advising him from the start. But they declined his offer to invest in his business. They had their own company to run and risks to handle. But they were willing to trade factory space, tools, and an engineer, worth the equivalent of one million dollars, in exchange for a 15 percent equity stake in Local Motors. Months later Rogers returned to Lehrman, who gave him a million dollars in cash at the same valuation.

Eventually, Rogers would raise seven million dollars.

The Rally Fighter

On an early June 2012 day in the desert, 110 degrees in the shade, I'm chilling on the outskirts of Phoenix, Arizona, in a Rally Fighter, Local Motors' flagship vehicle, when the driver asks if I want to go airborne.

"Hell, yeah," I say. I mean, who wouldn't?

He tells me to pin the back of my head against the seat (to protect against whiplash), revs the engine, and in seconds we're up to eighty miles per hour, screaming toward a ramp outside the Local Motors factory. The car sails upward until gravity asserts itself. We don't stay airborne long—maybe a couple of seconds. The landing feels like getting jostled in a mosh pit. Not something I would try in a Ford Explorer.

Inside Local Motors' thirty-thousand-square-foot, spick-and-span factory I join Jay Rogers. With short hair, freshly pressed khakis, and ramrod-straight posture and military bearing, he looks like he could still complete boot camp. We're in the cleanest factory I've ever seen, well lit, with none of the telltale signs that automobiles are being born and serviced here—no oil splotches on the ground, heavy machines, or assembly lines. Tools are neatly organized on shelves. A tower of potted plants winds to the ceiling—there, Rogers informs me, to help offset the factory's carbon footprint. A half-dozen Rally Fighters in various states of undress lay around. One is earmarked for a customer in Poland, another is just a shell, a third is about to be wrapped in the vinyl Local Motors uses instead of paint. Customers have spent eighty thousand dollars and want a fully customized vehicle that rubs against much of the conventional wisdom coming out of both Detroit and Japan.

After Rogers made the decision to build cars he realized a hybrid or electric car was beyond his technological capabilities and would take too long to develop. Besides, he didn't think he could sell a car based on its having less impact on the environment. The Prius, for example, sold for only four thousand dollars more than a comparable make with a standard gas-guzzling engine. He also concluded that the conventional wisdom coming out of Detroit was wrong.

Automakers claim that heavier cars are safer, but that isn't true. Bigger cars are safer, because in a crash energy is dissipated throughout the car's body. But bigger doesn't necessarily mean heavier. If Rogers jettisoned the heavy steel used in most American cars and created bodies out of much lighter composites, he could manufacture an automobile that was large and weighed a lot less, with a wide wheelbase for stability. Composites provided other advantages. They cost less because steel tools are expensive and require vast amounts of energy, and working with composites enabled Local Motors to be nimble and instantly respond to customer tastes. He could quickly and easily change the look of a car by asking customers what they wanted. And he could wrap the vehicle in nylon wrap, which means there's no need for toxic paints.

Rogers leads me to a black Rally Fighter etched with red flames, which the buyer had put on. "Is this a small car?" he asks rhetorically. The wheelbase stretches as wide as an SUV's. "Is it a short car? It's frigging long. And is it lightweight? About eight hundred pounds," less than half the weight of a similarly sized car from Detroit. "It's hugely lightweight compared to other cars in its class."

He runs his fingers along the roll bar arcing across the reinforced cabin. Thus far two customers have suffered major accidents, he tells me, and both walked away without a scratch. In the more serious crash the driver hit a boulder field at fifty miles an hour, rolled over three times, and landed on the roof. Upside down he opened the door and crawled out unhurt. The car was totaled on the outside, yet the inside was virtually untouched. In February 2013 a Rally Fighter in the Parker 425 off-road race in Arizona flipped over and kept on racing, finishing fourth that day.

During his due diligence phase, before he started the company, Rogers wondered about potential lawsuits. He questioned the Factory Five owners, who create car kits for classic automobiles, and they told him seven people died operating their cars. If that were true, Rogers wondered, how could they still be in business? Easy, they said, because their customers built the cars themselves. If you're dead, you don't sue anyone, they explained. It's the families who would. But at a wake or funeral friends and relatives would say, "That Bob, he loved cars and he died doing what he loved." Suddenly he's a hero, a man who lived by his own rules.

Before Rogers started his business, within this protoplasm of ambition there lacked a strategy for creating designs guaranteed to sell. Designing and manufacturing any car was a risk. It was always possible that no matter what focus groups told you or how good you thought your design was, consumers might not want it. Who could forget the Ford Edsel, a $350-million dud that became synonymous with product failures in the late 1950s? Three and a half decades later Ford squandered six billion dollars on a "world car" that it could sell in multiple countries instead of tailoring vehicles for different tastes across multiple markets. Marketed in the early 1990s as the Ford Contour and Mercury Mystique in the United States, the car took eight years to develop—double the time it typically takes to design and manufacture a vehicle from scratch—and sold poorly until it was discontinued. One thing Rogers wouldn't do is get smacked down by abrupt changes in consumer taste like his grandfather did with Indian Motors.

Then he came across Threadless, a T-shirt maker in Chicago. Threadless was up against Gap, Old Navy, and the like—the clothing equivalent of the big carmakers. On the Gap's profit-and-loss statements is a multimillion-dollar write-down of unsold inventory from either mispricing products or simply missing the market. That was its Achilles' heel. Because Threadless founders didn't know how to outsource production to China, and were reluctant to risk precious start-up capital on designs that might not appeal to consumers, they had them designed by members of their community. This would in effect market-test the T-shirts before they were produced. Then they manufactured them with hand presses in Chicago, which was more expensive than having them made and shipped from China, but they sold every single shirt they made. What if, Rogers thought, he applied that model to cars?

Relying on large groups working toward their own ends while simultaneously attempting to achieve mutual goals to design and manufacture a car is not as farfetched as you might think. While America has always thought of its innovative heroes as lone wolves—from Thomas Edison to Albert Einstein, Henry Ford, and Steve Jobs—many of science's greatest advancements have arisen from the work of tightly knit groups of thinkers and doers: the Manhattan Project, the space program, the Human Genome Project. More than sixty years ago a collection of Bell Labs scientists invented the transistor, which proved to be the foundation for all the digital products that followed. Commingling in one place, they developed the programming languages Unix and C, which are the building blocks for all computer operating systems today, as well as the silicon solar cell and the first fiber-optic cable, communications satellite, and cellular telephone system.

Bell Labs owed much of its success to its leader, Mervin Kelly, who strove to create an "institute of creative technology" where a "critical mass" of talented people could foster a heady exchange of ideas, according to Jon Gertner, author of *The Idea Factory: Bell Labs and the Great Age of American Innovation*. Kelly even relied on architecture as a conversation catalyst, with Bell Labs' main building characterized by hallways so long a person couldn't see all the way to the end. This made it virtually impossible for someone ambling down the hall to avoid getting pulled into conversations with colleagues and acquaintances, or running into diversions, which could help provide inspiration for the next great thing. "A physicist on his way to lunch in the cafeteria was like a magnet rolling past iron filings," Gertner wrote. Steve Jobs, offering input on Apple's headquarters, demanded the same approach. Another group of researchers at Xerox Parc built on this work to divine the graphical user interface that has characterized decades of personal computing, and two groups of physicists in Switzerland worked together and competed to seek proof of the elusive Higgs boson, which, because

it may explain mass, tells us why our atoms don't zip around the universe at the speed of light.

Nowadays the real and virtual worlds are melding. Harvard research fellow Neal Gabler says we are heading toward a more globalized understanding of innovation, one buttressed by ever more powerful connectivity. Collaboration is no longer a product of physical proximity; collaboration can occur over vast distances and yield the benefits of bringing great minds and skills together. And these participants need not be so-called experts. They can simply be those driven by keen interest. Yet their labors, when combined with others', can create a whole far greater than the sum of its parts.

Not surprisingly, collaboration thrives online, where physical distance is dissolved by constant connectivity. Wikipedia is the ultimate crowdsourced project. An open-source collective of programmers coded Mozilla's Firefox browser. After a contest Netflix handed out one million dollars in prize money to BellKor's Pragmatic Chaos, a seven-person team comprised of mathematicians and computer engineers whose members hailed from the United States, Austria, Canada, and Israel. They produced software 10 percent better at predicting which movies customers would like based on past preferences than Netflix on its own had. Entire businesses have sprouted up based on the concept. ChallengePost allows organizations, including government, to challenge the public to solve big problems through competitions. On Kickstarter, artists, musicians, filmmakers, and entrepreneurs crowdsource funding. Kaggle's community of scientists and engineers—some professional, others capable hobbyists—compete for money to solve vexing scientific problems like predicting the outcome of the World Cup, the likelihood that Allstate would have to pay for bodily injury in the event of a crash, how much shoppers will spend at a grocery store, the progression of HIV in patients, and the location of dark matter in the universe. The contests with the most commercial impact are invite-only, and Kaggle doesn't disclose who sponsors them or what research questions they have posed.

Waze is a smart phone map app that alerts drivers to the latest traffic tie-ups by soliciting up-to-the-minute information from other users. Mechanical Turk crowdsources microtasks. Even news is being crowdsourced: the *Guardian* crowdsourced the expense reports of British politicians. The *Washington Post*, *New York Times*, and others asked readers to scour an ennui-inducing trove of Sarah Palin e-mails written when she was Alaska governor, and *Gawker* looked for help in deciphering financial statements that purportedly came from Mitt Romney when he was running for president. CNN and other news media harvest tweets and Facebook posts for on-the-ground eyewitness accounts from places reporters can't be and ask viewers to submit user-generated content such as photos and video. Crowdsourcing has even spread to law enforcement. The FBI crowdsourced cryptography in a murder investigation, requesting the public's help in deciphering two encrypted notes found in the pocket of a victim dumped in a field.

Rogers, recalling Bill Joy, founder of Sun Microsystems, who famously said, "No matter who you are, most of the smartest people work for someone else," envisioned a community around automobile design that he could learn from. Why would people come and design for him? "They design to win a prize if they get it, but they design to gain notoriety and hopefully to get a job," he says. Rogers knew less than 30 percent of car design students ultimately find work at auto companies, with the remainder finding other careers. But that didn't mean they didn't have a yen for designing cars. They were exactly the pool of talent he sought. These auto enthusiasts would join because they could work on their own inspirations. Maybe on their day job they couldn't, but at night, on weekends, and during their spare time they could. Then they could share their ideas with others, maybe even bring them to market.

When the community was thriving he would hold design contests. The incentive to play would come from sheer competition and the thirst to win. This would result in participants trying to outdo one another with better designs. Not everyone would participate, of course. Some would be content to just offer feedback, and they would receive credit in the community for their input. This, too, in a sense, derived from competition, because don't we all want to be recognized as particularly astute by our peers? But there would be a spirit of teamwork, of people congregating because of a shared passion for automotive design. Those who didn't enter the competitions would be just as valuable as those who did. They would offer know-how, suggestions, and feedback on designs, and act as members of a vast focus group.

Rogers set up shop in a three-thousand-square foot microfactory in an industrial park in Wareham, Massachusetts, down the street from Factory Five Racing. When the community grew to thirty-five thousand members exchanging designs and ideas on the Local Motors Web site, and there were six thousand designs to choose from, Rogers sat down at a table with his small team—which included a couple of engineers, his chief technology officer, and a few others—to discuss what the company's first car would be. With so many designs, all covered by creative commons licenses, each had an opinion. At one point they coalesced around an ecofriendly commuter car for city dwellers, but Rogers nixed it.

"Here's the deal," he told them. "It's going to be large, it's going to be lightweight, and it's going to be cool looking. That's all I know. It can be any kind of car you want to make but this one's out." Of all the designs they liked only one met this criteria.

The designer, Sangho Kim, a thirty-year-old graphic arts student at the Art Center College of Design in Pasadena, California, had modeled his illustrations on the P-51 Mustang fighter plane, a staple of World War II and the Korean War. It proved a popular choice among community members, who proffered secondary features and components such as a light bar and side vents. It was designated a kit car so buyers would be required to come to the factory premises to assemble the car under the watchful eye of Local Motors engineers. That way Rogers was able to skirt federal and state regulations like equipping his car with expensive air bags.

While the community crafted the exterior, Local Motors designed or selected the chassis, engine, and transmission. This combination—have the pros handle the elements that are critical to performance, safety, and manufacturability while the community designs the parts that give the car its shape and style—allows crowd sourcing to work even for a product whose use has life-and-death implications.

Rogers' engineers built the vehicle, and when the souped-up off-road Rally Fighter (sticker price then seventy-nine thousand dollars; now closer to a hundred thousand dollars) rolled off the assembly line in late 2010, it had been forged from parts cobbled together from Chevy, BMW, and a host of other automotive companies. A reviewer from *Popular Mechanics* took it for a spin and completed an off-road course in less than half the time a standard four-by-four could do it. He raved about the Rally Fighter with its "daddy-longlegs suspension," comparing it favorably to a Lotus; *Jalopnik*, the auto blog, called it the "coolest looking car ever." *The Car Throttle* blog calls it "the most badass car you've never heard of."

Rogers takes me out to the factory floor. "I could spend forever out here," he says, pointing to a first-generation Rally Fighter. "It has all kinds of crowdsource-based decisions in it. Many are right; some are not. The only way you learn what works and what doesn't is by building a car and getting it out there."

He was echoing Lean Startup methodology, first conceived by entrepreneur Eric Ries (author of a bestselling book). A core feature is "the build-measure-learn feedback loop." This requires developing a "minimum viable product" (MVP), quickly getting it out to market, then adjusting it on the fly once feedback rolls in. Of course, as Rogers put it, it's never fun when customers call "to bitch and moan," and at the beginning of production he wondered how did he and his engineers get things so wrong. But they had created a customer feedback loop that empowered their customers to tell them what they liked and disliked about the car, and virtually every new piece of data that came in made the Rally Fighter better.

Rogers shows me a car from Local Motors' first batch, a rugged, mostly well-designed mishmash of parts. The engine is a General Motors–sourced, 6.2-liter V8 often found in a Chevrolet Corvette. The steering column and wheel are from a Ford F-Series pickup. Mercedes-Benz made the fuel tank. The side mirrors come from a Dodge Challenger, the rear tail lamps from a Honda Civic Coupe, and the door handles from a Mazda Miata. It's a brawny, muscular street-legal vehicle with knobby thirty-three-inch tires.

He flicks at the door handle. "This was a bad decision given that this is a desert racing car," he says. "Heat that up to 110 degrees outside in the Arizona heat and you'll burn your hand. But we really couldn't have known that no matter how much computer simulation we did."

Leaky windows were another issue. Stop in a storm and rain hit the domed roof, rolled down the front, slipped down the strap, and snuck inside, dripping on the driver's knee. Local Motors solved this by adding a mini gutter to redirect the water. Then there was the time Rogers took his wife and three kids on a seven-thousand-mile summer vacation drive in one of the first Rally Fighters. They arrived in Maine and his wife caught her eye on a sharp edge that held a strap on the inside of the door. "I almost took out my wife's eye," he says. "I'm not going to take out other peoples wife's eyes." This, too, changed.

After manufacturing twenty-five Rally Fighters, Rogers shut down the factory to institute two hundred changes to the vehicle. Six months later a much better car emerged. As he looks back, Rogers says, "We shouldn't have sold twenty-five and taken six months off. We should have sold five and taken two months off, and then sold another five and taken two months off again." Again, he's talking the language of lean start-up methodology. Analyze users' feedback, fix the product, try again, rinse, repeat.

He relocated the factory to Arizona in 2010 because, he says, the Rally Fighter is a desert racing car and it makes no sense to manufacture and sell microfactory-made desert racing cars in Massachusetts.

Then DARPA's Regina Dugan called.

The XC2V

Local Motors was awarded a $639,000 contract it hadn't even bid on and set to producing a drive train and chassis based on a set of specifications that DARPA would provide for what the agency was calling an "Experimental Crowd-derived Combat-support Vehicle," or XC2V. It had to be a high-speed recovery and resupply vehicle—it wouldn't be armored and wouldn't be designed for infantry. DARPA issued a challenge to the community of car buffs that frequent Local Motors' message boards: design a ground combat vehicle with the capability to medevac two people and resupply troops in combat, and offered a total of ten thousand dollars in prize money, with first place winning seventy-five hundred dollars.

In four weeks more than 600 submissions came in, of which 162 were deemed buildable by Local Motors and DARPA engineers. The crowd voted on the best design and the winner was Victor Garcia from Aubrey, Texas, who held a degree in transportation design. He exemplified the talents of Local Motors' community members. As a contract worker for Peterbilt, a truck maker in Texas, the thirty-four-year old learned his health insurance wouldn't cover his son's birth. When he heard about the seventy-five-hundred-dollar prize for first place, he jumped at it. The money would just about cover his wife's doctors' bills. A military history buff—he still has his G.I. Joe collection from childhood—he was excited about the prospect of designing a military vehicle. Garcia spent almost every spare moment that month working on his 3-D models.

In his presentation, Garcia listed several inspirations for his design. It had to be agile like a jet fighter, leopard, and race car; purposeful like a honeybee and medieval armor or reinforced exoskeleton; and aggressive (think scorpion and wolf). He called his SUV on steroids Flypmode, partly because it could be almost instantly reconfigured for combat, to carry wounded soldiers from the battlefield or through thick jungle, or to transport supplies. For such a large vehicle it was surprisingly lightweight and thin yet well protected, and offered clear sightlines for soldiers to return fire. Designed to carry four people, the vehicle's back could slide out to transport two or even three wounded soldiers. The exterior had what he called "aggressive aesthetics" to better "intimidate the enemy."

Garcia worked with Local Motors' engineers during the building phase, and they communicated with car buffs in the community, some who were competing and many others who were providing feedback. They started with the chassis to the Rally Fighter, which they modified to account for larger wheels while the one-piece fiberglass body was cut differently to account for much more glass. The seats came from MasterCraft, which makes off-road race car seats with more robust suspension. Hinges originated from the Jeep Wrangler, the axle could be found on a Ford F-150 and some F-250 pickup trucks, and General Motors manufactured the transmission. The rollers and sliders for the tailgate, which was reinforced with a cable when pulled out and had to be strong enough to carry half a ton of human cargo over rocky terrain at breakneck speed, were used on factory assembly lines.

The engineers received the design on March 15, 2011, and delivered the finished vehicle by June 20. "It was a lot of work getting the glass made, getting all of those body structures to work, fit, and function, as well as incorporating the hinges, latches, and door jambs," Daid Riha, Local Motors chief engineer, says. At a key time Victor Garcia disappeared for a few days—it turned out his house had been hit by a tornado (no one was hurt). Despite all that, two days after Garcia's son was born the Flypmode, or as Darpa called it, XC2V, was ready for the road.

The XC2V was unveiled in June 2011 at Carnegie Mellon University's National Robotics Center in Pittsburgh, Pennsylvania. President Obama hailed it as a way to get products "out to theater faster, which could save lives more quickly," and said the technology would transfer faster to the private sector. "It's good for American companies," the president said. "It's good for American jobs. It's good for taxpayers. And it may save some lives in places like Afghanistan for our soldiers."

For Garcia, though, the best part of the ceremony was hitching a ride in his own creation. The vehicle, with its Corvette engine, was so powerful it practically lifted off the ground. "It's one thing to look at drawings," he says, "but to feel it, to experience it, was just awesome." His newfound notoriety also helped him wrangle a job out of it. Peterbilt, the truck manufacturer, promoted Garcia from contract worker to full-time senior designer with health benefits.

The XC2V had passed its first test. Dugan proposed to roll out this ambitious, more open process across DARPA to improve weapons systems, train soldiers, and even change the way the military does business. But then she left the agency for Google, where she is a senior engineer. Time will tell if the agency builds on her work or continues to conduct business as usual.

By the beginning of 2013 Local Motors has manufactured and sold more than a hundred Rally Fighters and its community participated in dozens of company-sponsored design competitions offering prize money. On The Forge, which is the name of Local Motors' community Web site, there was the BMW urban driving challenge, Domino's ultimate pizza delivery truck competition, and the Peterbilt truck design battle. There were competitions for motorcycles—the winner was built by DP Customs, a motorcycle maker from nearby Fall River, Arizona—a foldable three-wheeled bicycle with electric motor, custom car skins, and door handles. Shell Oil has sponsored "game changer" competitions for fuel-efficient cars designed for various cities around the world, including Amsterdam, Bangalore, Houston, and Sao Paolo. The community has created designs for vehicles to transport hunters in Texas and another for braving Alaskan blizzards. Reebok sponsored a contest for a new kind of shoe.

Designs for vehicles, at least, have the potential to end up as the next car that Local Motors produces, after the two hundredth Rally Fighter rolls out of the factory. But Rogers doesn't intend to stop there. He wants to help users who have designs they're passionate about build their dream cars from scratch at a Local Motors microfactory. Rogers would rent them the space and provide tools and engineering assistance, if needed. He even has a tag line: "Empowering a World of Auto Makers."

It's a long way off, he admits, the power to completely democratize the design, creation and sales of cars. But you can't change the world if you don't dream big.

CHAPTER 5

ANYONE CAN BE AN INVENTOR

On most Thursdays Ben Kaufman, the twentysomething founder and CEO of Quirky, a New York City industrial design firm (or, as he prefers, "a social product development company"), channels his inner game show host. That's when the office, located in a former factory hugging the western edge of Manhattan, is transformed into a makeshift theater with Kaufman acting as master of ceremonies. On this particular early June evening, forty Quirky-ites sit in rows of folding chairs situated on old wooden floors, facing a dais holding Kaufman and a handful of designers. Behind them is a projection screen. Out of the thousands of product ideas submitted to Quirky that week they're debating the top ten (as voted on by Quirky's users). Of those, Quirky will build products out of a few and sell them at major retailers and over the company's Web site, sharing the profits with the inventors and anybody who helped along the way.

Most inventions Kaufman ends up taking to market are "born in the bedroom, not the boardroom," as he is wont to say, and emerge from common, everyday struggles. Really, though, most Quirky products address a classic Seinfeldian-like question.

As in, don't you hate it when . . .

You can't get all your plugs into your surge protector?

Then there's Pivot Power, a flexible power strip that bends and folds so that large adapters fit in every outlet.

You make yourself a cup of tea at the office and the communal spoons are dirty?

Try MugStir, a set of three stainless steel teaspoons that hang on the side of a mug.

Dust balls and grit get tangled in the end of your broom?

Sample the Broom Groomer, a dustpan with rubber teeth that rakes debris from the bristles.

Cords on your desk connecting your laptop, printer, external hard drives, and phone cords become a rats' nest of cables?

Why, there's Cordies, which neatly organizes those wires.

You are preparing an egg-white omelet and try to separate an egg yolk from the white only to make a complete mess?

Check out Pluck, an easy-to-use yolk extractor that gently sucks the yolk from the liquid.

It's freezing outside, you're wearing mittens and need to make a call on your iPhone or send a text message?

Whip out Digits, mini conductive pins that attach to your gloves and let you use electronic touchscreen devices.

You get the idea.

The product ideas that are bandied about this June evening continue in this vein. One is a portable rack to dry clothes, an ecofriendly salad spinner cum serving bowl and tongs, and a tape dispenser to attach to bulk rolls. Another invention involves a Post-it Note inserted into a pen. A third is a foldable stool that can collapse completely. The wackiest idea is a facsimile of a military tank that shoots water into your garden. Perhaps the worst: a single-use combustible charcoal chimney for picnics and tailgating that entailed lighting a bag of charcoal on fire. It prompts one Quirky designer to ponder potential lawsuits. "I don't like this," he says. "It's like a Ford Pinto."

The brash, oft-profane Kaufman, perpetually in need of a shave and dressed in his usual black T-shirt and jeans, acts as if he'd guzzled a half-dozen bottles of 5-hour Energy before hitting the stage. He's not trained in design; in fact, he seems proud that he isn't trained in anything. Nevertheless he views most things through the prism of design. He doesn't consider himself a that-came-from-the-famous-designer-Angelo-Castiglioni-in-1956-and-is-part-of-his-late-works kind of guy. But if he sees something that intrigues him, he can't resist touching the material, looking at the seams, and trying to figure out how it was manufactured. And when he likes something, he *really* likes it. Weeks later I'm sitting with Kaufman in a conference room and he shows me a Web site for a relatively high-end specialty shop based in Los Angeles called KILLSPENCER, which makes men's bags, luggage, and accessories. Kaufman loves these bags so much he buys one of each new product. KILLSPENCER has his credit card on file and as soon something becomes available it's shipped to him. One of his favorites is a bag made of recycled Korean War tarp. Others have screws from World War II planes from Japan.

He keeps a lid on his own opinions, and that must be hard because he seems to have opinions on just about everything, preferring to let the group—and voting members of Quirky's community—decide which products get to the next step. For most of the people who submitted ideas, it's back to the drawing board. On the evening of the product slam, the duct tape dispenser and gargantuan toy tank are the only two to make the grade. Which doesn't necessarily mean that Quirky, after performing its due diligence, will take them to market. Then again it might, and that's the whole point. Because Kaufman's sincere wish is to make invention accessible.

"We're all born inventors," Kaufman says, "and we're put on this earth to leave it better than we came. Unfortunately this creative instinct is stripped away from us as students: read a book, take these tests, go to college." Then we go to college, get a job, buy a home, and take on a mortgage. On the job, we have to listen to whatever our bosses tell us, do what they say, pick up our paycheck, and leave. "We get stripped of all these collaborative and creative instincts and just become worker bees."

With Quirky, he aims to change all that. By layering game mechanics into its community platform and driving participation and engagement, he's well on his way. Actually, the game mechanics *are* the business model. They protect the company from risk, since ideas bubble up from below; for an idea to become a product it has to show it has market potential. Part of the reason it's so powerful is that people don't *have* to make anything. They *want* to.

All of this has resulted in an intriguing crowd-based work flow. As with Local Motors, it begins and ends with an online community populated by several hundred thousand armchair inventors—students, teachers, restaurant owners, hobbyists, firefighters, graphic artists, and the like. They guide an idea for an invention from the back-of-a-drink-stained-napkin sketch through brainstorming and testing. At that point the company's design team jumps on board and, working with the inventor, they create a 3-D-printed model to further refine the concept.

Quirky is essentially panning for gold. Any member can post an idea and if the community votes it up, the company sifts through the sand and mud to locate the few valuable nuggets. Once a prototype is conceived, Quirky records a video and, based on the cost of development, will market test the product in the community, setting a target for presales. If enough community members pledge to buy it, which helps defray the cost of development—on average, it costs about two hundred thousand dollars to take an idea from sketch to prototype, according to Kaufman—the company manufactures it in China then sells it through its online store or at large retailers such as Amazon, Bed Bath & Beyond, OfficeMax, Staples, Target, Toys "Я" Us, and a couple hundred others.

Like Local Motor's Jay Rogers, Kaufman dislikes the term "crowd sourcing" because it implies the Quirky community is smarter than the experts. He likens it more to a "push and pull" dynamic. The community feeds designs and responds to them and Quirky provides expertise to make things happen. It is, he says, "more a conversation, collaboration, or cocreation" that makes it possible for Quirky to shepherd a product to market much faster than traditional approaches. The record: 39 days from the initial sketch to being sold at Bed Bath & Beyond for a simple device you stick into a piece of fruit to siphon out the juice. The average is about 120 days.

Unlike Local Motors, which uses principles of gamification to cull ideas for how to build cars, Quirky simply could not exist without its outside creators. It's not trying to revitalize an industry and the problem it's solving doesn't lie with one invention or idea but in the process of bringing inventions to market. Several aspects drive community participation. First, there's a good possibility of cold, hard cash to motivate users not only to submit ideas for products but to "influence" others. Each member profile page is a kind of leaderboard where anyone can see how many product ideas someone has created, how much money they have earned and revenue they are partially responsible for generating, and the other products they have influenced by providing feedback or voting on, say, a color scheme, a price, a special feature. Because most of us harbor ideas for inventions.

The inventor receives a piece of the action, as does everybody who contributes, whether it's by voting, offering feedback, or achieving more substantial influence. Then they're awarded a sliver of "ownership" in the finished product and receive a kickback from each sale. If the doohickey is sold through Quirky's store, Amazon, Thinkgeek, or other partners, those who contributed share 30 percent of the revenue; if it's Target and the others, they get a 10 percent kickback. It can add up fast. In 2012, Quirky paid its community about two million dollars of its projected twenty million dollars in revenue. Perhaps equally important, their participation means that one day they can walk into a Target or Walmart, pick up a surge protector, broom, or plastic mug off the shelf, and on the back of the package read their name listed as one of the inventors.

From the company's perspective, if this large and engaged community of professional, amateur, and wannabe inventors thinks a product has legs, it probably does.

"The ideas that we see on retail shelves these days aren't the best ideas in the world," Kaufman says. "They're just the ideas that companies had the wherewithal to bring to life."

While Kaufman doesn't view the Quirky community as being gamified, it possesses similar elements to Trada, a crowdsourced paid search marketplace that did gamify its platform, leveraging "concepts pioneered by video game makers into a new construct called crowd mechanics," which it defined in a company release as "the incentive and engagement system designed to drive outcomes in a crowd through individual and group incentives that include both monetary and non-monetary rewards, levels, and achievements." A community member working as an "optimizer" in Trada-speak does what any advertiser would do on Google AdWords. He researches the client's Web site, creates a clickable banner ad, enters keywords, and creates a budget to automatically bid on placement. It can be painstaking work to find just the right strategy that will get more people clicking on these ads (what's known as conversion rate).

But Trada discovered that cash alone wasn't enough, even though a top earner at Trada could earn nine thousand dollars a month. So it layered in multiple motivation systems designed to foster competition, communication, and cooperation among its marketplace members. Its platform features:

- Points, which users earn for generating conversions at or below an advertiser's target cost;
- Levels: The higher the level, the greater a member's earnings potential;
- Grades that are calculated by looking at a member's overall performance—beating a client's targets for each click, and click-through and conversion rates;
- Leaderboards, which compare community members' performance across the platform.

On Quirky these features are disguised, but they are here nonetheless. Each member profile page shows a list of inventions, total earnings, the number of ideas submitted and a separate category of products influenced, how many ideas someone has created or "influenced," how many are in development, and the number of sales at stores. As with Twitter, Quirky community members have followers and can follow others. With this level of transparency, and the way the information is expressed on each member page as a chart, the information as a whole is similar to a leaderboard. Total earnings operate as points. The number of inventions created and influenced are akin to levels. Any Quirky community member who visits another member's page will likely feel a smidge of competition. *Look how many inventions he's created or influenced. Look at how much money he's made. Maybe I can, too.* These are subtle game mechanics, but game mechanics they are, appealing to natural motivations in us all.

Kaufman has been out of high school just seven years. Growing up on Long Island, New York, he was a "bad student, about as bad as they come," cutting class and harassing teachers, so much so that he was forced to repeat eighth grade. He says he made it his mission to push boundaries. When his school assigned each student a laptop, Kaufman repeatedly dropped his just to see how much abuse it could take. After it was duly dented and cracked he duct-taped it back together.

His precociousness paid off. At seventeen, he came up with an idea for his first invention: a pair of lanyard headphones with concealed wires so he could listen to his iPod Shuffle in class without his math teacher's finding out. He mocked up a model with ribbon and wrapping paper and asked his parents for money, which they scraped together by remortgaging their house. Kaufman's mother, Mindy, owner of a small local factory, proved to be a tough negotiator and demanded 90 percent of the founder's equity, giving her son the chance to earn back up to 50 percent of the company if and when he paid them back. Kaufman, who thus far has attracted more than a hundred million dollars in venture capital for Quirky, claims this first seed round was the hardest.

Even before graduating high school in May 2005 he had launched his new company, Mophie, which he named after his dogs Molly and Sophie. With his paper and ribbon prototype, he flew to China to locate a manufacturer. It didn't take Kaufman long to blow through much of the $185,000 his parents loaned him, which, he says, disappeared in the crowded streets of Shenzen when his engineers and the factory ran into trouble perfecting the product and manufacturing process. Finally, though, he had a workable product: retractable headphones for an iPod shuffle, which he dubbed Song Sling. After returning stateside he sold ten thousand of them before almost running out of money.

At the same time Kaufman took note of an emerging iPod user behavior. People were buying more accessories—armbands, belt clips, speaker systems, chargers—but before they could use them they had to take their iPods out of the protective cases. He decided to develop a line of iPod rechargeable cases, clips, and other accessories that would add functionality to these cases and rounded up a small amount of seed capital from some local Vermont entrepreneurs, which he spent on one final Hail Mary: booking the cheapest booth he could find at the 2006 MacWorld, the gigantic trade show dedicated to all things Apple. His booth was tiny and staffed by a skeletal crew of three, surrounded by hundred-million-dollar companies with splashy exhibits. To Kaufman's amazement, Mophie won a Best in Show award at MacWorld for his Relo series—a line of a dozen cases outfitted with FM transmitters, rechargeable batteries, and a host of other features. Back in Vermont it took several months to hustle $1.5 million in venture funding at a $1 million premoney until valuation so he had the resources to manufacture the Mophie product line.

Then it was time for another MacWorld and Kaufman knew he had to make another splash. Not long before, he had been riding New York City's subway and noticed a woman wearing a pair of headphones he had designed. Flushed with pride, he realized he was in a position to help others feel that same sense of joy and satisfaction. In a taste of what was to come with Quirky, Kaufman paid $250,000 for a bigger MacWorld booth and doled out pads and pencils bearing his company name, then invited conference attendees to help design his next line of products. He put each of these 150 product ideas for a vote on the Mophie Web site with the promise the company would produce the winning prototypes within seventy-two hours. Three concepts made it into production. One, the Bevy, ended up a popular iPod shuffle case that doubled as a key chain and bottle opener, selling tens of thousands of units in twenty-eight countries.

Soon Mophie was clearing millions in revenue. But Kaufman also experienced the pitfalls of raising venture capital when his investors, claiming he was too young and inexperienced to lead the company he had created, brought in a chief executive officer. Disillusioned, he sold Mophie for "not very much" shortly after launching the Juice Pack, the Mophie case cum charger that ended up a $120 million bestseller for the company's buyers.

Kaufman doesn't regret leaving Mophie, though. In fact, he claims he was relieved. "I didn't want to end up selling iPhone condoms the rest of my life," he says.

He couldn't get the image of the woman on the subway wearing the headphones he had designed out of his mind. It had been the "best feeling in the world," yet he realized he wasn't unique. Everyone has ideas. But the best ones don't always make it to market. Good ideas require luck, circumstance, and pedigree. That didn't seem right. He realized his true passion was figuring out how to make invention accessible to all.

So he founded Quirky, paying one hundred thousand dollars for the quirky.com domain. He didn't choose the name to describe the products the company develops. No one, after all, wants to buy a quirky refrigerator; consumers want one called Frigidaire that works and will last a long time. Instead, he says, the name is a tribute to the unconventional process of bringing inventions to market. In its first year selling products the company took in one million dollars in revenue and within three years was selling more than one million units of community-developed products that would never have existed otherwise.

At Quirky, a design with potential goes through rapid product development. First a project manager is named and responsibilities are doled out to various teams, with tasks divided into a dozen overlapping mini-projects: industrial design, mechanical engineering, materials, finishes, colors, and product naming. It's a rigorous process, even for something as chintzy as, say, a toilet brush. In this case the Quirky team conducted intense research, handing out a block of clay to Quirky employees and asking them to take an impression of the inside rim of their toilet bowls. This way they were able to calculate the precise geometry for a brush to work in almost every toilet. Then Quirky, which has a bevy of 3-D printers and laser cutters on the premises, creates prototypes until they end up with what its designers believe will be a successful product.

Once Quirky's designers decide a product is ready to demonstrate they post a video, which is really an argument for why the product should be produced. Then it's the community's turn to weigh in on price. How much would people pay for it? Based on the cost of development and the ultimate retail price, Quirky sets a threshold for how many units must be presold before it will go through with manufacturing. Throughout the process Quirky tracks, to a fraction of a percentage point, how involved in the creation of a product each community member is. The average product that Quirky brings to market involves input from a thousand people; every time one sells at Bed Bath & Beyond, Target, or through Quirky's online store, a thousand people are paid based on their contributions. In 2012 two Quirky products were awarded Red Dot Design Awards—Pivot Power and Verseur, an all-in-one wine opener. The judges wanted to commemorate the names of the inventors on a plaque. Kaufman submitted the names of everyone who'd had a hand in developing them, which amounted to a couple of thousand inventors and influencers.

Those who have scored with Quirky products are a diverse lot and an integral part Quirky's story. Take, for instance, Jake Zien, the inventor of Pivot Power. He came up with the idea for a telescoping surge protector when he was sixteen, after struggling one too many times with cramming plugs into a power strip. He threw up his hands and muttered, "Damn, I wish I could just stretch this thing and make them all fit!" then wondered how hard it could be. At the time he was attending a precollege program at the Rhode Island School of Design and created a mock-up out of modeling foam and wood. A family friend advised him to patent the concept, which would take years and cost twenty thousand dollars. He was coached to approach companies with similar products and try to sell them the intellectual property. Like, "Hey, I'm a teenager and I have a cool idea. Please don't screw me." That meant even if he succeeded in patenting the device, he would still be at the mercy of deep-pocketed corporations, which didn't sound like a recipe for success.

Then in 2010 a family friend forwarded Zien an article on Quirky from an in-flight magazine and he checked it out. A week later, while bored in class, Zien decided to post his invention. At the time, it cost ninety-nine dollars to enter a product into the Quirky contest (it's now ten dollars; the entrance fee discourages spammers). A week later the community voted his idea up and the company informed him it would work on it.

Quirky back then was a fledgling business with about a dozen products in various stages of development. One was Cordies, a cable organizer, another Click n Cook, which was a modular spatula. There was a key chain tripod for a camera and a gizmo for collecting rainwater into old water bottles. To Zien they seemed like one-shot molded plastic or silicone products. His changeable surge protector strip would be more complicated.

After Quirky's designers got ahold of Zien's idea it took on a different shape. Originally Zien had called it Telescope Power, a power strip that not only pivoted, it expanded. To simplify the concept the company decided to scrap telescoping so that each plug pivoted, which Zien agrees was a more elegant solution. It proved popular with Quirky's community, which offered feedback and voted on everything from the color scheme (white and blue) to graphics, packaging, and pricing.

Zien's face and name are on every box, which, he says, "kind of weirds me out" whenever he goes to Target. At least it's not a body hair trimmer. The time between when he submitted the idea and when it appeared on store shelves was less than a year. Zien takes in roughly 10 percent of each direct sale and 3 percent of each retail sale, and has earned more than $350,000 thus far. Pivot Power has also spawned other versions, including a mini surge protector, one in green for Christmas, and another designed for sale in European Community countries.

Another Quirky inventor is Judi Sigler, who is from a small Nebraska town. She first heard about Quirky during a blizzard while killing time, catching up on news online when she came across an article about Quirky. After she checked out the site, she thought, "Gosh, I should send in an idea." Sigler, a school counselor, was on Christmas break, and with the weather so horrible and being cooped up inside, she had ample time to become acquainted with Quirky's site. What drew her to ıys, was how easy it was. You didn't need to create a prototype ın a lawyer to file a patent application. And you could throw in ɾwo cents about other people's products.

ike Zien's, her idea was born out of frustration. Being a teacher, she d her coworkers shared a communal kitchen, and when she made tea or coffee she had to hunt around for a spoon and hope the previous user had cleaned it. Then after she used it she needed to wash it. Plastic stirrers and spoons were frowned upon because of the cost and environmental impact. Her initial idea, which she posted on Quirky, was for a bracelet that held a spoon and that could be wrapped around a favorite cup or mug, which she mocked up in clay then Photoshopped. It didn't go live right away; it was in the system for a week. "The whole time I'm thinking, 'Oh, why did I do that?' You have this kind of remorse like, 'Oh, it was silly. Why did I even do it? I should just take it down.' Then I thought, 'What do I have to lose? It's in there.'"

The next morning Sigler logged on to Quirky and found that a community member had shot and edited a video, which brought her idea to life. Members of Quirky's community offered feedback. Some of it was good, some wasn't. For example, a few members advised Sigler to create a mug with a minipropeller on the bottom to stir drinks, which she rejected as too complicated. Sigler ended up with a set of three spoons that clip to the side of a mug and posted an updated product photo. It won.

It took Quirky's designers fifteen months to bring the product to market, with community members contributing the name MugStir, color schemes, and logos. In the meantime they kept Sigler and the 503 Quirky community members who helped influence MugStir apprised of its progress through blog posts and a video taken from the factory in China where they showed off a working prototype. While MugStir has been a modest success—the company told her it plans to update it—she has two other inventions winding through Quirky's developmental product cycle, including a portable plug-in lamp that has additional outlets and a plug-in hot pot that can heat up ramen noodles or macaroni and cheese.

Altogether Sigler has made about five thousand dollars, which includes other products she's influenced, like Pivot Power. "Not enough to retire on," Sigler says, "but it's fun to get fifty dollars here and there, and I've made a number of friends through Quirky."

A third Quirky inventor is Bill Ward, whose idea came to him while he was sweeping his garage. He cut his finger on a shard of glass as he cleaned off the broom's bristles. It wasn't serious but it got him thinking. A few minutes later he figured out a solution. All he needed was a dustpan with tines to comb through the bristles and remove dust bunnies, glass, dirt, and anything else. That's when he came up with the Broom Groomer.

Ward, who operates a toy invention company and owns two restaurant/hostels in Quito, Ecuador, where he once worked as a nature guide, has been inventing things since he was thirteen, when he came up with a toothbrush to automatically spread toothpaste evenly across the bristles. In college there was the Dog Frisbee, which he cooked up on a beach while tossing the eponymous plastic disc to his Labrador. It would land and she couldn't lift it up. She would just scratch at it. So Ward retrofitted a Frisbee with a stick coming down from the bottom so it flew, landed, and tilted, which gave a pooch a way to pick it up. He licensed it but the company didn't invest in marketing and the production quality was poor. Still, Ward made a little money. He admits he's obsessed with inventing things. One of his favorite activities is browsing convenience stores searching for the perfect piece to help him complete an invention prototype—like the white enema he used to test an air-powered rocket.

Over the years Ward has conceived of hundreds of inventions, although precious few have gotten anywhere. He has no set system for generating ideas. Sometimes he'll come across a product that makes him think of other potential products. Other times he'll address a specific challenge a company has. He's found that just when he's about to give it a rest is when "something magical happens." Basically the process works like this: Ward has an idea, he writes a brief description, and discusses it with his agent. If he believes Ward has a viable idea, they figure out the best way to present it. Renderings and a working model are optimal but can be expensive.

Inventors also need a thick skin. Just before the economic crisis of 2008, he signed a license agreement with a top toy maker and received "a huge advance." The idea that one of his inventions would sit on store shelves had him "walking on clouds." There was even talk of a series of television commercials. But it was canceled. Another time he devised a concept for a new toy, built a model, tested it, and readied himself for a meeting at Fisher-Price, only to learn the product already existed. Because ideas are easy to steal, he won't describe them. All he'll say is being a professional inventor is hard, and he faces constant rejection. Convincing a toy company to create a product is at best a long shot. Inventing one that becomes a hit is as likely as winning the lottery.

But Broom Groomer wasn't a toy, and Ward wasn't sure what to do with it. On one of his trips to Quito he met with an Ecuadorian supermarket chain. His wife, who is Ecuadorian, knew somebody who knew somebody. The store executive told him the only way his broom cleaner could sell in Ecuador is if it retailed for $1.35. Ward took his hand sketches of the Broom Groomer to a local molding company, which created drawings and estimated it would cost $3 per unit to make. This, Ward knew, was a common challenge for entrepreneurs: A too-low price point and the necessity for economies of scale, which was well beyond his abilities.

Back in the States, he contacted dustpan and home goods companies, and spent months dickering over nondisclosure agreements until he was able to show his CAD drawings. Every company turned him down. Then he read about Quirky in the same in-flight magazine that Jake Zien had and decided to submit his broom-cleaning device. He had a firm he relied on for the toy industry create a video to show the Broom Groomer in action with some music, which he submitted with the CAD drawings. The first time he almost won, so he resubmitted the idea and a couple of weeks later came out on top.

During the product refinement stage Quirky designers, who gravitate toward simplicity but also try to offer separation from competing products, made some changes to Ward's initial idea. They added a step-on feature so the dustpan wouldn't move, while a Quirky community member suggested "fins" to catch the debris of a broom's bristles. Some Quirky-ites were unhappy that a pole or stick—like movie-theater dustpans—wasn't included so a user wouldn't need to stoop. In Ward's initial CAD drawing he had included a hole for just such a stick but it didn't make it into the final product.

After arriving at a retail price of $9.99 there was the matter of presales. In his case, Ward was obligated to sell 690 Broom Groomers before Quirky would put it into production, which not only would indicate a market for the product, but would bring in almost $7,000 to the company. He reached out to friends and family over Facebook and via e-mail, promising they wouldn't have to part with money unless it was made. In the end, Ward bought the last hundred Broom Groomers, which he gave away as gifts. From when he first joined Quirky to his invention hitting store shelves was less than nine months. "Fast," Ward says. "A toy takes at least a year and a half to two years." Over three years more than forty-five thousand units have been sold, generating more than $36,000, of which Ward has collected a little more than $18,000.

A sign that Quirky might have hit the big time was Ben Kaufman's appearance on *The Tonight Show with Jay Leno* in early 2013. He demonstrated several Quirky products such as Bill Ward's Broom Groomer, Jake Zien's Pivot Power ("It has more plugs than Joe Biden," Leno quipped), as well as the Stem, the company's compact fruit spritzer, the egg deyolker, and a motorcycle helmet that displays turn lights and brake signals. Kaufman also demoed a couple of Quirky products that had "bubbled up from the community" that were decidedly bad—a muzzle for quieting crying babies, for one, and something he called the Fruity Tush. On the Quirky community Web site the inventor described it as "a Men's/Women's panty liner that wraps around the back of a thong and fits in the crack of your bum."

"We get thousands of submissions a week," Kaufman said. "Not all are winners."

Leno held up the garishly patterned panties to the camera. "What is this?"

"People have gas," Kaufman said.

"Is this a fart filter?"

"It's an air freshener. Turn that thing around."

Leno showed the audience the back, where two air deodorizers hung.

"Fruity Tush is the marketing name," Kaufman riffed. "The technical term is Fart Filter."

"Guys," Leno said. "*Not* a good Valentine's Day gift."

But if Fruity Tush garners enough community support, if enough people vote and rate and comment on the idea, Kaufman promised that Quirky would make it.

It's up to the crowd.

SERIOUS PLAY

Michael Fergusson, a forty-two-year-old game designer from Vancouver, British Columbia, creates games with a serious purpose. He wants to modify human behavior.

Through his company, Ayogo, Fergusson fashions games for positive social impact, applying the behavioral psychology of games to help users manage chronic health conditions. One game he designed is *HealthSeeker*, a Facebook game Ayogo developed for the Diabetes Hands Foundation in conjunction with the Joslin Diabetes Center, which is affiliated with Harvard Medical School. The game helps people living with diabetes to habituate healthier behaviors around diet and exercise. It uses conventional techniques of social game design such as "compulsion loops" built around achievements as well as reciprocal social obligation, because a player's progress can be shared with her social network of friends on Facebook. Instead of rewarding players with greater health, which creates little motivation in most people—"if we were motivated by better health, we'd all be healthy," he says—*HealthSeeker* relies on game mechanics. The aim isn't to cure social ills like drug abuse or overcome addictions by persuading smokers to quit. It's about the little things. "We're trying to leverage what we understand about how our brains work and motivate very small actions by giving very small rewards," Fergusson says.

The game is comprised of a collection of modest missions. Grab a coffee at Starbucks but forgo milk and sugar, you receive points. Measure your insulin levels, get points. Take a walk instead of riding an escalator, more points. Each time a player successfully completes a mission, which occurs outside the game but has real-life consequences, she's rewarded with a squirt of dopamine. The game then becomes its own reward. "You could take all the health aspects out of the game and replace it with watering plants," Fergusson says, "and it would operate the same way."

Players seem to not only like *HealthSeeker*, they appreciate the health benefits—exactly what Fergusson was aiming for. Lea Bakalyar, a stay-at-home mom from Atkinson, New Hampshire, says it helped her make incremental changes that taken together have had a big impact, like modifying how she serves food to her family. Instead of putting the whole meal on the table she now offers portioned plates from the stove. "It has helped take away the feeling of 'If it's in front of me, I'll eat it,'" she says. Tanya Ortiz, a homemaker from Queens, New York, with Type II diabetes and high blood pressure, likes the social-networking component, which creates "a comforting atmosphere with people who share similar dilemmas."

Fergusson designed *HealthSeeker* with two main objectives in mind. He offered instant-gratification rewards for healthy activity and he made those instant-gratification rewards something that players could use to share with and influence the healthy behavior of others. When you see that your friend has scored more points than you, and undertaken more missions, you may want to alter your behavior to catch up. "Our premise is that these two compulsion loops, one of pattern completion, and one of reciprocal social obligation, would reinforce each other and make our game more effective in producing action," he says. Meanwhile another game, *The Great Race*, is a mobile scavenger hunt for kids, who solve clues that lead them through a five-mile course, which promotes exercise while showing them the various parks and public spaces their respective cities offers. And in the *I ❤ Jellyfish* game players navigate a dangerous aquatic world while they're taught how to regulate their heartbeat. The faster a player's heartbeat, the more his avatar glows.

Naturally, serious games—defined simply as games designed to have a purpose beyond simple entertainment—aren't just for health. They've also been seeping into education, contributing to science by helping biologists learn more about proteins and RNA, and assisting astronomers in charting new stars and solar systems. Games have been developed to aid in city planning and assist in emergency management response. The military uses games extensively to recruit and train soldiers. Lockheed Martin reports that in 2012 it trained twenty-two thousand military commanders and support staff with *Warfighters' Simulation* (or *WarSim*) in a fourteen-war game exercise, and, as we saw in a previous chapter, DARPA has been experimenting with them to foster crowd sourcing. *Peacemaker* is a commercial game designed around the Israeli-Palestinian conflict, promoting greater understanding between the warring sides. The United Nations sponsored a humanitarian game called *Food Force*, which involves delivering emergency supplies by air and truck in rebel-held crisis zones. Students in Europe and the United States can assume the responsibilities of a prime minister or president when they play *Democracy* in school, introducing policies that affect the economy and foreign policy, and confronting crises in crime and homelessness while trying to satisfy competing political factions.

All of these are examples of simulations, which are roughly defined as the imitation of real-world events in a virtual space, and they have become part and parcel of training. More than a thousand colleges and universities assign students an IBM "sim" called Innov8 to practice running virtual businesses. Etcetera Edutainment in Pittsburgh sells a line of game-based learning products to teach everything from safe practices for electricians—make a mistake and your avatar gets toasted—to avoiding sprains and strains, slips, trips, and falls in factories, to properly using a dialysis machine. Simulations have also become staples in medicine, not only in training but in surgery.

In this section we'll look at serious play phenomena such as "edutainment," when learning is offered within the rubric of games. I'll talk about the ways I've layered games into graduate courses I teach at New York University—not for fun, but to promote learning—and look at ways that game mechanics are being unleashed in high school classes. We'll visit a clinic in Virginia where patients rehabilitate severe injuries with the help of the Nintendo Wii. We'll look at simulations in medical training, where advanced robotics have been embedded in mannequins to improve learning, and the use of simulators in an actual operating room on a patient undergoing surgery.

"Fun is functional," Fergusson says. "We learn better, socialize better, work more productively, and gain greater satisfaction from work that [derives from] play, and there are so many opportunities to use this to make the world a better place."

CHAPTER 6

THAT'S EDUTAINMENT!

One day in the fall of 2011 I decided to experiment by layering game mechanics into one of my journalism courses—a rigorous six-hour writing and reporting class that meets once a week and works on the fundamentals of hard news and deadline reporting, with a business focus, for newspapers, wire services, and online news. Over a fourteen-week semester students undertake more than twenty assignments, plus they work on a class publication, taking turns as editors, and keeping track of the site's metrics and participating in social media.

It's a tough class, the linchpin of the Business and Economic Reporting program at New York University, a challenging three-semester graduate program that leads to a master's in journalism. Students take half their courses at the Stern School of Business, where they are thrown in with hypercompetitive MBA students, and the other half in journalism. More than 90 percent of our students land jobs in journalism, often at major news organizations—the *Wall Street Journal*, *Forbes*, CNN, Bloomberg, Dow Jones, Reuters, Business Insider, *PandoDaily*, *TechCrunch*, and many other places.

As any teacher will tell you, it can be difficult to engage students for an entire semester, especially in a class with such a big course load. Burnout, in the past, has been a problem. After one particularly brutal semester, I decided to make a change, and as I started researching this book I figured the classroom would be an ideal testing ground for introducing game elements into the curriculum. What are grades in school but a kind of game anyway? And no less an authority than the Federation of American Scientists has endorsed video games as a potential means for teaching "higher-order thinking skills, such as strategic thinking, interpretive analysis, problem solving, plan formulation and execution, and adaptation to rapid change."

I wasn't dumbing down the course for the millennial generation. Indeed, there's evidence to support the use of game elements in education. A growing number of academics, led by James Paul Gee at Arizona State University, believe that gaming can drive problem-based learning, in which students develop skills as they work collaboratively to confront challenges. Gee is quick to point out that he's not advocating for the likes of *Call of Duty* in the classroom.

"The problem is that our schools are focused on relating facts and how well students retain this info," Gee says. "Teachers are teaching to the test."

When Gee began playing video games seven years ago, he was struck by the fact that games are often long and demanding—not nearly as dumb as stereotyped—yet designed to be so intuitive that no manual is ever needed. You learn by playing. That's precisely what students at Quest to Learn, a public school for sixth to twelfth graders in Manhattan, are doing. The school bases its entire pedagogy on game design. It seeks to have children assume the roles of truth seekers—explorers and evolutionary biologists, historians, writers, and mathematicians—and engage in problem solving. There are no grades. Students are rated "novice," "apprentice," up to "master." A class might be devoted to engaging in a multiplayer game and working in teams to defeat hostile aliens or becoming immersed in a "sim" game and running an entire city. The kids even code their own games, which involves math, English, computer science, and art.

In Singapore, China, and Finland, where children do better in math and science than in America, problem solving is the key to learning. In America, we take the opposite approach. We teach math as a theory, then throw in problem sets as homework to reinforce what students have learned. The schools are in essence teaching the manual without exposing children to the game. Gee reasons that kids would learn more if they had to confront challenges that required them to use hard skills. Indeed, the 2006 Summit on Educational Games by the Federation of American Scientists found that students recall just 10 percent of what they read and 20 percent of what they hear. If there are visuals accompanying an oral presentation, the number rises to 30 percent, and if they observe someone carrying out an action while explaining it, 50 percent. But students remember 90 percent "if they do the job themselves, even if only as a simulation."

This reminded me of perhaps the best educational experience I had attending public school, which happened all the way back in fifth grade. My teacher, Gary Crew from Elmsford, New York's Alice E. Grady grammar school, had created a self-paced history curriculum. As twelve-year-olds we covered European history from Christopher Columbus through the beginning of the nineteenth century. To this day, decades later, I remember much of what I learned about Columbus; the conquistadors, including Hernando Cortés and Francisco Pizarro and the terror they wrought on the Aztecs and Incas; Vasco Núñez de Balboa, who "discovered" the Pacific Ocean; Bartholomeu Dias, the Portuguese explorer who was first to sail around the tip of Africa; the Dutch East India Company and its chokehold on trade; the Lewis and Clark expedition; and much, much more. I can't say that for any other history class I have ever taken.

The difference wasn't what we learned. It was how we learned it. Because we had the option of teaming up with a friend, I worked with a classmate, who became as obsessed as I was. Today this type of pedagogy is referred to as social teaching, but back then I don't think there was a name for it. All I knew was that we weren't forced to sit down with old, moldy textbooks. Instead we read a chapter out of a book on, say, Cortés, and then took a multiple-choice exam to gauge our comprehension. If we earned 80 percent or higher, we leveled up to the next assignment, which might mean listening to an audiocassette of a brief lecture on mercantilism that Mr. Crew had taped, heading to the library to locate books on Pizarro, or reviewing an atlas reflecting the European sense of the world in the sixteenth century to plot out explorers' journeys.

Every class meant exposure to a different medium and a different way of learning. In a sense, it was visual storytelling expressed as a treasure hunt that lasted an entire school year. And it wasn't simply our thirst for knowledge that drove us. We were competing with each other. I didn't want to slow my friend down by not scoring high enough on the plethora of exams we took and he felt the same. That meant being prepared and truly absorbing the material. But we were also competing against others in the class. There was a spiritual reward in being ahead of everyone else, so every time we worked on history, we focused. Best of all, it was fun. Three and a half decades later I wanted to bring this kind of approach, in a limited way, to my journalism class. So I contacted a local tour guide company in New York City called Stray Boots to see if it would help me out with a Wall Street treasure hunt, in which students learned the history of the area by playing a walking game.

In the second week of the semester I met my fifteen students in front of Manhattan's Trinity Church, just a few blocks from Ground Zero. I divided them into three teams of five, and each chose a leader to operate a smart phone to receive each question. The students padded around lower Manhattan, collectively trying to answer questions, which ranged from how many floors below street level are the gold vaults of the New York Federal Reserve Bank (five) to the color of the World Financial Center's roof (green) to who is buried in a particular pew in Trinity Church (Alexander Hamilton). They had to furnish their answers before receiving the next question. It took each group about an hour to answer fifteen of them. The following week I gave students a written test. I wanted to find out what they would better recall: the answers to ten questions from the treasure hunt from a week earlier, or a short reading passage (about 450 words that I cobbled together and distilled from Wikipedia) on the history of Wall Street, which they read twice in the span of four minutes. Then I took away the piece of paper.

The results, albeit unscientific, were nevertheless notable. Collectively, my fifteen grad students correctly answered 77 out of 150 questions (or 51.3 percent) from the reading passage but for the treasure hunt they got 89 of 150 right (or 59.3 percent). In other words, students had higher recall of a game they had played a week earlier than the short passage they read a few minutes earlier. Sure, 8 percent isn't a huge difference, but I think it's significant.

More striking, the students who operated the smart phones did the best on the treasure hunt questions. One student got ten out of ten on the treasure hunt but only six right on the reading passage; another answered seven correctly on the Wall Street game but only two right on the passage; the third did equally well on both tests. The people most engaged in the game had the highest retention rates.

Avi Millman, the twenty-eight-year-old cofounder of Stray Boots, told me he wasn't surprised. A former math teacher of his used Stray Boots to help her design a mathematics walk. In one instance she took a group of middle-school students around Greenwich Village and had them, for example, measure the Washington Square Arch's area in square feet. She also found that students were more engaged and seemed to enjoy learning more.

A Princeton graduate, Millman came up with the idea of gamified walking tours in the summer of 2008 while visiting Rome. Like many travelers he relied on a drab guidebook but realized an interactive tour would be much more fun. Today Stray Boots charges twelve dollars for gamified walking tours in ten cities, including New York, Philadelphia, San Francisco, and a tour of Portland, Oregon's microbreweries. Millman and his cofounder, Scott Knackmuhs, initially bootstrapped the company and relied on some family money. Now headquartered in a one-room office in downtown Brooklyn with five employees paid "ramen noodle low salaries," it's profitable, and in November 2012 announced a series-A round of two million dollars.

Of course, my little test that Stray Boots helped me concoct is by no means scientific, but it does show promise for serious games. Sebastian Thrun, founder of Udacity, a company that offers interactive classes, takes this further. He views traditional methods of teaching with its reliance on lectures and fourteen-week semesters as relics of a bygone era. Instead he points to video games and Twitter as ideal models. Children are shaped by their environment and culture and learn quickly through the mechanics of video games while also gravitating toward smaller and smaller "slices," as with Twitter and its 140-character limit. He wants to make video games the core of education, where students go at their own pace and bite off smaller chunks of knowledge, which would, he says, "transform the medium."

GameDesk, a Los Angeles–based educational nonprofit founded by Lucien Vattel, has already been doing this. It has been building "the classroom of the future" at a high school for at-risk students. Supported by $3.8 million from AT&T, as well as donations from the

Gates Foundation, Motorola, and Samsung, GameDesk, which touts Bill Nye the Science Guy as a board member, designs games to teach students subjects like geoscience, math, and physics.

Aero, a game Vattel and his team developed, focuses on aerodynamics and the physics of flight. Students strap on wings made of fabric and repurposed Wii controllers and soar through the sky, watching their activities on a large screen. When kids take off the first thing they notice is they start drifting down to the ground. This introduces the gravity factor. Then they fly through various different hoops and notice that no matter how they fly—straight up, down, or do loop-the-loops—gravity always pushes them toward the center of the earth. A student can also transform the air into thousands of tiny marbles that represent invisible molecules dancing around the plane. They express the interaction of the wings and various mechanics as they respond in space to forces of gravity, lift, thrust, and drag.

With another game, *MathMaker*, underwritten by Motorola, students design their own games and in the process of tapping into their creativity learn core mathematical concepts such as factoring, fractions, parabolas, linear and quadratic equations, and ratios. According to Vattel, 80 percent of students at a school where less than two-thirds ultimately graduate increased their math scores an average of 22 percent during the program.

"The best way to learn that is not by reading a stale paragraph or looking at a still 2-D image with a diagram," Vattel says.

Lee Sheldon, codirector of the Games and Simulation Arts program at Rensselaer Polytechnic Institute, has created courses that double as multiplayer games. In one he conducted at the University of Indiana, he instructed students to choose avatars and join "guilds" comprised of six or seven members. Sheldon divided class time among "fighting monsters" in the form of quizzes and exams, "completing quests" such as presentations or research, and "crafting" game analysis papers and video game concept documents. In the first week students began their semester-long journey as "Level One" avatars and leveled up as they amassed points. Just showing up to class earned one 10 points. The student received 50 points for writing a game proposal and 25 for presenting it to the class. Acting as a "guild leader" added 100 points. Completing the midterm exam, which entailed defeating a "Midlevel Boss," was worth 400 points. Sheldon based final grades on students' total tallies. A grade of C took 1,460 points, a B 1,660, and an A 1,860. Since turning his courses on games into actual games, Sheldon reports that students are more engaged, get more out of classes, and are far more likely to show up.

A course on games seems a natural fit for a semester-long game, but what about other disciplines? In his book *The Multiplayer Classroom: Designing Coursework as a Game*, Sheldon shares examples of teachers in other disciplines—biology, computer science, education, history, and math—who have layered games into coursework. Denishia Buchanan, a biology teacher at a school in Arkansas where the families of 80 percent of her students live below the poverty line, created a multiplayer classroom, fueled in part by virtual currency that students earn for completing "quests," after reading about Sheldon in the *Chronicle of Higher Education*. "Questing," Buchanan concluded, increases student motivation, attitude, and performance. "Students in my classroom are doing three times the amount of work that students completed in previous years," she says, "and they are doing it with joy and without complaint."

But not everyone is convinced that turning education into a game is for the best. "Who said education is supposed to be fun and not hard work?" says Alexander Galloway, a media, culture, and communication professor at New York University. "At some point, you have to buckle down and memorize facts."

He's right about that. I certainly wasn't going to jettison my syllabus and create a completely game-based approach to journalism. I could just imagine the expressions on the faces of hard-boiled master's candidates if I were to suddenly tell them they had to choose an avatar, go on quests, and slay monsters. If I inundated students with games, would they tune them out like, say, banner ads on the Internet? Would they grow wise to this manipulation and walk away?

"If you follow human desire and trigger dopamine response, everyone eats Twinkies all day," Galloway says.

Library Treasure Hunt

The success of my Stray Boots experiment emboldened me to try another later that same semester, this one designed for library research. I make it a rule to push my students to conduct face-to-face and/or phone interviews with living, breathing humans (I require a minimum of two sources per story, and assign at least one a week) and invite a research librarian to class to run a seminar on research databases. In addition, students cover live events, go into the field to conduct reporting, and file stories on tight deadlines, and every semester I organize a press conference with an economist from the Conference Board, a private think tank. But I also want them to become experts at pulling up information quickly over the Web.

To teach them how, I have students conduct an in-class research exercise to underscore the wealth of information available to an enterprising reporter. Students have half an hour to pull up as much data as possible on a public figure. I usually assign the former CEO of Experian, the credit report company, because of a comment he once made. He was complaining about the government requiring credit companies like his to provide consumers one free report a year to check for inaccuracies and monitor for fraud. He called the legislation "unconstitutional" and said giving away reports was not "the American way." Here's a man whose company's primary function is to amass and traffic personal information, and he was miffed a consumer had a right to see what was in it without being charged?

I wondered what kind of information about him resided online. Lots, it turns out. My students learn all sorts of things about the man. His work history (including salary, bonuses, and stock transactions), the boards he serves on, home address, value of the property, blueprints, and much more. Since his home is not far from Experian headquarters someone could, if he wanted, plot the best route to work, or use Google Earth for a birds'-eye view of his land.

Nevertheless, one challenge facing journalism educators in this age of instant-access Internet is prodding students to leave the warm glow of their computer screens to conduct primary-source research. It seems if they can't find something through Google it doesn't exist. I'd be remiss if I didn't expose them to research beyond the Web.

This led me to team up with Alexa Pearce, a research librarian at New York University's Bobst Library who works with the Arthur L. Carter Journalism Institute, to create a mobile, interactive treasure hunt. The idea behind the hunt was to send my graduate journalism students scurrying into parts of the library where they'd never set foot before, seeking bits of information that couldn't be located online. In the process students would learn something about Bobst Library and its vast storehouse of knowledge—its 2.5 million books in open stacks, 500,000 government documents, and 80,000 audio and video recordings.

For the first seven years I taught at NYU, I assigned an in-class research test (the precursor to this interactive treasure hunt) that required students to answer ten questions without using the Internet. The test was not easy. Over the years I've posed questions such as: "How many nations are represented by the combined student body of New York City's public schools?" (150.) "How many languages are spoken in New York City's five boroughs?" (Anywhere from 180 to 200, depending on how you define a language versus a dialect.) And "What is the most popular T-shirt sold at NYU's bookstore?" (Champion gray T-Shirt with NYU written in blue.) I've also asked what kind of reddish stone makes up Bobst Library's facade (sandstone), the number of New York City council members (fifty-one), vice presidents who died in office (seven), and the number of countries represented in the summer Olympics (around two hundred, depending on the year). For each answer students were required to provide an unimpeachable source, either a person (with contact information) or a bibliographic citation for a book or periodical.

At the beginning it was relatively easy to create questions whose answers weren't online, but starting around 2005 the rate of information migrating to the Web picked up considerably. It also became more common for the people my students called for answers to point them to Web sites. Then there were the complaints. The third year in a row I asked for the value of Columbia University's endowment ($7.8 billion, give or take), an administrator, irked with fielding their queries, yelled at several students. After that I limited the scope to information sitting in the library. But I figured a treasure hunt would be more fun, and threw in an incentive: I informed the class that students with the top three scores could redeem their points for the right to buy their way out of a future assignment. This proved a popular motivator.

On a Tuesday morning in winter my students congregated in Bobst's cavernous atrium. All of them were required to carry a smart phone with a preloaded QR code reader app. Alexa Pearce, a Bobst research librarian who helped me concoct questions for the test, had customized fifteen different tests because we didn't want a horde of students inundating the same location at once and hoped to make cheating if not impossible at least very difficult. The test was composed of nine questions, each worth 1,000 points, and if a student requested help or a hint it would cost 250 points. They had three hours to complete it.

Students were given just one question to start. We had designed the game so they had to level up to advance. In other words, the only way to get to the next question was by answering the current one correctly. This way there was no looking ahead, which kept the mystery intact. For example, the first question could require a student to wade into the stacks to find a volume associated with a specific call number. When she found the book, there could be a note inside with the next clue instructing her to go to page 28 and locate the second word that starts with a "C." The word could be "concomitant" and the student might have to find it in the *Oxford English Dictionary* and identify its first recorded use, then e-mail the answer to Alexa. She then replied immediately with the next clue.

We also threw in acrostics so students had to unscramble a set of letters leading to a specific periodical (say, the *New Yorker*), then have them consult the *Readers Guide to Periodical Literature* to find the right microfilm, which they would have to scan. When they came upon the article they were seeking they might have to create a PDF and e-mail it to Pearce, who would send back the next clue, which might entail listening to a speech by Amelia Earhart or Franklin Delano Roosevelt and filling in the blank to a phrase three minutes into the speech. Or perhaps they had to venture into a special collection of rare cookbooks and snap a photo of a recipe to text to Pearce, who would text back the next clue that could lead to a QR code hidden in the stacks, which might instruct them to head to the lower level of the library, where I was waiting with coffee, doughnuts, and another clue.

Over the years, scores on my research tests have varied quite a bit, and the students have, truth be told, expressed a sense of dread about them. On this particular Bobst Library Research Treasure Hunt, three students earned perfect scores—and gladly collected their free passes on a future assignment—while most of the others lost points by buying hints or making careless mistakes. One student, for instance, lost a hundred points because she located a book based on its citation but chose the wrong word to look up in the *Oxford English Dictionary*.

Still, as a class, the scores were higher than they ever were for the static research tests I used to give. Subsequent classes have also excelled, with students telling me how much they enjoy the interactive element.

I imagine students could glean all this from a tour of the library, but that's a passive way to learn and they likely would retain little. By adopting elements of game design, suddenly a challenging exam becomes edutainment. And you can discern from the questions it is by no means dumbed down: it's a rigorous exam, but one in which the students have fun, gain knowledge, develop a greater appreciation for what Bobst Library has to offer, and tend to retain what they've learned.

And there's no app for that.

CHAPTER 7

Wii-HAB

Mary Clark liked to exercise by walking the hills near her home in Arlington, Virginia. A naturally competitive person, she would try to beat anybody she encountered on her route to the top. As she entered her sixties she began to notice pain in her left Achilles tendon. It started as a pinch that slowly but progressively got worse. She saw a podiatrist, who fit her with orthotics, assigned her some exercises, and told her to take it easy. This didn't help and eventually she found that she couldn't stand for more than five minutes before the pain became unbearable.

Clark is the director of instrumental music at a church in Bethesda, Maryland. She also sings in the choir and performs with hand bells. In rehearsals she could sit, but during performances had to stand, and this was excruciating. Clark returned to her podiatrist, who put her in a boot up to her knee, which she kept on for an entire year. Still, the pain, which she says ranged from a five to an eight on the pain scale, didn't go away. Discouraged, she set up an appointment with Dr. Steven Neufeld, an orthopedic surgeon at the Orthopaedic Foot and Ankle Center in Fall Church, Virginia, who specializes in surgeries on the foot and ankle, performing between seven hundred and eight hundred of them each year.

After examining her, Neufeld told Clark that her Achilles tendon was so badly damaged he advised replacing it. The big, wide Achilles tendon is the strongest tendon and muscle in the leg, but he could swap it out with the flexor hallucis longus tendon from her big toe, which sits right behind the Achilles. By moving it to where the tendon inserts onto the heel bone, it could be retrained and strengthened through physical therapy, and she wouldn't lose range and motion in her big toe because she, like all of us, is blessed with an extra tendon called the flexor hallucis brevis that can adapt to take on the extra responsibility.

When Neufeld performed the surgery in March 2010 he found that 75 percent of Clark's Achilles had been damaged. Over the years she had suffered numerous tears that caused bleeding and built up scar tissue that had to be scraped away. While replacing her Achilles he also removed a bone spur on her heel.

After six weeks in a cast and not being able to put any weight on her foot, Clark was fitted with a boot and started rehabilitation. The goal of her rehab was to strengthen the muscles and retrain her tendons to perform different functions. Within the ligaments and tendons there are little nerve fibers called proprioception responsible for sensing the foot in space and helping the body react to particular stresses. If the foot hits the ground at a certain angle, there's a little nerve fiber that hits the floor and tells the brain, *Okay, the foot is hitting the floor at a certain position. I need to tell the tendon or ligament or muscle on the other side of the foot to act appropriately.* Physical therapy and rehabilitation are key because the tendon has to be trained to fire differently, and that involves timing and altered reflexes. The usual recovery time is about a year, but rehab starts shortly after the operation so muscles don't have a chance to atrophy. By getting patients up and moving quicker and sooner, the muscles get bigger, the tendons get trained faster and become less likely to tear again down the road.

In recent years, the physical therapists at the Foot and Ankle Center have been supplementing rehabilitation with games from the Nintendo Wii—and they aren't the only ones. Since its 2006 release, Nintendo's Wii has become a staple in rehabilitation, so much so it's been dubbed "Wiihabilitation" or "Wii-hab." A growing number of clinics around the country have adopted the Wii for rehabilitation. Patients like Clark recovering from surgery or who have suffered strokes, paralysis from workplace accidents, torn rotator cuffs, or broken bones, and soldiers returning from Iraq and Afghanistan with combat injuries have used the motion-sensitive controller to control animated characters on a screen. This way grueling rehabilitative exercise becomes a game, a competition (if it involves playing against another person) so engrossing that patients almost forget they are exercising. And because they earn points, they can chart their progress.

It's not just private clinics that have been experimenting with video-game controller systems. Wakemed, an 870-bed hospital in Raleigh, North Carolina, has been using it as a physical therapy tool to help patients redevelop the coordination they lost, while the Hines Veterans Affairs Hospital in Chicago uses the Wii in its spinal cord injury unit. Before it closed, Walter Reed Army Medical Center prescribed the Wii to soldiers injured in Iraq during combat, a group that grew up playing video games.

Hector Romero, an occupational therapist, told *Soldiers* magazine, "When the body is hurt, it tries to stop movement because all it wants to do is heal. With the Wii, patients overcome their fears and the body's reaction to movement. It is a positive distraction, and is extremely effective in improving dexterity and eliciting an increased range of motion."

He and other therapists employed by the military have experimented with techniques to make Wii-hab even more productive as patients got stronger and more agile: for example, strapping weights around wrists and elbows to further challenge certain muscle groups. One of Romero's patients, SPC Matt Bell, who was shot in the clavicle by a sniper in Iraq and suffered nerve damage to his shoulder and left hand, was quoted in the same article: "I might notice the pain in the first minute. But then I get into the game, and I totally forget about it. Then it just becomes fun, and I just try to focus on the game."

While anecdotal evidence in support of the Wii as a rehabilitative device abounds, Nintendo does not market it for this purpose, and there are few formal studies. One, carried out by the Stroke Outcomes Research Unit at St. Michael's Hospital in Toronto, found improvement in eleven stroke victims with weakness in their arms after two weeks of playing Wii games, while eleven other stroke patients who played card or block games experienced no change in arm strength. A second looked at a thirteen-year-old boy with spastic diplegic cerebral palsy who played Wii sports games such as boxing, golf, and tennis over eleven training sessions of sixty to ninety minutes. The researchers found improvements in the boy's mobility, postural control, and visual perception. A Medical College of Georgia study indicated that the Wii could help treat symptoms of Parkinson's. Researchers at Elon University in North Carolina carried out a study on eleven elderly patients and found that Wii Fit dramatically helped improve their balance. A nursing researcher from Michigan State University College of Nursing, with the help of a $379,741 grant from the National Cancer Institute, has created a program that involves Wii-based walking and balance activities for patients recovering from cancer.

Orthopaedic Foot and Ankle Center physical therapist Matthew Bernier introduced the Wii to the clinic after catching a demonstration at a conference. He was intrigued because there are balance trainers on the market that cost ten or fifteen thousand dollars, which was out of his price range. Yet the Wii Fit came with a complete set of games and a balance board and ran, with a television to play them on, around a thousand dollars. He identified several games he was sure would translate well to physical therapy of the foot and ankle. "A lot of the Wii stuff that we do is balancing and proprioception, sensing the foot in space to teach the tendons and muscles to fire at appropriate intervals," Bernier says. "Our patients are working on two things: They're working on muscle strength to get that muscle bigger and stronger, and they're retraining the reflexes so that the brain tells the muscle to fire sooner to prevent injury."

I visit the clinic on a day Mary Clark has physical therapy. She begins with a suite of exercises that has her balance on one foot. "I hate these," she says, especially one that has her hop on her so-called bad leg across the room and another that requires her to shift side to side for twenty repetitions. Then she gets on the Wii balance board for soccer and her whole demeanor changes. Acting as a goalie, she leans left and springs up to head the ball before it can end up in the goal, then quickly resets to do it on the other side. Back and forth, the pace quickening, she's able to do this for several minutes, moving spryly and racking up points.

Under Bernier's watchful eye, she switches to the *Penguin Slide* game, controlling the movements of an animated penguin trapped on an unstable iceberg, having to slide and move to catch fish that jump nearby. This also requires Clark to be nimble, to move in quick bursts. "She sees with her eye where the penguin is going and that teaches her brain to signal her foot to fire a muscle to get her foot in position to balance to get to the fish," Bernier says. The games he chose for her require weight shifting laterally and interiorly, and force her to use her calf in what he calls "an endurance type of method." The balance board gives her brain feedback from her feet.

Bernier likes the penguin game for this because it spruces up a mundane type of traditional rehabilitative exercise and poses it as a challenge with an additional speed component. "The patient not only gets the exercise that we were doing before, laterally weight shifting back and forth, but they're able to get the visual feedback seeing the iceberg move back and forth so they know how much weight they're putting on their leg," he says. This visual feedback—seeing on the screen what your body is doing—allows the brain to make those connections to the muscle or to the nerve ending that controls the muscle that much quicker. "Having that visual feedback and seeing yourself or seeing the icon that represents you allows the body to relearn, retrain, or restrengthen those areas that are deficient much faster than just having somebody do a mundane set of exercises," he adds.

In Bernier's opinion *Penguin Slide* and others like slalom skiing and another that has the user act like she's walking on a tightrope are in some ways superior for rehabilitation than traditional exercises, which can't replicate the reaction time or the variety of quick movements. Unless somebody's standing in front of you saying, "Okay, jump left. Okay, jump right" and mixes up the pace, it would be difficult to get the same kind of workout.

Home exercises are an integral part of rehabilitation. Clark was dedicated to doing the exercises that Bernier assigned but found without the Wii that it was a hard slog, so she had her husband buy her one for Christmas and now spends an hour a day, five days a week, working out.

"The Wii is actually, well, it's cartoons, which kids watch, but you're doing something and it keeps track of how long you've been doing it, it keeps track on how many calories you spend on each one," Clark says. "When you're in the game you're willing to do things that you would never do otherwise."

Other patients at the clinic report similar success with the Wii. Faye Morrissette was hiking with a group of women in Great Falls Park when she slipped on gravel and fractured both ankles, winding up with a plate in one and nine pins in the other. She also was prescribed exercises on the Wii. "They take your mind off of what you're doing because you're concentrating on trying to get the points," she says. "You're not thinking so much about rehabilitation, you're thinking about winning." Four decades ago Gail Swinson fell off a rope and injured her ankle so badly doctors almost amputated. After she recovered she had limited mobility but little pain until about ten years ago. When she couldn't bear it any longer she underwent ankle replacement surgery. She, like Clark and Morrissette, found the Wii to be an effective rehab aid. She's become a devotee of Wii's yoga program, finding that the feedback from the balance board ensures proper technique, but she's also become a fan of the skiing game. "It works my peroneals, my anterior tib, my gastroc, and soleus for stabilizing," she says.

As for Mary Clark, she reports that she's back to normal but continues to work out five days a week on her Wii. She performed a concert with hand bells at Christmas, standing for more than three hours without any pain.

For this, she thanks her surgeon, her physical therapist, and the Wii. "If the Wii tells you to stand on one foot as part of the game and move a certain way, you do it because there's an objective," she says. "Your mind is focused on attaining this goal. If I just tell you to stand there for thirty seconds on one leg, it's boring."

The game makes something usually thought of as grueling and challenging into something fun.

CHAPTER 8

BLINDED ME WITH SCIENCE

Scientists had long been searching for the keys to a protein-cutting enzyme from an AIDs-like virus in rhesus monkeys. Called the Mason-Pfizer Monkey Virus Retroviral Protease, its enzymes aid in the virus's replication, and if scientists could crack their structure, they believed they could one day formulate drugs to hobble the disease's virulent spread. It would require folding its protein, which is a difficult and complicated procedure.

In all living things proteins are molecules made up of long chains of amino acids. They have been called "biological workhorses" that "carry out vital functions" in a cell. How a protein does its job is determined by how it folds into shape—much like a key's shape determines whether it can open a lock. When these pieces of protein lock together they form a *Tetris*-like puzzle, and the way they fold can form the fibers in your hair or the motors that run your muscles. A well-folded protein origami can help cure diseases. A misfolded protein, however, can help HIV replicate and lead to cancer or less severe afflictions like asthma. Understanding protein shapes is vital to understanding life, but techniques for determining their shapes can be time-consuming and costly, requiring specialized training and equipment.

Researchers in Poland working for a lab affiliated with the University of Washington had experimental data that could confirm the existence of a perfectly folded protein, but this wouldn't tell them how to fold it—kind of like knowing the answer to a question without being given the question. Colleagues at the university in Seattle had for years tried running this molecular mystery through an automated program that could fold thousands of proteins an hour but had come no closer to a solution.

The program was the brainchild of biochemist David Baker, a professor at the University of Washington, who had created Rosetta@home, a downloadable screen saver that borrowed time and processing power from tens of thousands of home computers whose owners had donated their machines' processing power. This brute-force approach proved effective for simple proteins, but was far from ideal. All this distributed computing power wasn't enough to handle more complex protein shapes because there are simply too many possible configurations to calculate. A protein consisting of a relatively short train of a hundred amino acids could have ten to the thirtieth power possible conformations. That's a one followed by thirty zeros, a number so big there is no name for it; it's so large it could take a hundred *billion* years to run through all the combinations.

Baker finessed this problem by limiting the potential area a donated computer addressed, which cut down drastically on the number of possible solutions. Now, an obvious strategy might have been to throw more computers at the problem. But Baker and his team had already roped in eighty-six thousand PCs from around the globe, which, combined, was roughly equal to a supercomputer. Nonetheless, Rosetta@home, even with its vast computational reserves, was fooled by protein-folding puzzles that Baker believed humans, with their superior spatial reasoning, could solve just by looking at them.

To further this goal, Baker's lab sought to tap the combined efforts of thousands upon thousands of users to help solve scientific riddles. This wasn't exactly a new idea. More than twenty years ago a puzzle game called *Atomix*, a commercial game for the Commodore Amiga and other PCs, had players concoct genuine molecules from a pool of atoms. And scientists had already figured out they could harness immense computing power at low cost by organizing vast networks of interconnected computers.

This distributed approach can be powerful, and necessary for the amount of processing power needed to fold millions of proteins in this brute-force technique. In a sense it's how Google operates, by spreading mind-boggling processing power across hundreds of thousands of machines strung together rather than relying on a few supercomputers. In essence, researchers take traditionally unproductive time and energy, when computers that are plugged in stand idly by, and harness their excess capacity for productive ends. While Google owns its PCs, researchers must rely on the kindness of strangers. This distributed approach not only yields vast processing power to throw at intractable scientific problems, it encourages the public to contribute to science, although these contributions are largely passive. That's because all they are doing is donating computer processing power. They aren't actually engaging with the science.

The first mass-distributed computer network sprung from failure. In 1997, two researchers divined a plan to win a ten-thousand-dollar prize for the first person or team to crack a fifty-six-bit encryption algorithm. They rounded up ten thousand computers for the task but were sabotaged by rival factions who went to war over Internet chat, leading to a series of massive denials of the service attacks that ended up scuttling the project. A couple of months later, a different set of researchers undertook a new effort, which they named distributed.net, and within 250 days claimed their prize. The second contest, which dealt with decrypting sixty-four-bit encryption, took almost five years before the secret message could be decloaked. It read: "Some things are better left unread."

Two years after distributed.net went live, another massive volunteer computing project was spawned, this time at the Space Sciences Laboratory at the University of California, Berkeley. Called SETI@home (for "Search for Extra-Terrestrial Intelligence") it was—and continues to be—an open-source program that relies on users donating excess capacity on their personal computers to analyze data from radio telescopes. Since then, more than fifty other projects have launched based on the same open-source code, with missions like simulating beam dynamics and modeling for epidemiology of malaria in Africa.

There have been several other projects that stretch from the vast reaches of the galaxy to Earth's deepest oceans and that require varying levels of participant engagement. In Galaxy Zoo, conceived to aid astronomers in classifying "deep sky objects"—planets, solar systems, and the like—designers estimated it would take a year for players to classify one million galaxy images. After its first day, players classified some

70,000 objects an hour, and in the first year 150,000 players amassed 50 times that, contributing 50 million classifications. One player named Hanny van Arkel discovered a mysterious blob in a faraway galaxy that scientists now think is part of a gas cloud heated by a black hole. With MilkyWay@home and Einstein@home volunteers help investigate interstellar space. In Planet Hunters anyone with a personal computer can help classify Kepler Space Telescope light data, while in Moon Zoo, users zoom in on high-resolution photos of lunar craters and take note of rocks that NASA might want to further investigate.

Down here on Earth, WhaleFM, through its Whale Song Project, has rounded up legions of citizen oceanographers to listen to orcas and assist researchers in matching similar-sounding calls. Out of MIT comes EyeWire, which looks to an online community to map connections in the retina to help neuroscientists learn more about how it assists visual perception. From DARPA came a contest to piece together documents that had been shredded into ten thousand pieces, which the winning team solved by customizing algorithms to suggest puzzle pairings and then having humans put them back together. In *Ancient Lives*, armchair archaeologists channel their inner Indiana Jones without leaving the comfort of their desk chairs to help decode text fragments from ancient Egypt. Phylo, out of McGill University, assists researchers in locating sections of DNA that are similar across species and that contribute to traits such as eye or hair color, and medical conditions (heart disease, diabetes, and high blood pressure).

In 2007, over lunch with Zoran Popović and another computer science professor, David Salesin, David Baker discussed adding a human layer to Rosetta@home. Baker suggested they encourage sharp users to order their screen savers to try different folding approaches if they saw what the algorithm was doing wasn't effective. Popović shot it down. No one would care about that, he said. To get people engaged, he suggested putting people at the center of the experience.

That's when the idea of turning this protein origami project into a game started to take shape. People already spent millions of hours every year playing video games. Like the excess computational power of idle PCs, however, all of this mental energy was wasted.

What if, they wondered, instead of massively multiplayer online games there could be massively multiplayer online science? Then they could advance science by rewarding problem solving and creativity to solve real-world problems. It would be a form of "distributed thinking," which Baker saw as a way to present scientific problems to the masses and attract a crowd that could contribute to solutions. Effectively, it would combine the power of computers—and what they excel at—with the creativity and spatial reasoning of humans, which is what we do well. Somewhere along the way the game picked up the name *Foldit.*

They would need game designers and that's when Popović brought on board two of his graduate students, Seth Cooper and Adrien Treuille. Cooper, a PhD candidate in computer science at the University of Washington, was halfway through the program, studying computer graphics, specifically motion trackers and real-time animation, when he got the invitation to join. As a kid growing up in Columbia, Missouri, he had been deep into gaming. He got his first computer, a Mac, when he was in elementary school, which he used to teach himself basic software coding and to create primitive games. In high school, he took college-level computer science courses and enrolled in various summer programs, then attended Berkeley for college, majoring in electrical engineering and computer science. While his academic research had pulled him away from games and toward computer graphics, "I never forgot how much joy I got from playing and designing them," he says.

He joined a postdoc, Adrien Treuille, as a colead game designer on *Foldit.* Like Cooper, Treuille, who got his undergraduate degree in computer science at Georgetown, had always been fascinated by games, and had been making them since he was twelve, when he was recovering from appendicitis. After that, whenever he was bored, he'd invent a game. Sometimes the games involved cards, but he often used whatever was available. If he was at a diner, he'd create a game using the condiments on the table.

They quickly identified the crux of the problem as being one of image recognition: humans are adept at reading words in images and determining objects in a scene, while computer-driven methods were not. They were well aware of Luis von Ahn's work on the *ESP Game*, and Google's licensing of it to label millions of images for search.

Because of the project's visual nature, Treuille suggested they view their game as more of a toy. A game has predetermined rules, but a toy is something you want to play with, poke at, flip in the air to see what it does. The act of folding proteins was not dissimilar to twisting and turning a Rubik's Cube to get the colors to match. Part of it is mechanical, but the other involves intuition and spatial reasoning, seeing how the pieces fit together.

They also had to keep sight of the ultimate goal. With *Call of Duty* or *World of Warcraft*, designers create enjoyable experiences for their players to maximize engagement and retention. Their game, on the other hand, had to accomplish all that *and* advance scientific inquiry. There was tension between the freedom to design for engagement and the realism of scientific constraints. The game's architecture had to foster the coevolution of the players and the game itself. By solving progressively challenging problems, players gained experience (i.e., they got better at it), while the game adapted to the players by "learning" how they used it and therefore became a more useful tool.

Another open-ended question involved the essence of scientific discovery, which has no predictable end. In the game, players had to be motivated to seek the best possible protein structures but game makers could not know in advance what those structures (or answers) would be. So they organized the game around a standard competition, with players simply trying to best other players at the same tasks. Their goal would be simple: to boost your score you had to follow the rules of protein folding, which meant making a three-dimensional protein compact and avoiding empty spaces. The more compact a player made a protein, the more points he could rack up.

Scientific inquiry often consists of a series of setbacks, and creating a game like this was no different. Within three months Cooper and Treuille had a demo, but like most complex, freshly coded software it was buggy. In one of the first play tests they conducted with real players the game crashed after people played for a certain amount of time. The problem, they eventually realized, was that play testers were having such a good time that they were making many more moves and playing for much longer than Cooper and Treuille did in their initial testing. That taxed the system's memory. They fixed it by limiting how many moves the computer could save at a time.

This, they realized, was a good problem to have. Sifting through data they took note of some unexpected game-tester behavior. Many users persisted despite a woeful player experience. (In some ways, all that bugginess contributed to the creation of a control group.) Instead of giving up they adapted by saving their shapes every minute so they wouldn't lose them every time the system caved in. The game had a magnetic hold on users. Thus absorbed, they put up with all manner of irksome inconvenience as long as they could continue folding their proteins.

Energized by the level of engagement the game conjured, Cooper and Treuille worked out a system to afford constant improvement. While another student worked on the underlying code, they organized a testing protocol to gather user data. Three to five players were brought into a lab and asked to reveal what they were thinking as they played: What is fun? What is frustrating? Where do they get stuck? What do they not understand? "Even with just a few people, if there was something obviously wrong, if three out of four people said, 'I don't understand this thing,' then we would have a pretty good idea that that was a problem," Cooper says.

Cooper credits these "think-alouds" for helping improve the game experience. In early designs players could only indirectly manipulate proteins. Once players could do it directly, engagement shot up. The game designers made liberal use of pyrotechniques like fireworks, cartoonish protein figures, and sweet-talking pop-up windows, tweaking colors and words until they maximized their impact.

Slowly the game took shape. It had a profound scientific purpose at its core, but it was also a toy, a three-dimensional puzzle displayed on a two-dimensional screen. It just cried out to be played with. *What happens when you fold that line to meet this line? That line should probably go here. Maybe twist it in this direction. Look at that; it folds perfectly.* Cooper and Treuille made a concerted effort to present rewards to players across different time scales and organized the game around leaderboards to tap people's competitive drive.

Meanwhile, Popović created an interface that rendered these proteins as playful animated loops and spirals. Players manipulated the cursor to snatch, guide, and shake anywhere along the chain of amino acids, folding a protein into its optimum shape. The rules of our universe applied, meaning players operated in a world beholden to physics. The more efficiently a protein was folded, the more points a player would receive. The game's score would also serve as a proxy for how the protein might work in the lab—whether it catalyzed a reaction, stuck to part of a virus, or even itself.

Then these player-created proteins would be presented for analysis. Any solutions showing promise would be synthesized in the lab, going from the realm of two-dimensional shapes on a screen to reality. It has to be done in a lab because proteins can fold amazingly fast. Some can do it in a millionth of a second. But the process is so complex that it can take quite awhile for the computer to simulate it. Fifty nanoseconds (50/1,000,000,000 of a second) can take a computer a full day to simulate.

On May 8, 2008, Baker's lab released its massively multiplayer competition in speed origami. *The Economist* wrote about it the same day, and readers and many others, fascinated by the concept, drove so much traffic to the servers they crashed. From there the game spread by word of mouth, which was buttressed by occasional media coverage. Players studied the tutorials to learn the basics of protein folding and how to play the game, and, playing with test proteins for which Baker already possessed structures, players learned the ropes, made friends, asked questions, shared insights, and partially completed puzzles. In addition to the Contenders, players congealed into teams named Folders for Obama, Freedom Folders, and Richard Dawkins Foundation to better their chances, and one player created a wiki that was converted into a manual for the game. The designers even started a "mini-Facebook" for players. Over that summer, roughly a hundred players a day signed up to play and tens of thousands of users folded proteins, with the game ultimately attracting a diverse fan base in the hundreds of thousands.

The quest to advance science was just one reason players gave for their interest in the game. Others were keen for the competition, while still more enjoyed the social interaction that online games provide. Two-thirds of top scorers had no background in biochemistry, and only one out of eight players had ever worked in science. This lack of a scientific background was not a hindrance. In fact, it might have offered an advantage. How did *Foldit*'s primo players stack up to the scientists in Baker's lab? "We are nowhere near as good as the top players that come up with these amazing solutions," says Firas Khatib, a biochemist who joined the lab as a postdoc six months after the game was released. "Unlike scientists, they have the freedom of not having all of these restrictions in their minds about how proteins fold."

By deconstructing players' movements within the game, the game makers recognized specific instances when humans' superb pattern-recognition skills offered them an edge over computers. As John Timmer explained in *Ars Technica*, *Foldit* players "were very good about detecting a hydrophobic amino acid when it stuck out from the protein's surface, instead of being buried internally, and they were willing to rearrange the structure's internals in order to tuck the offending amino acid back inside. Those sorts of extensive rearrangements were beyond Rosetta's abilities, since the energy changes involved in the transitions are so large." Similarly, "Rosetta was good at linking up stretches of protein through charge interactions and hydrogen bonds, but it would often get things slightly off (think of a zipper that's off by a single tooth). Shifting every bond by a single partner was beyond Rosetta's abilities, but it's something a human can do trivially."

This trove of user data helped researchers identify players' strengths, which varied from user to user. Some players were adept at making necessary large-scale adjustments. Others opted for subtle tweaks over wholesale changes. This made *Foldit*'s social communication tools, which had been built into the game, vital, since they enabled players to work together, tapping each person's expertise and interests.

Foldit players were better at the game than scientists, but how did they compare with the world's best protein folders? In 2009 Khatib aimed to find out by entering top players into a biannual protein-folding competition called CASP (Critical Assessment of Techniques for Protein Structure Prediction). Each team tried to accurately predict a protein's shape based only on its amino acid sequence. Until then, winners had almost always been professional scientists. At the start, as *Foldit* players lagged behind, it looked as if they would do it again.

So Khatib stepped in by messing with the proteins offered to contestants to spawn a whole bunch of wildly terrible solutions that gamers could then refine. By stretching the canvas—and their minds to greater possibilities—Khatib opened up a different approach for the *Foldit* players, who ended up breaking the top one hundred in the world and came up with the best-ranked answer to the most difficult challenge in the entire competition.

Then something amazing happened: a group of *Foldit* players contributed to an important discovery, solving a puzzle that had stymied researchers for more than a decade.

The Contenders

For years, the researchers in Baker's lab in Poland had been trying to fold the protein for the Mason-Pfizer Monkey Virus Retroviral Protease. Thus far, Rosetta@home had not even formulated a nibble. In a last-ditch effort, Khatib presented the protein to *Foldit* players. Ten days later a group of players solved it.

Michele Minett, a self-described "lowly lab technician" from the United Kingdom, is credited with having solved the 3-D puzzle while working with members of the *Foldit* group the Contenders. The group is informally comprised of about three dozen players from all walks of life. Some have a background in science, others don't. A few may code but many don't. After reading about *Foldit* in *New Scientist*, she figured it would be a "more productive way of wasting time" than, say, *Minesweeper*. She started playing in November 2008, six months after its release. On her woefully out-of-date computer, the game ran slowly and the display was jerky. At the time, manipulation of the protein was done manually by studying the shape of the protein and using the game tools to pull parts together or apart and change the position of side chains. Initially she played for short periods, gradually learning the techniques by experimentation and reading the conversations in the global chat window. She found the internal chat facilities "a vital part of creating and maintaining the *Foldit* community without which the game would not work."

She says she asked to join the Contenders because she liked how members comported themselves in game chat and was looking for a relatively small and friendly group where she could make a contribution. A year after she started playing, she upgraded her PC, which made it possible for her to work more easily on protein puzzles. Over that period advances in the game meant it was possible to leave the program to run a sequence of instructions programmed by the player on a protein instead of making manual adjustments every few minutes. This function, called "scripting," arose out of a function in the game called "The Cookbook" and enables players to script or code their own strategies in the game. Players can share and modify their recipes with other players. This way they can pick up strategies from other players and then automate them. The most popular recipe, "Blue

Fuse version 1.1," was made up of just a few lines of basic code that anybody could learn to write. According to Cooper, a biochemist from Baker's lab remarked that it was an algorithm that they had independently been developing in the lab but hadn't published yet. "Organically," Cooper says, "the community of *Foldit* players had come up with the same algorithmic moves that the scientist in the biochemistry lab had come up with independently."

Between December 2010 and January 2011, Khatib unveiled the Mason-Pfizer Monkey Virus puzzle to *Foldit* players with the comment: "The Folded monomer of protease from Mason-Pfizer monkey virus is currently unsolved by protein crystallographers." As usual, they were given a deadline, this time three weeks, and provided with ten alternative starting points. Khatib added: "We hope you can help us solve this structure!"

At that point, all Minett could see was "a remarkably ugly shaped protein." In fact, Contenders' players agreed it was ugly and their intuition told them it looked wrong, although no one could say why. In a sense, everyone was simply trying to make the protein look more aesthetically pleasing, more compact and organized. Some players used brute force, threading and rethreading, banding things together and rebuilding, using quake scripts to settle, and so on. The way they collaborated didn't vary much from one puzzle to the next.

Minett's first step was to look at each of the ten starting points and attempt some manipulation to see which might have the most potential. In each of the options, she noticed a loop sticking out at one end, like a tail. To make the solution as compact as possible, she attempted to get the "tail" to move closer to the protein's main body. But she didn't have any success doing that with solo attempts. Meanwhile, she downloaded solutions produced by team members in the hopes of improving on those options, which in game parlance is known as "evolving." One of these solutions had been worked on initially by a teammate, whose handle was spvincent. Subsequently, another Contender, grabhorn, also contributed. (Citing a desire for privacy, neither would reveal his real name.)

She tested out the same manipulation on the evolved solution she had used unsuccessfully on her solo solutions. In this case, it worked, due to changes her associates had made to the protein. Suddenly she was able to tuck in the flap that had been sticking out. At the time

Minett wasn't aware that she had solved anything. No alarms went off, no balloons, no fireworks. In fact, the move that involved tucking in the flap didn't even result in an increase in points nor was the solution one of the highest scoring that had been submitted.

After three weeks, Khatib and his biochemist colleagues analyzed the data. Of the millions of solutions generated by the six hundred players who played this particular puzzle, Minett's protein-folded model was the only one accurate enough.

It had taken her and her two Contender teammates ten days to succeed at something that had eluded scientists for more than ten years.

"We could then say that this was the right structure for that particular protein," Khatib says. "The cool thing is that now that we know the shape of that protein we can try to design another protein or a drug that would prevent the protein from folding properly, thus effectively deactivating it. We could make a drug to fight against the disease."

The researchers in Poland were thrilled their decade-long quest had ended. "One of them said it was the greatest day of his life," Cooper says. "We had to open bottles of champagne simultaneously over Skype to celebrate." Cooper and Khatib also set up a chat with Minett and the other Contenders' players to inform them of the importance of their discovery. They told them they intended to publish a research paper about it and asked if they would like to share authorship. But the players declined and asked if the team could be listed instead. That, Cooper says, reflects "the social camaraderie aspect of the game. People are really connected to their teams and teammates and the friends they've made in the game. And they're from all around the world." The paper was published in the distinguished scientific journal *Nature*. It was the first time to Khatib's knowledge that gamers had solved a thorny problem that had stumped scientists.

For *Foldit* the hits kept on coming. Not long after the Contenders cracked the Mason-Pfizer Monkey Virus Retroviral Protease, the scientists in Baker's lab were working on an enzyme that catalyzes something known as the Diels-Alder reaction, which brings together two molecules to form a particular kind of bond that if fabricated could assist in the formation of drugs. The scientists and players went through numerous rounds of puzzles. Ultimately, Baker's lab was able to create an enzyme that was twenty times more efficient in catalyzing the reaction than the one they had started with. All this was made possible because players inserted thirteen amino acids, which in the protein game is a significant departure from the structure scientists began with. In fact, it was so drastic a departure it would never have occurred to them it could work.

"But the players didn't know that, so they just tried something that they thought would work, and it turned out to work really well," Cooper says.

If things continue along this path, it won't be the last scientific discovery that *Foldit* players make. According to Khatib, they plan to make a game to actually shape a drug that binds and blocks the retroviral protease and could do the same to a closely related enzyme on HIV. That way *Foldit* players wouldn't simply be folding proteins. They would be shaping the drugs that could come from them.

"That's the really exciting next step," Khatib says.

CHAPTER 9

MED-SIMS

Dr. Carla Pugh was a first-year surgical resident at Howard University Hospital, working the night shift in the emergency room, when a man was carted in with multiple stab wounds. The patient was unconscious, yet Pugh noted there wasn't a whole lot of bleeding, certainly not enough to account for his mental state. "Something's going on," she told the chief resident leading the ER team. His heart, she feared, might have been nicked in the attack.

She advised cracking his chest, but her superior disagreed. He didn't see the classic textbook signs, namely distended jugular veins and muffled heart sounds. The patient had been drinking, Pugh pointed out—on his way in he had vomited on them—so he was likely dehydrated, which could account for his skinny jugular veins; and it was a busy night in the ER, so they might not hear his heart over the hubbub. While he didn't have all the symptoms he seemed to have two or three.

Her chief cut her off. Hospitals are hierarchical and since he outranked her, his word was law. By the time he gave the order to open the man's chest, it was too late. He died on the operating table.

This haunted Pugh. She ran through all the possible scenarios, performing mental simulations of how she could have changed the outcome, and promised herself if she were ever again faced with similar circumstances, she wouldn't hesitate to act. Two years later, she got her chance. Pugh was on the same night shift at the same hospital when a man leaving a friend's bachelor party had been stabbed and robbed. He was a John Doe: no wallet, no credit cards, no identification, and he, too was unconscious. The difference was his wounds appeared significantly more serious.

Paramedics had placed a bath-mat-size piece of gauze on his chest, and when Pugh peered underneath she saw a deep slice in his right chest and a lung hanging out. With such extensive injuries there should have been a lot more bleeding. With so little blood, the man, despite the savage wounds, should still be awake. This time she was the doctor in charge and ordered the patient flipped over so she could look at his back. She didn't find any other cuts or punctures. They turned the patient again and stripped off all the gauze and bandages when Pugh spotted a tiny hole.

Holy crap, Pugh thought. "Put in a chest tube," she ordered the resident on her team. "If we don't get a gush of blood, we'll crack his chest." When no red geyser was forthcoming they prepped the patient for emergency surgery, inserting a breathing tube to get him oxygenated and help his heart beat. They rushed him to the operating room and just as they were transferring him from the stretcher to the operating room table he flatlined.

The anesthetist readied paddles to shock his heart.

"No!" Pugh shouted. "Give me a scalpel!"

There was no time for niceties. She poured sterile solution right out of the bottle, soaking her gloved hands and the knife—she wasn't even wearing a surgical gown—and ripped open the man's chest. Shoving her hand inside, she rooted around until she located the hole and plugged the leak with her finger. His heart jumped back to life.

It was 2 a.m. and there wasn't time for the thoracic surgeon on call to get there. While Pugh waited for a rib spreader she marveled at the feeling of a heart beating around her finger. In all of her years of training she had never touched one as it pumped blood through a living, breathing human being. If a sharp object pierces a beating heart, the outer incision ends up wider than the one on the inner wall, which doesn't move as much. Because it results in such an unusual shape, under normal circumstances doctors would cover the hole with a special patch made of soft metal and shaped like a bullhorn. The nurses couldn't find any bullhorns that would fit, however, so they had to sew it closed the old-fashioned way. Pugh looked over to her resident, who was set to begin.

"You're not stitching with my finger in here," she said.

One errant move and he could poke a hole in her finger or stitch her to him. Who knew if the patient was HIV-positive or plagued by other infections? Thinking quickly, she decided to tag team it. Pugh would start each stitch, because she could feel where her finger was, then pass him the thread, which he would tie off. She would inch her finger over and they would repeat the process.

With the first stitch blood squirted out. They had to hurry.

A few days later Dr. Pugh was making her rounds when she entered her John Doe's room. She found him sitting up in a chair, smiling through a haze of painkillers.

"You look great!" she said, surprised at the transformation. "You almost died."

"I heard," he said. "You're the one who saved my life."

It was all over the hospital. Pugh had even earned a nickname: Magic Finger.

He told her the last thing he remembered were four men approaching him in a parking lot. He never made it to his car. When he didn't show at the wedding, his friends and family went looking for him. It took forty-eight hours to track him down. Now he was on his way to a full recovery.

She thought about how close a call it was. Over the past century, medical technology had advanced. Less than a hundred years earlier some doctors still bled patients with leeches, and the late nineteenth and early twentieth centuries saw the advent of antibiotics, sterilization, X-rays, open-heart surgery, chemotherapy, fMRIs, and now *Fantastic Voyage*–like cameras so tiny they travel through veins and arteries. Yet the way medicine was taught—still premised on the old "see one, practice one, do one, teach one" methodology—it hadn't kept pace.

A patient's survival shouldn't depend on chance, on the doctor in charge having experienced similar real-life emergencies. Pugh looked back at her own training. When she was a second-year resident on a rotation in urology she watched a patient undergo prostate surgery. To prepare she had stayed up all night studying anatomy and reading up on suprapubic prostatectomies. For the first thirty minutes of the operation, all she could see was the back of the surgeon's hand. He was teaching the procedure to a senior resident and Pugh, bursting with curiosity, wondered how his student could be learning if he couldn't see what the surgeon was doing. Junior-level residents weren't supposed to talk in the operating room, and Pugh was about as junior as they came. Nevertheless, she couldn't stop herself. "Can I feel what you're feeling?" she asked the surgeon.

The room fell silent. Finally, he said, "Sure," and guided her hand inside the patient's bladder until she felt something mushy. She had no idea what it was. Nonetheless, there was something powerful about this haptic connection.

There had to be a better way to train doctors. Pugh decided to make her life's work finding it.

Simple Sims

Carla Pugh was raised in a single-parent household in Berkeley, California, and because they lived on a limited income she learned to make do with whatever they had and to mend whatever didn't work. Anytime she came across a broken, abandoned Barbie she would clean her off and commandeer the parts to repair friends' dolls, performing her own surgeries, replacing errant legs, joints, and broken heads. She sewed stuffed animal eyes back on and sutured rips and tears, fixed bicycles, lamps, and radios, and even tried to improve the washing machine so it would never go out of balance (with mixed success).

Pugh can scarcely recall a time she didn't want to be a doctor, from the moment she first heard stories about her great-grandmother from the Deep South, a Jill-of-all-medicine who birthed goats, horses, and babies. After graduating from Berkeley with a degree in neurobiology Pugh attended medical school at Howard University. Along the way she recognized that she was a visual learner: She had a photographic memory of things she could see, and if things were presented in an artistic, aesthetic manner, whether it was human anatomy or the inner workings of a car, she intuitively grasped how they worked. In school she excelled in labs, less so in lectures or classes that prized rote. She remains to this day a person who can put together Ikea furniture without reviewing instructions and tailors her own clothing. When her three-year residency at Howard was up she enrolled at Stanford to pursue a PhD in education to explore ways to improve medical training. She was primarily interested in simulations—controlled imitations of reality (a situation or process) created for skills practice and problem solving while fostering judgment and increasing knowledge.

Medical simulations are almost as old as the metaphor. Since antiquity healers have relied on clay and stone models to represent human organs and bones, and in some cultures these simulations provided diagnostic tools when females were restricted from contact with male doctors. In the Middle East clay liver models etched with omens that date from the Late Bronze Age (1550–1200 BC) were used in diagnosis. Throughout history simulation-based instruction also involved plant models, human cadavers, and living and dead animals. In the ninth century, small wax and wooden figures illustrated reproductive processes, and later ivory, wood, and glass were used to simulate medical conditions. It wasn't until the 1700s, however, that the first intricate system of models—the first realistic medical simulation—was produced.

It was born of the belief that France's dwindling population posed a threat to national security. Actually, as historian Carol Blum reports in *Strength in Numbers: Population, Reproduction, and Power in Eighteenth-Century France*, the nation's populace grew throughout the eighteenth century, just not as fast as Britain's or the German states', all of which were potentially hostile. Nevertheless, the ruling elite's belief that the population was falling led to intense hand-wringing. French Enlightenment philosophers put forth various theories. Denis Diderot believed it was the king's penchant for war and favoring luxury goods over basic foodstuffs that were to blame. Voltaire claimed there were too many priests. Montesquieu took aim at the church's stance on divorce and celibacy. The church fired back, claiming libertine philosophers had adopted a dishonorable form of celibacy because they didn't marry and procreate—these "men of letters," it was said, were the first to take up masturbation—and proposed a tax to be levied on unmarried citizens, which would be used to assist fathers of large families and to raise abandoned children. Other proposals ranged from embracing polygamy (for men only, naturally) and out-of-wedlock births.

King Louis IV, who didn't help matters by expelling large numbers of Jews and Protestants during his reign, agreed with a relatively obscure midwife, Angélique Marguerite Le Boursier du Coudray, that an alarmingly high infant mortality rate contributed to the problem. To address it, France didn't need more surgeons; it required better-trained local midwives, peasant women and doctors; His Highness commissioned Du Coudray, at her request, to travel the French countryside to teach them, which she did for twenty-three years. Nina Rattner Gelbart, a history professor at Occidental College and author of the exhaustively researched *The King's Midwife: A History and Mystery of Madame du Coudray*, estimates that as many as ten thousand women received training across forty cities.

"I cannot say the number who opened up to me about their sad situation," Du Coudray wrote in 1756. "I made them go into detail about their deliveries, and by the accounts they gave me I could not doubt that they attributed their infirmities to the ignorance of the women to whom they had recourse, or to that of some inexperienced village surgeons."

Because she worked with a largely illiterate populace, Du Coudray couldn't assign trainees the obstetrics textbook she had written. She needed visual aids. This led her to design and construct an ingenious "upholstered machine" with a synthetic womb to simulate childbirth. Despite the primitive materials at her disposal in eighteenth-century France, the result was amazingly realistic: a life-size pelvis of a woman in labor—the womb, vagina, bladder, and rectum. Skin, organs, and umbilical cord were comprised of linen, leather, sponges, and padding, and her earliest models were partly constructed of skeletons to mimic various bones and the pelvis. (Later she incorporated wicker and wood.) Red and clear liquids squeezed from a collection of sponges replicated blood and fluids. Ensconced inside was a lifelike model of a baby, the joints flexible enough to be placed in different positions. Membranes filled with water to show a child swimming in the womb, and each body part was numbered, corresponding to a chart listing the anatomical names.

Du Coudray made her contraption flexible enough so that students would be exposed to both straightforward deliveries and those with complications. Traditional learning, she argued, depended largely on theory, but when difficulties arose, trainees were completely unprepared, and this was, as she put it, "the cause of many misfortunes." With her simulation, though, babies could be delivered from an almost infinite number of positions. She could mimic a cesarean, illustrate ways to extract a baby with instruments passed through malformed pelvic structures, or show how forceps used incorrectly could cause the head of an infant to cave in, and with them illustrate the loss of blood and fluids that accompanied each procedure. Du Coudray provided umbilical cord representations that could be swapped out depending on the scenario: in the one representing a cord tied to a healthy newborn, practitioners could feel the beating of the blood vessels; another represented a withered artery, while still another was inflated to imitate the cord of a stillborn. Then there was the model with a baby's severed head with a crushed cranium to show what could happen in a badly botched delivery, and a realistic-looking cancer-riddled womb made from a pastiche of cloth.

She aimed to shock for a reason. About the model of a baby whose head was crushed, Du Coudray wrote: "I thought that with a demonstration this tangible, if I could not make these women very skilled, I would at least make them feel the necessity of asking for help soon enough to save the mother and child, help that cities do not lack, but that would be very necessary in the countryside, where the skill of a surgeon called too late is often useless, and he can and he can only be the spectator of two expiring victims for whom his art and his zeal are by then fruitless."

In three months, Du Coudray boasted, "a woman free of prejudice, and who has never had the remotest knowledge of childbirth, will be sufficiently trained." Her visual approach to learning appears effective. Gelbart credits Du Coudray with contributing to a steep drop in infant mortality that helped make possible the rise in France's population during the second half of the eighteenth century.

Pelvic Exam in a Box

In this little-known, eighteenth-century French midwife Pugh had found a kindred spirit. As she pursued a PhD in education, Pugh enrolled in a graduate-level course on human-computer interactions where she began work on her first medical simulator. She chose the pelvis, not because she was an ob-gyn, but because a professor loaned her a pelvic mannequin model. It was an ideal test case because a physician giving a female patient a pelvic examination relies almost solely on touch.

Pugh taught herself C++ coding, ripped apart the mannequin, and placed sensors at various points, off-the-shelf microprocessors that measured pressure on a scale of one to ten. There was no textbook to tell her where to situate them. She guessed based on her own experience. The sensors embedded in the teaching mannequin enabled the simulator to offer feedback never before available on palpation—the use of touch in clinical practice for diagnostic and therapeutic purposes. The results were displayed on a computer screen, which helped guide a user's hands to the right places and apply a suitable amount of pressure. She realized that touch in medicine was not hard to quantify but difficult to explain. It'd be like telling someone unfamiliar with America's coin system to reach into her pocket for loose change and blindly extract a nickel from a stash of pennies, nickels, and dimes.

It was a propitious time for Pugh to enter the world of simulations, and not just because so many Americans grew up on a steady diet of video games, which by necessity take place in simulated worlds with their own set of rules. Already sims, which enable users to practice something so often and in real-world settings that it becomes second nature, had transformed aviation and the military, and they were becoming a staple in medicine, too. Modern sims went back almost as far as the Wright brothers. Six years after the Wright brothers lifted off from Kitty Hawk in 1903, a "Barrel Trainer" was created to train pilots in flying the Antoinette, a new type of French plane. There was ample need. Surveys dating from 1912 found that 90 percent of flight accidents came down to inadequate pilot training. The rig, cobbled together from two half barrels atop each other, allowed a pilot to practice before taking the aircraft for a spin. He would operate a steering wheel and a rudder that controlled his pitch and roll, having to do everything correctly or the "plane" couldn't maintain balance.

It didn't take long for the interests of aviation and the military to converge. During World War I, there was ample need for pilot and gunnery training devices, and several were developed. Firing at a target from a fast-moving plane (called "deflection shooting") required practice and skill, and simulations were ideal for that. In World War II, more than half a million Allied pilots trained on Link simulators. Invented by Edwin A. Link, who developed the initial prototype in the basement of his father's Binghamton, New York–based piano and organ factory, he mounted the trainer on a pedestal and used organ bellows and a motor to mimic the sensation of flight. A student pilot would then climb, dive, pitch, and roll like a real aviator. At first, Link peddled his invention to amusement parks, until the Army Air Corps bought six Link trainers to train pilots how to fly blind in bad weather and at night, relying solely on instruments.

Winston Churchill, emerging from his bunker to offer his famous Battle of Britain speech—the one with the famous phrase, "Never in the field of human conflict was so much owed by so many to so few"—indirectly paid homage to Link trainers by lauding the courage and skill of the Royal Air Force. "All hearts go out to the fighter pilots, whose brilliant actions we see with our own eyes day after day, but we must never forget that all the time, night after night, month after month, our bomber squadrons travel far into Germany, find their targets in the darkness by the highest navigational skill, aim their attacks, often under the heaviest fire, often with serious loss, with deliberate, careful discrimination, and inflict shattering blows upon the whole of the technical and war-making structure of the Nazi power."

When Pugh started her PhD she had intended to develop Web-based teaching tools for surgeons, but this changed one evening as she prepared her pelvic simulator for a demonstration at a medical conference in London. Two medical students at the end of their rotations asked to try it. Pugh had been continually refining her pelvic simulator, and just by looking at the data she found she could tell how well someone performed. The gist of a pelvic exam is that a physician places one hand inside the vaginal vault, and applies pressure on the cervix. This pushes the whole organ towards the entry of the abdominal wall. Then she palpates the portion of the uterus opposite the opening, trapping the organ between her two hands. Pugh plotted the data representing the amount of pressure over length of time. When she did she could see where a practitioner touched on the cervix, for how long, and at what pressure. What's more, she could accurately track her movements. For example, one user touched several areas of the cervix, held constant pressure on the left, was not able to find the uterus to palpate it, switched positions, went on the right, then did left and right, back around the interior and still was barely able to touch one portion of the uterus. That indicated she was performing the examination incorrectly.

Both students gave the impression they understood how to give a proper pelvic exam. The graphic interface on the simulator's computer screen, however, told a different story. The first student performed a thorough exam, but the second barely touched anything of relevance. When they were done, Pugh shared the results, which prompted the second student to exclaim: "I've been doing this exam wrong for two months. Why didn't I have access to this before I did an exam on a patient?"

Why indeed? After that, Pugh placed sensors in all manner of mannequins, harvesting them from medical supply stores, then customizing them. She built one to mimic a prostate, another the rectum, a third, breasts. Then she came up with the idea to mimic specific diseases, because not all tumors are created equal, and these differences can throw off an inexperienced physician. Many of these models didn't involve the use of sensors. Pelvic models weren't equipped with realistic simulations of ovarian tumors and in various sizes, while some medical mannequins were simply inaccurate, like one model she encountered with the prostate in the wrong position and the rectum in the wrong place. Styrofoam penises were rendered in identical shapes and sizes.

On a quest for more realistic medical simulations to cover real-world scenarios she scoured art supply stores, fabric and hobby shops, hardware stores, and even Toys "Я" Us. She checked out porn shops to inquire about penises, circumcised and uncircumcised, erect and soft, in different sizes and shapes, which shopkeepers found hilarious. "Everywhere I go, anything I see, touch, and feel is fair game for building a human being or a part," Pugh says. Anywhere she went offered the potential for more materials for her sims.

Through trial and error she discovered that various tumors could be represented by anything from dried lima beans to glass beads or clay to hard rubber balls to pom-poms encased in oily condoms. Lentils embedded in rubber were particularly good for mimicking fibrocystic breast changes, a noncancerous condition, and she melted plastic to imitate cysts or thickened tissue. She filled simulated breasts with "tumors" and lumps represented by lentils, beans, and clay, and sliced the edges off of ice cube trays and embedded the slats in foam to make ribs. Squishy balls did a nice job of representing ovarian masses; hard, wooden balls worked well for ovarian cancers. "I use lots of water balloons, lots of condoms, lots and lots of arts and crafts," Pugh says. "I take my team on field trips to the hobby shop and tell them I need a rock-hard tumor of various sizes."

Building human beings out of common, everyday parts earned her a reputation as a "medical McGyver." Then Pugh decided to tackle an even more unlikely medical area. Because nowhere was touch more important than in surgery.

Inside an Operating Room

When Dr. Patrick Borgen was named chief surgeon of Maimonides Hospital in Brooklyn, New York, his first objective was to change the culture. Maimonides is a large urban medical center, one of Brooklyn's largest employers with 6,000 staff, and New York State's largest Medicaid recipient. In 2011 it served more than 130,000 patients and delivered 8,500 babies—about one every hour. It's also a training center, the largest non-university-located training program for residents in the United States, second only to the Mayo Clinic, with 525 doctors in training.

Borgen is tall, a little heavy, and suffers from a bum shoulder, courtesy of a motorcycle accident, although that doesn't stop him from racing vintage bikes on weekends. He grew up in New Orleans wanting to be an engineer like his father, who worked at NASA. When he was eleven, he, like millions of other Americans, watched Neil Armstrong take a giant leap for mankind with man's first step on the moon, something his father had a hand in. Ultimately Borgen gravitated to biomedical engineering and attended medical school. He spent two years in a genetics lab at Sloan-Kettering, joining the faculty in January 1991 and becoming chief breast surgeon from 1993 to 2006, when Maimonides recruited him. As a doctor he has a stellar reputation, named one of the best doctors in America by Castle Connolly Guide and one of the best in New York by *New York* magazine, and is a recipient of a 2012 humanitarian award from OHEL, a local children's home and family services agency that serves the Jewish community.

At Maimonides, he took over a department of surgery that had a storied history. The first heart transplant in the United States, and the second in the world, was performed in the building where Borgen's office is located. Maimonides was also one of the centers that developed nodes surgery, which entails going through a body orifice like the mouth with a scope to take out, say, a gallbladder. But it operated as a macho good ol' boys club with nurses and residents afraid to challenge orders. Some surgeons wore cowboy boots and strutted around Borough Park, Brooklyn, a working-class neighborhood home to one of the country's largest Hasidic and Orthodox Jewish populations.

Borgen believed the best surgeons were self-critical. He wanted to create a culture that would encourage surgeons to wonder, "If I did that again, how I would do it differently?" At Memorial Sloan-Kettering, Borgen worked with Dr. Murray Brennan, whom he called "the greatest cancer surgeon of the last century in this country." In February 2009 Brennan performed a Whipple procedure on Justice Ruth Bader Ginsberg, removing then reconstructing parts of her pancreas, small intestine, bile duct, gallbladder, and duodenum, an operation that for most surgeons would have taken six or eight hours. Brennan did it in two hours and twenty minutes. "My kids used to talk about beating a level in video games," Borgen says, "and they would get up to these astronomical levels. Well that's where Brennan was playing: at level gazillion."

Over dinner Borgen asked his former colleague, "Gee, were you a little nervous operating on one of the Supremes?"

"I wish I had that operation back," Brennan said. "At this point in the operation I usually put three stitches, but this time I put two, and I worried . . ."

Here Brennan was, seventy years old and still striving to improve. That's how he was able to complete an enormously complex and difficult operation in a little over two hours, which helped enormously in the septuagenarian justice's recovery time. Borgen wanted to instill that level of self-critical behavior in the next generation of surgeons.

It wouldn't be easy. One week into his new job one of his surgeons ran into a complication. Afterward Borgen asked what went wrong. The surgeon replied, "It's none of your business."

Borgan thought he was joking. "No, I'm serious," the surgeon said. "It's none of your business."

"What do you mean it's none of my business?" Borgan asked.

"It's my patient, it's my operation. I don't need you looking over my shoulder."

“The world is looking over your shoulder,” Borgan said. “They’re looking over all of our shoulders.”

A week later he fired the surgeon.

In his first thirty-six months, Borgen recruited twenty-five cutters and ended practices like having outside doctors in private practice sweeping in to perform surgery. Instead, he mandated they become employees of the hospital and operate as part of a team. He was a big believer in *The No Asshole Rule* (“I love that book!” he says), looking for personality traits like self-awareness, critical thinking, and self-effacement, choosing surgeons not just for what was on their résumés but for how they meshed with the supportive yet self-critical culture he was inculcating. To further this, Maimonides became one of the first hospitals in the United States to institute a formal time-out before each operation, the way pilots do, and a formal debrief after. “That caused about ten surgeons to leave,” Borgen recalls. “They said, ‘I’m not doing this. This is bullshit.’ Okay, fine. See you later.” Borgen would have been happy to pack their bags.

There’s an abundance of literature on the deleterious effects of fear and intimidation in workplaces. An experienced copilot might be reluctant to speak up if he’s afraid of the pilot—even if the plane is about to hit a mountain. Borgen set about hiring people who could bring a sense of camaraderie and dissolve the hospital’s traditional rigid hierarchies. They wouldn’t become defensive if asked, “Why is this fluid this color?” or, “Why is this red light blinking?” If challenged, they would stop and, through teamwork, seek the best solution. The result, Borgen says, is that performance improved. Since he constituted a new cardiac surgical team, patients stand a better chance of surviving a heart attack if taken to Maimonides than at 98 percent of hospitals in the country, according to government statistics.

That didn’t mean there wasn’t the occasional blemish. Two years after Borgen took over as chief surgeon he was informed that a “wrong-sided procedure” had taken place. Doctors were supposed to inject dye and take a picture of a vein on the left but instead took one on the right. There was no harm to the patient, but surgeons had broken several rules that Borgen had instituted. He got rid of the entire team, but not because they had committed several errors: “It was their reaction to the mistake,” he says, “the inability to take criticism and to learn from their mistakes.”

He likens the feedback that each surgeon receives to that of a game. In a video game, a player receives immediate feedback on every shot, gesture, or movement. He constantly learns from his mistakes or he doesn't get to the next level. At Maimonides Hospital, if a surgeon or staff does something wrong, he has to acknowledge it then correct it the next time. "If you play the game the same way every time, without ever criticizing how you play the game, you're never going to reach the highest level," Borgen says.

Through the use of simulations, games are also a mainstay of surgery. It begins with training. Until recently, medical students practiced surgery on live animals, standard practice for more than a hundred years. Borgen remembers the first time, as a sophomore at Tulane, he operated on a small cat set to be euthanized. It was a simple procedure but he nicked an artery and the animal began to bleed to death. "The room started swaying, and I felt clammy and someone caught me or I would have completely passed out," he says. "I was so distressed."

Maimonides shut its animal research center in 2010 in favor of more modern training methods. Nowadays each medical student practices over the Internet by manipulating instruments: stacking blocks, tying knots, putting square pegs in square holes. A proctor observes on her own computer screen at home via a Web-based Skype-like technology. To ape the chaos of a large urban ER, the hospital purchased lifelike mannequins that respond to medical emergencies as humans would. For a bit of theater and verisimilitude, while doctors are in the middle of an acute trauma case a pizza delivery guy might walk in and try to distract the team, demanding payment for a pepperoni pizza while doctors see how the trainees respond.

Even surgery is, at its essence, a simulation—at least from the vantage point of the doctor performing it—and more often than not involves minimally invasive, video-assisted techniques and a robot. The surgeon operates by watching a computer screen and manipulating levers, while another doctor inserts instruments through multiple small incisions. To show me, Borgen leads me down Maimonides' corridors until we come to an operating room. After handing me a "bunny suit"—shoe covers, rubber gloves, and a mask with instructions to put them on—we head inside.

There, Dr. David Silver is performing a robotic prostatectomy, which involves removing cancer from a patient's prostate. He sits on a stool, his eyes locked into a 3-D, high-resolution viewing scope, manipulating levers like he's the operator of a bulldozer. The robotic system is called da Vinci, and runs about $2.5 million. Borgen estimates the equipment in the room costs about $4 million. Across the room lies the sedated patient, covered from head to toe except for the small area being operated on. Silver's assistant stands over the patient, changing attachments, needle holders, scissors, cautery, and staplers. Ten feet away sits the anesthesiologist, lounging in a chair and playing a game on her iPhone. Soft rock plays in the background: "Hotel California," by the Eagles. Like the driver in a car, the doctor chooses the music.

Borgen, in whispers, explains what's happening. In a traditional operation, the kind portrayed on old TV shows like *ER*, there was a doctor, an assistant, a resident, and a nurse, all circling the patient. It's very different today. Now a doctor isn't even looking at the patient anymore. He's looking at a screen. But he sees so much more and can do much more detailed work with far greater precision and speed. "In the chest," Borgen says, "we go in with the robot and lymph nodes look as big as a cabinet. We see things we didn't see before." There are areas of the body—deep in the pelvis, for instance—where a doctor's hands simply won't fit. A robot, however, can perform surgery in these extremely tight spaces. The electric arms move in ways that human hands can't, so a surgeon's stitches can defy logic, and this benefits patients. In colorectal surgery, which involves excising cancer, robots have eliminated the need for colostomies. Before, 80 percent of patients used to get them.

"Oh yeah, baby, right in, there it goes," Dr. Silver says. "Okay," he tells his assistant. "Do the other side." A few seconds later: "Good, good job. Go, go, go, go; whoa, whoa, whoa, whoa, whoa, whoa, little jump. Good, good; little more. Good."

Borgen translates: "This is a resident doctor and his assistant, so she's watching on the screen. As he needs different attachments for the robot, she changes those out. Right now, she's moving the catheter back and forth as he sutures this up."

I find the operating room profoundly serene. I tell Borgen I've been to health spas that seemed tenser, but he disagrees. He's performed hundreds of minimally invasive operations and tells me the robotic arms are so strong they could snap a metal bar, so there is no such thing as a small mistake. If you're removing cancer-containing lymph nodes there's the fear of missing one, and one misstep could nick a blood vessel or primary organ. But for patients it is far superior to traditional surgery. It means a much speedier recovery. One patient, Borgen tells me, came in with a ruptured thoracic aortic aneurysm. In the past, he would have been under the knife eight to twelve hours and endured a long, slow recovery involving a month-long hospital stay—assuming he survived. With minimally invasive surgery doctors simply deployed a graft, and he went home in two days.

Learning to simulate operations took some adjustment. "I remember the first time I did laparoscopic surgery it felt so foreign," Borgen says. "It took a while to coordinate the movements and get used to the fact there was a human being across the room while you're essentially watching a TV screen. But all of this is so much better."

Several studies indicate that simulated, minimally invasive surgery is clearly superior to the old way when it comes to patient recovery. Operations are shorter with less blood loss. Data on laparoscopic colon cancer surgery versus open indicate there was a faster recovery and better patient experience. Whether long-term cancer operations are as good as traditional surgery is still unresolved. To further test this, the hospital board has been pushing doctors to conduct more traditional operations, but the surgeons have resisted.

"You want to leave the hospital and see your family in two days," Borgen says of patients. You don't want to needlessly make them endure a seven-hour operation and six weeks of painful recovery simply to aid in the collection of data.

"Like if you're in a study, you don't want to be the placebo group," I reply.

"Placebo, yeah, I used to have a cartoon that had a tombstone that said 'John Doe: Member of Placebo Group.'"

Borgen does have one concern, though. In this age of minimally invasive surgery, younger doctors may go through their entire careers without ever feeling a gallbladder, liver, or stomach, or touching a beating heart. "In laparoscopic axillary node dissections, which are part of breast cancer treatment, it's critical what you feel," he says. "It's so easy to miss a lymph node embedded in fat that you would only know was there by touching and feeling that tiny spot, knowing that it feels like a BB."

But, he adds, "It's really hard to simulate that."

Human-made Human

I'm in Carla Pugh's lab at the University of Wisconsin hospital finishing up a hernia operation. Just about done. All I need to do is put in the last few stitches. The miniature camera attached to the end of the two long needles I'm manipulating doesn't lie. I'm a lousy surgeon. My stitches look like an abstract expressionist made them. Fortunately the patient isn't alive. In fact, he never lived, since it's little more than a cloth box with different layers of mesh, which look like the internal organs of a human, and laparoscopic tools, all of which sit on a base consisting of two Frisbees.

This is Pugh's laparoscopic ventral hernia simulator, a decidedly low-tech device that exists in stark contrast to the hospital's high-definition surgical simulations. But that's precisely the point. Pugh built it to mimic how surgery feels from the vantage point of a surgeon. It deploys the same tools used in a typical laparoscopic procedure: the same scope, mesh, suture, and instruments. Residents and other trainees are tested on their decision making. For example, how they locate the hernia defect using the laparoscopic camera, determining the appropriate measures to repair it, judging the best stitching methods and the selection of the appropriate size and type of repair mesh. After completing the "operation," the trainee can pull back a flap and look closely at the stitching. As with her training simulators, Pugh cobbled it together from off-the-shelf parts procured from various stores and cloth: cotton, silk, burlap, polypropylene, and other synthetics.

Dr. Jacob Greenberg, a surgeon in his midthirties who specializes in minimally invasive techniques for surgery of the stomach and esophagus as well as bariatric surgery, has trained on Pugh's simulator, which cost about a hundred dollars to produce, and claims it is more realistic than the twenty-thousand-dollar sims available elsewhere in the hospital. Pugh's surgical simulator offers a "real, actual 3-D space, not a 2-D space virtually created," and "visual feedback." You can take the top off and see how well you have sewn up the defect where you can't with other simulations. "The students love it," he adds, "and so do the residents."

Pugh has created other sims for surgical procedures, all made from layers of different types of cloth to mimic humans' insides, none of which have sensors in them. There's one that mimics part of the Whipple procedure for patients with pancreatic cancer, others to simulate the removal of a tumor from the colon and an operation on large or small intestines, and another that simulates another kind of hernia procedure. She has these high-touch simulators made by a fabric vendor whom she trained and who keeps all the proceeds. Thus far she has sold about a hundred of them to hospitals and training centers around the country. Channeling her inner Madame du Coudray, Pugh also added a baby delivery simulator to her line of sims. She formed the birth canal out of liquid latex shaped into a pelvis and performed surgery on dolls purchased from Toys "Я" Us by widening their shoulders and using a metal frame to extend them. "I made their heads bigger or smaller," she says, "because different sizes and shapes may make it difficult for them to be pulled through the birth canal."

Most of her time, however, is taken up with running the six-million-dollar Clinical Simulation Center, located in another wing of the hospital, where I meet Susan Olson, a registered nurse in her fifties who doubles as a senior education specialist. Olson, who started her nurse training in 1976, is old enough to remember practicing intramuscular injections on oranges before being allowed to stick a real-life patient.

She takes me on a tour, showing me training rooms chock full of crash-test-dummylike figures in various sizes and shapes, which she calls "low-fidelity mannequins." Some are partial bodies. In one room there are rows of models with just a head and neck for CPR training and lessons in performing tracheotomies. In another a mannequin has different colored vessels for arteries and veins. Trainees perform palpations, locate the proper vessel to puncture, then thread a catheter into the heart. In a separate room there's a mannequin with a lumbar puncture. A trainee would practice checking the spinal cord fluid to see if it's infected.

"There's a big difference between reading about something and doing it," Olson says. "You need to experience the sensation about how deep do you go, what does it feel like when you pop in to that space, and we can have that connected to the spinal cord fluid and simulate that."

Trainees would first view a video explaining the procedure, get a lecture, then engage in hands-on practice. They are also taught about hygiene.

"I certainly would not want an infection because somebody bumped and contaminated the needle that is going into my spinal cord," she says. "You can't just set down a needle in an area that is contaminated and expect to pick it back up. Anything between the chest and the waist is the only sterile area. They can't scratch their nose while they are doing the whole procedure."

Next, Olson introduces me to TraumaMan, a staple of hospital training since it was developed in 2001. TraumaMan is actually a limbless trunk—somewhat like a dress dummy—made up of simulated human tissue comprised of what the company calls an "elastomeric composition designed specifically for surgical dissection." There's an accompanying kit that allows trainers to create realistic-looking wounds with moulage.

The result is a set of ghoulish mannequins with serious injuries, which look like they belong on a horror movie set. She leads me to one with a serious stomach wound with "blood" oozing out.

"Looks like a traumatic farm accident," Olson says. She's seen a lot of those in Wisconsin.

She shows me another partial mannequin whose forehead has been pierced by a large screw. Probably a construction accident, Olson explains. She's treated a lot of those, too.

Little is left to chance. We pass a bank of sinks where trainees practice scrubbing and putting on gowns and gloves. When administering to mannequins trainees are required to follow strict protocols as if they were taking care of real-live patients. There's a room with arcadelike games and toys to build skills for laparoscopic surgery. One is inspired by the Claw Crane arcade game, in which a player picks up stuffed animals and other prizes with tongs controlled by levers. In this iteration the user looks into a monitor and has seventeen seconds to pick up a ring with long forceps, place it on a peg, switch to his other hand, pick it up again, and transfer it to a different peg. In the corner is a box holding different kinds of cloth that allow a person to practice suturing. Nurse Olson picks up one and says, "Pretty sutures, but he sutured the bowel closed. Not good." There's a practice ultrasound machine that provides a realistic image of an embryo. Even the hallway we walk down is wider than usual, designed to be like those in a hospital that handle gurneys.

Stan, the Man

Really, though, I'm here to meet Stan D. Ardman, or just Stan, the world's most advanced medical mannequin. (His name is a play on "standard man.") When Nurse Olson and I enter his room I suppress the urge to apologize for barging in. Stan is lying in a hospital bed with the usual assorted medical contraptions around him. He has light-brown hair, blue eyes, is five foot eleven, and weighs 170 pounds. His skin is a composite of urethane-silicon, under which sit a rats' nest of wires, hydraulics, pneumatics, and other hardware driven by powerful microprocessors and software. He has a circulatory system comprised of hoses that mimic synthetic veins and arteries that transport fake blood and has a pulse and a heartbeat. As anesthesia starts to take hold his eyes flutter shut and open gradually when he comes out of it.

When Stan is turned on he reacts just like any other patient. He blinks, breathes, pulses, and speaks. Actually a doctor or nurse speaks for him from the control room through a speaker in his throat—or Stan has a number of preprogrammed expressions and statements. He also cries out in anguish, coughs, and even passes gas. If he goes into cardiac arrest, trainees can perform CPR or shock him back to the living with defibrillator paddles. Air bags in his chest enable him to breathe like a human and doctors can reinflate his collapsed lung with a long needle and a chest tube. An IV can be shot into his right arm and a catheter plugged into his urinary tract. Attendees can insert a needle into his thorax to draw fluid and gauge internal bleeding.

Stan, a high-fidelity mannequin, is no six-million-dollar man—he runs about two hundred thousand dollars. But he comes from a long line of medical mannequins that stretch back more than five decades. The first, dubbed Resusci Annie, was hatched in 1960, designed to simulate mouth-to-mouth resuscitation, which explains why her inventors based her face on a famous drowning victim in the river Seine in Paris. In the late 1960s, two doctors at the University of Southern

California, working with aerospace engineers, built the first computer-controlled life-sized robot they dubbed "Sim One." Far ahead of its time, Sim One's heart beat, it had a pulse and blood pressure, and its chest moved as if breathing. At a cost of a hundred thousand dollars, only one was constructed and the computers that operated this complex piece of machinery took up an entire room. The 1970s heralded the arrival of "Gynny," a partial (waist to midthigh) plastic mannequin for pelvic exams, equipped with a vaginal vault, cervix, uterus, ovaries, and a rectum. It wasn't until the late 1990s, when computers simultaneously got smaller and more powerful, that more realistic medical mannequins became available.

Stan's sensors discern whether a doctor's technique is correct. "They will show us if I've got my hands positioned correctly," Olson says. "When we are giving him breath, it will show that air going into his lungs—or not, if I'm not doing that correctly." He is also programmed with several different lung sounds to simulate a patient with pneumonia or asthma. When Stan goes into shock he sweats, too, which Olson says "adds to the realism." The only major limitation is that a nurse can't put saline in the mannequin because of the electronics (he'd short out). Instead the syringes inject air.

Olson can tell by the way the mannequin is set up that Stan has been prepped for an afternoon training session that will involve a patient with heart problems and abnormal rhythm. Students will have to quickly diagnose what ails him while doctors observe from the control room behind one-way glass, manipulating the controls of the computer. In other scenarios, Stan might be having complications from a liver transplant. Paramedics might be administering to a car accident victim. A heart attack victim could have a dangerous reaction to anesthesia. The room is rimmed with four cameras to catch all the action. Afterward trainees watch the video and receive critical feedback.

Olson hears the stories from trainees who have undergone simulation training. A physician from one of the outlying communities told her that after completing her simulation training she came upon a three-year-old with a heart rate of 220. Because of the training, she knew exactly what to do, since she had practiced the maneuvers in class.

Trainees also come to view Stan as much more than a mere amalgamation of plastic, circuits, and wires. Says Olson: "They will say, 'Is the patient breathing?' and we'll say, 'Did you check his chest? And see him breathe? Did you check for a pulse?' 'Oh yes,' they'll respond, 'there it is. It feels kind of fast.'"

Sometimes trainees become emotionally attached. Stan is so life-like that residents have been known to sob when he dies, which he does, without complaint, several times a week. One trainee at another hospital became so distraught she even had to undergo post-traumatic stress treatment.

Carla Pugh doesn't discourage trainees from developing a deep level of empathy with inanimate objects. Even when she's using a basic sim that is little more than a disembodied plastic breast in a box and hooked by wires to a computer, she insists that trainees refer to it as "she" and that "she" be covered with a blue cloth when not in use just like they would place a blanket over a patient on a gurney.

"Because it's a human being," Pugh says. "She's sitting there on the table with her breast exposed, so when we're not examining her we cover her."

PART III

GAMES AT WORK

In one of his stand-up routines comedian Chris Rock explains the difference between a job and a career, revealing that he once worked a minimum-wage job as a dishwasher at the Red Lobster on Queens Boulevard in Queens, New York, scraping shrimp off of plates. He advised people with careers to shut up around people with jobs. "Don't let your happiness make someone sad," he said. Because "when you got a career, there ain't enough time in the day. When you got a career, you look at your watch, time just flies. Like goddamn, whoa. It's five thirty-five. Damn, I gotta come in early to work on my project. 'Cause there ain't enough time when you got a career. When you got a job, there's *too* much time."

Anyone who has held a stultifying job can attest to how slowly the day passes. It's a completely different story for most of us with careers. Doing what you like doing is good for engagement. The trick is transferring some of this to jobs that are just that: jobs. "Work can be tough. It can be boring, repetitive, complex; you have to collaborate," says Stanford professor Byron Reeves, who studies the role of multiplayer online games to improve collaboration, innovation, and productivity, as well as customer and employee engagement. "If you are not engaged, it doesn't go well."

Reeves predicts that game design will eventually insert employees *inside* video games. He posits two scenarios for a mythical call-center employee named Jennifer. In the first, Jennifer spends eight regimented hours a day at a typical corporate cubicle farm. She fields seventy-five calls a day. Her performance is tracked on a gargantuan lighted board that lists data such as handling time, number of calls on hold, and projected versus actual call volume. She must log out for lunch, so the exact start of her break can be recorded. If she's late, she can be suspended. Turnover at this office is high, and there's scant opportunity to get to know coworkers. For the three months she works there, she's talking constantly, surrounded by a sea of other people. Yet she's lonely, bored, and feels undervalued.

In the second scenario, Jennifer works from home. When she logs in, she's greeted by her own personalized avatar and joins her twenty-person team. While they congregate on a pirate ship (this week's theme), they are in reality spread across three different time zones. But they can chat with one another, so Jennifer forges friendships. Her team competes with others and her success depends on the success of her teammates. As calls are routed to her screen, she accumulates points for inputting data accurately and following company protocols. There's even voice stress-analysis software, so that if Jennifer handles a caller deftly, she scores more. The higher she scores, the more she helps her team, whose progress is expressed by how quickly its ship sails to an island, where they are rewarded with a real-world perk: free holiday airline travel.

Jennifer performs the same core job functions in both scenarios. In the second, though, even mundane tasks seem fun, and the constant feedback she receives in the form of points gives her a growing sense of accomplishment. She's become a motivated, loyal, productive team member.

This far-out scenario may not be as far off into the future as you might think. At IBM, Chuck Hamilton holds the curious title of V-learning strategy leader. (The "V" stands for virtual.) One of the stranger parts of his gig is to manage the tens of thousands of avatars that IBMers have created for themselves. Like Cisco Systems and other large companies, IBM saves on travel and hotel expenses by holding the occasional convention in a virtual space; a couple of hundred employees, each represented by an avatar, can attend. "In the early days," Hamilton says, "people showed up as whatever they chose—dogs, cats, penguins. It was a playful, exploratory time." Now that these virtual conventions are common fare, however, IBMers' avatars have gotten, well, more traditionally IBMish. "They modify their avatars to get as close as they can get to the way they really look," he says. "I do get e-mail from people in Japan and China asking where they can get a particular eye shape or skin color."

In this section we'll explore why businesses in this increasingly social media–fueled world must better engage workers and customers or confront potentially dire consequences. We'll look at a company that has achieved a "self-fulfilling cycle of benefit" for both customers and its business, another that has deputized users to handle complicated questions about software coding, and a third that deploys game mechanics to encourage customers to act as customer-service representatives. We'll visit a restaurant outside Boston that has added a game layer, which creates customer feedback loops and increases monthly revenue 2 percent to 4 percent. And we'll travel to Microsoft to spend time with Ross Smith, who has been experimenting with introducing games into the company's famously challenging workplace.

There's a lot more to gamification than offering users, employees, and consumers badges and other virtual trinkets, of course. Rewarding Tropicana orange juice drinkers with redeemable points, for instance, is "Taking the thing that is least essential to games [points] and representing it as the core of the experience," as game designer Margaret Robertson put it. She's even coined a neologism—"pointsification"—to describe the phenomenon.

Sebastian Deterding, a German game designer and academic, decries "the badge measles" as an "infectious disease currently spreading across the Internet." Starting with Foursquare and other geolocation services, it jumped to Yelp, *Huffington Post*, Google News, and now afflicts sites of all stripes and sizes. He quotes Will Wright, creator of the megahit *The Sims*, who once said, "Game elements aren't the monosodium glutamate of fun that you can simply add to an activity to make it motivating and engaging."

Businesses, Deterding says, "engage in a very flawed pop behaviorism" by treating games "as Skinner boxes that dole out points and badges like sugar pellets every time we hit the right lever." People play games because they enjoy the tension that is presented when they are overcoming challenges. Games are intrinsically motivating. We play them for ourselves, not because they offer rewards like points or money. In other words, "games are not fun because they are games," he says, "but when they are well designed."

Robertson and Deterding are right, and you rarely hear about the gamification failures, which, if the designers don't engage users, slip quietly into the night, just another corporate expense on a balance sheet. But the companies I write about in the following chapters have judiciously incorporated gamification into their workplaces, products, or services, motivating employees or even their own users to perform tasks they normally wouldn't want to do. This is true of those working at a virtual call center, trawling online message boards for queries to field, serving at restaurants, and bug-testing software. While the recipes may be the same—engage, encourage competition, offer instant feedback—they play out in vastly different environments.

Virtual call center LiveOps, British SIM card provider giffgaff, and EngineYard, which offers software in the cloud, all maintain large, distributed workforces that either field calls from their homes where they can only be monitored remotely or offer customer service over the Web. The use of game mechanics helps these companies solve the problem of cheap labor while maintaining better quality of service. With restaurants deploying Objective Logistics software, waitstaff—the frontline employees who are the ones to deal with customers directly—compete for the privilege of naming their schedules, which turns out to be a powerful motivator. They aren't ordered to be friendly to diners, push more expensive entrees, or nagged to keep refilling water glasses—and they can't look forward to raises or promotions—but they're graded on their ability to upsell (sell more items), which leads to bigger checks and ultimately more generous tips. At Microsoft, the workforce is comprised of highly skilled, well-paid employees, many of whom are on career tracks at a hugely profitable, mature company that may very well be on the decline. It has to navigate a generation gap between younger engineers and Microsoft veterans and induce already harried, overworked people to take on even more responsibilities when new software must be tested in-house.

As varied as these work environments are, these companies all turned to the same solution, gamification, and it's been working.

To steal an idea from Gamification Summit Chair Gabe Zichermann, perhaps companies should create an entirely new management position: chief engagement officer. Her job would be to focus entirely on engagement. Zichermann proposed it as a customer advocacy position, but I think it makes sense to expand its duties to include all sorts of engagement—from customers and staff to freelancers and management.

Find ways to make work seem less like work, and everyone benefits.

CHAPTER 10

NEW WORLD ORDER

For centuries, humans congregated in small communities, with the vast majority of commerce involving small, mom-and-pop shopkeepers and modest local retailers. Citizens worked, lived, and socialized in these communities, and news spread fast. A bad customer experience could kill a store because everyone within walking or horse-and-buggy distance might hear about it. After the introduction of the automobile people took up commuting, and supermarkets with more efficient supply chains moved in and broke down these tight-knit communities. Mass media, that is the advent of newspapers and television, abetted this cultural change. People didn't share information so much anymore; it was pushed to them in the form of advertising. Consumer satisfaction became largely irrelevant because there was no efficient mechanism for people to disseminate their product experiences with one another.

As a result, for the past fifty years customer service has been the backwater of a business. Because it didn't add directly to a company's bottom line it was deemed as important to a business's ultimate well-being as the human resources department. Purchase a defective blow dryer or need help troubleshooting a problem with a new stereo and you dialed a call center, hoping you wouldn't be placed on hold in an infinite call loop and praying someone could help you. If you felt gypped, you might gripe to friends and family members or write the company a blistering letter to be filed away where no one would see it.

With the emergence of social media, however, where one bad experience can go viral via Twitter, Facebook, and YouTube, becoming the equivalent of a hit song and tarnishing a company's reputation, and the advent of consumer reviews on Amazon, Yelp, Apple's App Store, and others, there's far greater transparency. Suddenly the balance of power has shifted to the consumer, whose influence spreads far and wide, and companies are scrambling to keep up.

Almost one in five customers (17 percent) surveyed in a 2012 study commissioned by American Express used social media at least once over the course of a year to obtain a service response, a number that is surely growing. When these social media users encountered good service they told an average of 42 people about it (compared with just 9 for those who were not on social media). When they had a bad experience they were even more vocal, telling 53 people on average. Yet it took a customer roughly 4.4 phone calls to fix a problem with a company, while 21 percent had to call back 7 times. No wonder there are iPhone apps (one is called "Phone Rage") that will stay on hold for you until an operator answers. This is a by-product of the customer service quagmire, where a company has to cope with a veritable flood of complaints, sometimes on the order of tens of thousands a day.

The longer it takes to satisfy a customer, whose complaints are logged in a public forum visible to the world, the more likely the problem will snowball. The speed with which social media can affect a company's "trust factor" is leading to a focus on what Richard Laermer, founder of RLM Public Relations in New York and author of several books on viral marketing, labels "horizontal growth." In other words, "instead of pushing for new customers, focus on your current customers," he says. "If they have a positive interaction with customer service, or love your product, they'll tell other people and do your marketing for you, which will attract new customers."

I've been a willing instigator in this horizontal growth. As an iPhone user I was for years tethered to AT&T and often flambéed the company for its rickety network, which is notorious for dropping calls. But I softened my stance after returning from a short trip to Toronto. An AT&T customer service rep called to inform me I racked up hundreds of dollars in roaming charges because I had neglected to protect myself with an international-travel "data pack." She offered to retroactively apply one for $24.99, which effectively wiped the slate clean. You bet I tweeted my satisfaction.

This is precisely what the company that has become famous among iPhone users for dropped calls and other aggravations hoped I would do. Molly DeMaagd, AT&T's director of social media, told me the company monitors blogs, Facebook, Twitter, and trolls the Web for negative commentary. But it has also increased its watch over customers' usage, in large part because an unhappy Twitter user doesn't merely reach an audience consisting of a few friends. "It could be that hundreds of thousands or millions of people hear about it," she says, "and that could have a negative impact on AT&T's brand image." I've also taken to Twitter to badger Network Solutions into lowering the price of reregistering several domains I had parked there over the years. The company was charging $39.99 a year per domain to renew, but, as I pointed out, I could move them to another service provider charging $9.99, so Network Solutions matched it.

In the old days, it was about distribution, location, marketing spend, celebrity endorsement, traffic buying, or the black art of search engine optimization. Now it is about wooing consumers by wowing them and earning their respect, trust, and allegiance so they repay you with rave reviews, which reinforce your brand and affect your bottom line. How many times have you clicked "buy" in Apple's App store without thinking just because the app you were looking at had a flurry of five-star reviews or decided not to buy something from Amazon because other users had panned it?

Surveys bear this out. Market research firm Cone, Inc., in its 2011 Online Influence Trend Tracker, reported that almost 90 percent of consumers who were surveyed found online reviews trustworthy. What's more, 80 percent had changed their mind about a purchase when confronted with negative reviews, while 87 percent confirmed their decision of a purchase based on positive reviews. The survey noted that one driver of this trend is "near-universal" access to the Internet and consumers' embrace of smartphones, which allow users inside stores to pull up product reviews and information before purchasing. Indeed, almost 60 percent said they were more likely to research recommended products online because they could quickly and easily find information via their mobile phones.

A Nielsen survey from 2012 that looked at the level of trust in marketing tactics found that Internet users trusted online reviews posted by strangers more than they did editorial content in newspapers, magazines, and online news sites. Others indicate that one-star reviews of books on Amazon have a greater impact in dampening sales than positive five-star reviews have in increasing them, although there can be nuances. If detailed enough, negative reviews can actually bolster sales of a product if they are perceived as offering value to a consumer, who can then make up his mind. No wonder some companies have tried to put in the fix. New York State Attorney General Andrew Cuomo fined Lifestyle Lift, a cosmetic surgery chain, three hundred thousand dollars for "astroturfing"—having employees pose as satisfied consumers to publish positive reviews and comments to trick Web-browsing consumers. Amazon deleted reviews for a Kindle Fire tablet computer case when the company learned that the case maker was paying people to write positive reviews. Meanwhile Amazon reviews are rife with paid-for reviews, which the company does its best to delete. If Web 1.0 was the static Web, in which information flowed one way from Web sites to site visitors, and Web 2.0 heralded the rise of social media sites such as Facebook and Twitter—they let users post and share their own content—then Web 3.0 has been a complete shift in the relationship between companies and consumers.

A number of businesses—appliance makers, airlines, computer manufacturers, fast-food chains, retailers, telecommunication companies—have found themselves ensnared in nightmare social media scenarios, events that five years ago would likely not have pricked the public's consciousness. There's the uplifting tale of Salt Lake blogger Heather Armstrong and her brand-new thirteen-hundred-dollar Maytag washing machine, which had gone on the fritz. It was not propitious timing, since Armstrong had a newborn baby in the house. After a repairman made several visits but was unable to fix it, laundry was piling up and Armstrong dialed Maytag's help line, only to confront a decidedly unhelpful customer service representative.

Boiling over, she took matters into her own hands and jumped on Twitter, where, at the time, she had more than 1.5 million followers: "So that you may not have to suffer like we have: DO NOT EVER BUY A MAYTAG. I repeat: OUR MAYTAG EXPERIENCE HAS BEEN A NIGHTMARE." A few minutes later she tweeted:

"Have I mentioned what a nightmare our experience was with Maytag?" Within nine hours Maytag's owner, Whirlpool, pinged her over Twitter, and the next day not only was her Maytag machine fixed but Bosch, a competing appliance maker, offered her a free washer, which she donated to a women's shelter.

Companies aren't only forced to confront unhappy customers. These days the social-facing front of a business must field all sorts of brand-affecting issues. A jewelry maker accused Urban Outfitters of ripping off her designs, which snowballed into a full-blown social media–fueled crisis. Domino's Pizza had to put out a PR fire after two employees filmed a prank in the kitchen of the restaurant where they worked, posting a video on YouTube featuring one of them preparing sandwiches for delivery while stuffing cheese up his nose and wiping mucus on the order while the other provided narration. Over Twitter JetBlue, Virgin, Southwest, and other airlines have all had to combat legions of irate passengers, some trapped for hours on the tarmac, and in the case of Southwest, a kerfuffle with director Kevin Smith, who was kicked off a flight because the pilot deemed him too fat and therefore a safety risk.

The allegations don't necessarily need to be based on facts. On a Friday in mid-2011 a photo appeared on Twitter purporting to show that McDonald's required African Americans to pay additional service fees. Naturally the photo went viral. After the company declared it a hoax the company went full bore on Twitter, asking "influencers" to spread the truth and replied personally to individual Tweeters. The rumor was squelched and on Monday McDonald's stock price rose 5 percent. On the other hand, sometimes McDonald's has made a mess of social media. At the 2012 Olympics, London mayor Boris Johnson, addressing fast-food companies' sponsorship of the spectacle, called criticism of McDonald's "bourgeois snobbery," adding, "It's classic liberal hysteria about very nutritious, delicious, food, extremely good for you I'm told, not that I eat a lot of it myself. Apparently this stuff is absolutely bursting with nutrients." The public response? You might say McDonald's was flame embroiled and the mayor accused of selling his soul for money; the night before the opening ceremony an opinion tracker of the twenty-five official Olympic sponsors ranked McDonald's dead last, based on a formula mixing the volume of tweets, sentiment, potential reach of the tweeter, and reception of the tweets.

It's abundantly clear that customer relations have migrated to social channels and it makes little sense to try and funnel people to toll-free phone lines and automated menus when they are already massing on Twitter and Facebook. Joshua March, founder of Conversocial, a London-based maker of social media customer service software for businesses, estimates that almost a quarter of people become a fan of a company page to get customer service help and expert advice, and about half joined just to get product information and updates. What Facebook calls fans are really customers, and should be treated as such. "The conversations a company has with its customers over social media truly represent its brand," March says, "often at the dynamic moment when point-of-purchase decisions are being played out."

While many companies have for a while eavesdropped on customers, these businesses now have their own social identities, and people aren't just blogging about them, they are speaking to them as if they are, well, human. Unfortunately most companies have not adapted to these new rules of engagement. A study by Maritz Research found that 85 percent of people surveyed had never received a reply from a brand after posting positive or negative comments online or on social media despite the expectation of more than half of complainants that they would. What's more, 88 percent of consumers in another study said they would be less likely to buy from companies that ignore complaints in social media. The more successfully a company pushes a Facebook page or Twitter account for marketing, the more its customers will use it to ask questions or grieve their complaints. "These comments are public, for all to see, and swift responses are expected," March says. "Failure to deliver can alienate existing and potential customers."

It's not easy to separate the relevant customer-service queries from the chaff, mind you. If you printed out and stacked transcripts of every phone call the U.S. National Security Agency records over the span of a year, the resulting pile would stretch to the moon and back—far too much material for the agency to effectively monitor. There's a similar info-glut that characterizes social media, with 98 percent of it occurring on two channels: Twitter and Facebook (with almost all brand mentions there occurring in the news feed). Conversocial met with an American telecommunications company, which March would not name, that records four hundred thousand pieces of social content mentioning it every month. Typically, though, only 10 percent to 20 percent of social media chitchat between consumers and businesses relates to a customer service issue.

This is where the Conversocial software platform comes in. Through natural language processing and automatic keyword searches, it surveys Twitter and Facebook for customer service issues relating to its clients and filters them out so a company representative can quickly respond. Because of the sheer amount of data, companies simply don't have the resources to key in on relevant customer service queries, and customers do expect a company to respond—and quickly. In a survey conducted by New York University professor Liel Leibovitz, 30 percent of respondents said they expected companies to reply within hours after being contacted through social media, while 16.6 percent wanted a response in less than ten minutes, and 13.1 percent in under an hour. Almost a third demanded a response within the same business day. Meanwhile one in five used a mobile device to contact a company over social media while in a store. The Conversocial software provides a workflow so a team of people can process the comments, categorize, assign, and collaborate internally. If someone complains on a Facebook page, the company can see the full history of the complaint.

In a sense, Conversocial has taken the classic call center model and adapted it to the social media age. But others are bypassing a company's customer service department altogether by placing these activities in the hands of their own highly engaged customers. Think organization on a mass scale. Think the power of community, teamwork, and crowd sourcing.

In ancient Scottish English, "giff gaff" means mutual giving, the old custom of returning the favor of a gift with a gift, but it's also the idea for giffgaff, a small, fast-growing mobile phone service in the United Kingdom with an apparent fondness for lowercase letters. The company has a "share, share that's fair" approach to business. Its users participate in various company functions, namely customer service, marketing, and sales, and receive payback in the form of cash or additional minutes on their phone cards. Mike Fairman, the company's CEO, says the inspiration came from examples of mass collaboration across the pond in the United States: the 2008 Obama campaign, for one, and Wikipedia, except giffgaff is applied to a commercial environment. Redistributing duties allows giffgaff to keep down the cost of running the business and pass the savings on to customers. "It's a self-fulfilling cycle of benefit," Fairman says, "not just for customers but also for the business."

Giffgaff forged its community two months before launching the service. The first superuser, who spent hours reading through the company's terms and conditions—and any other material he could find—was waiting to answer questions when the site went live at midnight. From the beginning, Fairman says, "He was able to answer really tough questions." Since then it has consistently yielded prompt and able customer service: according to the company it takes an average of ninety seconds for a customer to receive an answer online, day or night, twenty-four hours a day from one of its forum members.

To motivate these ad hoc customer service providers, the company splits its profits fifty-fifty with users, giving back almost two million dollars in 2011, as well as millions of calling-plan minutes. In 2012 the top earner earned more than twenty-two thousand dollars over a six-month period. Users need not be tech geniuses; they can monitor other areas of the site, too. There's a section devoted to potential new users who can query existing customers about what they think of the business, how it operates, and to help them find the right SIM cards for their needs. Members also earn points for soliciting new members. About 40 percent of the company's customers participate in this loyalty program, which it calls a "payback scheme," with 2 percent donating their proceeds to charity.

Another company tapping the wisdom of its users to inform other users is Engine Yard, a platform as a service business that helps all kinds of concerns deploy and manage Java Script, Ruby on Rails, and PhP software. Because of the level of complexity of its offerings, a key aspect of Engine Yard's mission is educational. It offers all manner of video and podcast tutorials to assist developers with database creation and maintenance, platform architecture, and troubleshooting to name a few. When the answer to a particularly complicated question isn't apparent in its materials, users can pose questions to other users. Instead of the cold, hard cash that giffgaff uses to prod participation, Engine Yard relies on gamification (provided by Badgeville) to traffic in social capital in the form of recognition. (Some would simply call it bragging rights. Whatever.)

Users accumulate points for specific tasks—for example, contributing an article on a technical subject—that benefit the community. It not only furthers Engine Yard's educational goals, but community members view it as a badge of honor and the author gains greater peer recognition. Posting comments on the article can also help rack up points. "We set up tracking for these types of behaviors," Bill Platt, Engine Yard's vice president of worldwide customer service, says, "so we encourage greater participation by recognizing the behaviors known to help developers succeed, and help make a more engaging community where developers can shine." The company reports that the introduction of gamification to its community saved it at least 40 percent on operations costs, because it didn't have to scale up an entire customer service staff. And it can always scale back, if necessary, without having to lay off anyone.

All of this is simply a new twist on something that has been around since the advent of Web business in the mid- to late 1990s. In its early days eBay relied on volunteers to staff forums in a kind of information arbitrage: knowledgeable users provided customer service and guidance to those just starting out. The same for Amazon. When HotorNot, which hit the Web in 2000 and allowed anyone to rate the relative attractiveness of others through their photos, needed to monetize, its founders, James Hong and Jim Young, naturally turned to advertising. But the site had a porn problem, with some users throwing up nude pictures while pornographers phished for e-mail addresses to spam them, and advertisers would stay away unless the site was cleaned up.

At first they installed a community monitoring system by providing a button for users to click on if they found anything inappropriate. Any post tagged too often would be deleted. Still porn persisted. Figuring they required a more hands-on moderation system, Hong deputized his Taiwanese-born parents, who were retired. A few days later he asked how it was going.

"Oh, it's very interesting," his father replied. "Mom saw a picture of a guy and a girl and another girl and they were doing . . ."

"Dude," Hong told his partner, "my parents can't do this anymore. They're looking at porn all day."

They hit on the idea of tapping moderators within their community, requiring applicants for this nonpaying yet highly sought after gig to pen an essay (to discourage not-so-serious pranksters). Those chosen were tasked with expunging photos or posts with celebrities, minors, models, porn, group pictures, ads, or anything with contact information such as e-mail addresses or phone numbers. Assisted by hundreds of deputies riding herd and filtering content, they cleaned up the site in no time. With seven million page views a day and 130,000 photos posted on the site, HotorNot broke into Nielsen's top twenty-five advertising domains on the Web within three months of its launch.

Each of these Web-based examples seeks to replace the traditional call center with user-fueled solutions, but that doesn't mean call centers are fading away. On the contrary, they will likely be around a long time. Some have been adopting game mechanics to improve service, which too often in the past has been lacking, and reject outsourcing these jobs because they find that Americans prefer talking to other Americans. LiveOps, Inc., for instance, a virtual call center with twenty thousand independent contractors spread across thirty-eight states in the United States, has introduced gaming staples like points, badges, and leaderboards into its platform.

Its workforce consists mainly of women between thirty-five and forty-five who work part-time out of their own homes and on their own schedules, earning between eight dollars to ten dollars an hour. They are required to pay fifty dollars for a background check—operators handle sensitive information such as credit card numbers—and, if accepted, provide their own landline, computer with broadband connection, and a quiet place to work (no barking dogs or crying babies). A big chunk of LiveOps' business is handling inbound sales calls for infomericals, when phones ring off the hook ten minutes into a TV advertisement. One big customer is Guthy-Renker, which sells everything from Proactiv Solutions acne treatment to Malibu Pilates, Tony Robbins self-help DVDs to Dean Martin Roast DVDs, and skin care products fronted by Susan Lucci, Victoria Principal, and Leeza Gibbons. Another is Tristar, which peddles the AbRoller, Genie Bra, and Power Juicer, as well as Ronco—creators of the "As seen on TV!" Pocket Fisherman, rotisserie ovens, and knife sets. Then there's Beachbody, with its late-night, guilt-inducing infomercial workout systems "Insanity" and "p90x"; the Automobile Club of America, which depends on LiveOps operators to provide roadside assistance; Kodak; insurance companies; and more than two hundred others.

One such operator, Patti Walbridge, from Barre, Vermont, started at LiveOps in 2004, shortly after she gave birth to daughters fifteen months apart. Now almost fifty years old, she has a routine that goes something like this: she watches for the new schedule to "roll out" and clicks on the green spots that represent thirty-minute increments of her availability. Sometimes she'll log on in the hope of catching a green spot that somebody else let go. Then she simply waits for the phone to ring. Everything is scripted so that LiveOps is not only compliant with the law but newbies aren't as likely to be nervous. There's a science to these scripts, which are designed to maximize efficiency and help operators maintain control of a call. Based on the research of Robert Cialdini, author of several books on marketing and persuasion, each script attempts to answer frequently asked questions and confront possible objections before a caller can raise them.

When she picks up the phone, Walbridge announces what product she's representing (sometimes it's a wrong number), gives her first name, and states that the call will be recorded (about 2 percent of all calls are monitored, according to the company). "I don't think I've ever had a caller hang up, refusing to be recorded," she says. "They actually welcome it, knowing there's a third party verifying everything was done right." The script guides her through the sale, pushes additional products (it's called "upselling") to the point she is able to harvest the caller's credit card information and mailing address, or, if it's a "lead-generation call," garner a mailing address to send the relevant information.

Naturally, not every call results in a sale. If a caller asks a lot of questions (Walbridge draws the line at four or five, depending on the person and product), she refers him to the customer service number. "My job is to sell the product," she says. "If it sounds like there isn't going to be a sale, I need to delegate the call to customer service so I can take the next call, which might be an eager sale." It might be a complaint, as well. That is also delegated to customer service unless the customer has had no luck reaching anybody at any other avenue. She admits, "For very upset customers I'm not afraid to encourage them to contact a lawyer."

Operators are rewarded in a number of ways: the better Walbridge performs on a call, the more additional calls are funneled to her, which results in a higher call volume and better pay. Some programs have monetary incentives or commissions and drawings, and lotteries are offered to induce people to log on at specific times or on specific dates. Call volume tends to be better on nights and weekends when people might be home from work, so there are often incentives (a higher hourly wage, for instance) for people who can work those times.

Since 2010, LiveOps has been layering game mechanics into its system, offering virtual badges and points based on an operator's performance. Someone like Walbridge might tally points for keeping calls brief or receiving positive customer feedback, and there are also leaderboards that illustrate how well an agent is doing compared with other agents.

Sanjay Mathur, senior vice president of product management at LiveOps, says that gamification helps the company's widespread collection of operators to feel more a part of a community and identify with the team they're part of. Fifty agents might be servicing insurance giant Aegon, for example. "I will put you into this gamification portal to show you your relative performance, and show how the team is succeeding against the team goal as opposed to the individual goal," he says. "Then I'm going to start giving you points as individual team members to help you understand and showcase your performance against your peers." With these points, agents can buy virtual goods to dress up their avatars. It may not sound like much, but Mathur claims it has reduced call time, on average, 15 percent and helped increase sales by 10 percent.

Traditional call centers, with their low pay and almost endless rows of cubicles, are the quintessential dead-end job; many experience 100 percent worker turnover every year. Home Shopping Network, which runs its own call center out of Florida, has spawned numerous comment threads from disenchanted employees accusing the company of unfair labor practices and have described working there as torture.

But with a modest investment, companies can incorporate the characteristics that make games enjoyable into their workplaces. They won't spin a crappy job or dysfunctional environment into gold, but they can corral a largely decentralized workforce and encourage them to provide good service.

Better for their workers, better for them.

CHAPTER 11

CUSTOMER FEEDBACK LOOPS

Philip Beauregard was fourteen when he started his first job as a dishwasher and for the next seven years, until he graduated from Wharton with a degree in business, he worked virtually every job in the local restaurant business—from busboy to host to floor manager and more. Beauregard, whose father was a lawyer and mother was a social worker, was born and raised in New Bedford, Massachusetts, located sixty miles south of Boston and known as the "armpit of the cape" for both its geography and its economic happenstance. Once a rich whaling town—Herman Melville wrote *Moby-Dick* while living there in the 1840s—it had long ago fallen on hard times, characterized by a mix of once majestic whaler mansions and struggling, sometimes scary working-class neighborhoods.

Beauregard characterizes himself as the quintessential go-getter. Because he generally liked people and enjoyed interacting with everyone from teens on first dates to octogenarian ladies' clubs he made it a point to learn on the job. One day when he was sixteen he was waiting tables and approached a group of four women in their fifties.

"Hey, guys," he said, trying to be charming in an adolescent kind of way. "How are you today?"

After the women finished their meal he was surprised that they stiffed him on the tip and complained to the restaurant's manager. "Women," his boss explained, "do not like to be called 'guys,' especially women that are a little bit older. I know it's colloquial, but they just do not like it."

He took the criticism to heart and over time became good at reading customers. Although gifted in math, he didn't need to be a Nobel Prize–winning economist to know that if he casually offered appetizers or slyly suggested a drink instead of tap water, his average bill increased and so did his tip. Everything he said and did, he realized, influenced this performance, valuable lessons for the future entrepreneur.

A couple of years later one of the places Beauregard worked posted the weekly sales for each server, and he almost always won. His raw sales topped the rest of the staff and his tip averages were 20 percent to 25 percent while the others measured 17 percent to 20 percent. Yet older servers still wrangled the best shifts by asserting seniority, which meant the restaurant was leaving money on the table. Beauregard remembers one server filing her nails, the other lounging in a chair and gossiping while he raced around filling water glasses at *their* tables. One of their customers flagged him down, saying, "Could you *please* send our waitress over?"

Over time it dawned on him that restaurants were perhaps the biggest underperforming and unprofessional sales force in the world. At the same time, servers were missing out on vast opportunities to upsell. Instead of generic-brand vodka, get the customer to order Grey Goose, and while you're at it, an appetizer or two and dessert, all of which reap higher margins. Through experience Beauregard knew he could influence an entire party of six if he could key in on the influencer in the group. Gently persuade him or her to order the fried calamari or a beer and the rest would follow. Like the classic Sam Adams TV commercial, the one with a table of businessmen ordering iced tea at lunch until the head honcho says, "I'll have a Sam Adams," and everybody else changes his order.

Beauregard calls it "a social dance," and it is. Over the past half century, the nuclear family has taken the traditional Friday and Saturday night dinner from their homes to restaurants, which, along with bars, have become the social magnets, the places you go after work for a minivacation. Yet restaurants have put these vacations in the hands of eighteen-year-olds who may or may not be fully committed to the restaurant's success. Beauregard thought this was reckless. Restaurants want to convert every patron into a regular customer. To do that, service must be excellent. As restaurateur Danny Meyer often says, you go for the food, but return for the hospitality. But most restaurants didn't reward the excellence of their staffs. As an employee, though, Beauregard was merely one ingredient in the stew, so he put these thoughts behind him. At Wharton he pursued deep interests in mathematics and economics, although he did his utmost to hide his inner nerd, wrapping a *Maxim* magazine around a textbook on heuristics or statistics so frat-mates wouldn't look askance. Like many of his ilk, after graduating he slipped into a soul-snuffing job at a Boston-based investment bank, wondering if something better might come along.

One night in 2006, Beauregard battled insomnia. Some people count sheep when they can't sleep. Beauregard dissects mathematical equations—he found the work of John Nash, the Nobel Prize–winning economist featured in the book and movie *A Beautiful Mind*, particularly soothing. He thought back to his restaurant days and how behavioral science governed dynamics in workplaces. Then he pondered ways that microeconomics-rooted competition and natural selection could reward the best employees and motivate the rest. Ultimately he wanted to unwind all of these disparate behavioral threads and create a meritocracy based on a rewards mechanism. Eventually he settled on the restaurant industry as an ideal proving ground, with a powerful incentive rooted in scheduling: the best servers could claim the best shifts. The idea that this was gamification, a term not in wide use in 2006, didn't cross his mind, although later it would.

More to the point, he was righting wrongs that had once been perpetuated against him.

The Warez World

Beauregard decided to launch a start-up and knew the ideal partner: his friend and fellow "mathlete," Matthew Grace, who had also grown up on the Cape. While Beauregard's family was upper middle class, Grace, who was adopted as a baby, came from more modest means. His stepfather was a pipefitter who welded everything from heating systems to nuclear power plants, while his stepmother worked for a local credit union. Money was tight, and the precocious kid built Lego kits with thousands of pieces without consulting the directions to make it more challenging and slow himself down, although he got so good he could still do it within a few hours. In the early 1990s his mother got a computer and Grace, a latchkey kid, figured out how to use the dial-up modem to get online through AOL, where he frequented chat rooms. Then got into "warez," as in soft*wares*, where the latest releases were pirated.

It was heady stuff for a twelve-year-old. The warez world had an ethos all its own, a vitriolic culture oddly bereft of capital letters, where street slang was woven into the lexicon—"school" was spelled "skewl"; "the" was "da" (as in "da warez scene"); and anyone not on the inside was a "lamer." There were two main parts: release groups, which, since they located and cracked the software, sat at the top of the warez world, and couriers, who ferried the pilfered product to the masses. Each organization had a president, vice president, a council, and staff, including site operators and recruiters. Skirmishes among rivals abounded, decided not with guns and knives but by computer antics like taking over rival sites, sabotaging chat channels, spamming one another, and getting enemies booted offline. Grace loved that no one knew who he was; he was ranked solely on his skills (or "skillz"). The battle lines were typed.

At the time it didn't occur to Grace that the warez world was the essence of a multiplayer game, with each player rewarded not with points but with online cred, but it was. As soon as a piece of software was uploaded to a warez site, within minutes a "cracker" would grab a copy and expunge any serial numbers that could be used to trace the software back to its original user. Encryption or watermarks were likewise eradicated and the software was compressed. The cracker would go so far as to supply a user ID, registration number, and the release group's imprimatur, its cyberlogo: this guaranteed quality control. No group wanted a reputation for shoddy merchandise. Meanwhile, couriers were watching, waiting. When the cracked software hit the Web, they immediately moved it to any and all sites they were affiliated with, the idea to redistribute the software to as many places as possible, as quickly as possible. Sometimes "racing" occurred, which meant rival couriers were upping the same release onto the same site at the same time. But this was generally frowned upon, since it could screw up a release. Word also got out on IRC (Internet relay chat) and through private warez chat networks, or via e-mail or even word of mouth.

Within hours this expensive, proprietary software that had taken years to design and manufacture became available, free for the asking, over the Internet. No money changed hands, no profit was made. Because for those in the warez scene it was about things other than money: speed, conquest, the high of defeating rival couriers by uploading a fresh piece of software to a site seconds before they could, being the first release group to crack a new program, maintaining a site with the largest warez cache. It was like turning over the scoreboard on an arcade game. It was about ego and ephemeral glory, about being "the man" in a world that didn't even really exist. Mostly, though, it was about having your fifteen seconds of fame.

Grace's role in this online hullabaloo was to crack the passwords of rival group members and get them tossed off of AOL, which he did with great regularity and hilarity. He taught himself to code and the more time he spent online, the less he devoted to school. All night he'd stay up, learning the ins and outs of the computer and this emerging virtual community, skipping school. His stepmother, who by this point was separated from her husband, would routinely confiscate the computer, but the incorrigible Grace would find where she stashed it, and because she worked long hours snuck back online. Just another bored, uncooperative pupil bouncing from school to school in the real world, Grace had vast powers in the virtual realm, cracking AOL's proprietary code and posting it online and harvesting millions of e-mail addresses. At seventeen he was paid sixty thousand dollars by a shady character to fly to Atlanta to set up a server farm to blast spam and install a poison pill to wipe the drives clean if cops raided the owner.

When he entered his senior year, Grace learned that to graduate on time he had to cram three years of math into four months, and for the first time applied himself to school, taking algebra 2, trigonometry, and calculus, and acing all three. With his newfound work ethic he breezed through computer science at the University of Massachusetts at Dartmouth and as a sophomore was driving a BMW X5, which he paid for in cash. By 2006 Grace was working as a software engineer at Oracle, designing scheduling optimization applications. He created software for Best Buy's Geek Squad that told callers what hours they needed to be at home and Coca-Cola Enterprises that dispatched repairmen to vending machines, as well as programs for Boston's gas company and other utilities. Not only did Beauregard trust Grace implicitly, his friend had the perfect skill set.

It took a while, however, for Beauregard and Grace to jump into their new start-up. In fact, Beauregard made the move only after he was laid off from his investment bank job at the onset of the 2008 financial crisis. Looking back, it was the best thing that could have happened to him. He moved in to his parents' basement and plotted his future while Grace continued with Oracle, working on their new venture on the weekends and at night.

Starting a Start-up

Beauregard compiled a forty-page PowerPoint deck crammed with regression analysis and statistics from the food services industry. He designed a logo for Objective Logistics: a globe with a text box on top, which was so ugly, he says, it makes him cringe today. Then in January 2009 he and Grace were ready to advance to phase two of their plan.

They incorporated their new business and scheduled meetings with owners and managers of local restaurants. They wanted to know if their idea would actually hold water. While traditional employee incentive programs involved cash bonuses or Employee of the Month awards, theirs promised an automated system plugged into a restaurant's point-of-sale terminals (those touch-pad screens you see your waiter using). Their most basic function is to transmit orders to the kitchen, but they also track inordinate amounts of data: the name of server, the number of guests and what time they were seated, when the order was taken, what everybody ordered and when the food was served, and the check amount and the tip.

Through their research they learned that the top 10 percent of restaurant servers add an average of $8.54 to every check, while the bottom 10 percent subtract $7.21. They projected that MUSE, the poetic name they dubbed their system, would raise sales between 2 percent and 4 percent overall. To accomplish that would raise everyone's game. Automatically tracking each server's performance, it would display the results on a leaderboard. With performance-based scheduling staffers would compete to be among the leaders, earning better shifts and higher pay, and because shifts were automatically scheduled, it would save a manager time—about eight hours a week, they estimated. There would be an educational component, too, because they could offer suggestions on how to sell more and provide greater customer satisfaction. This put waitstaff's fate in their own hands. No more favoritism, politics, or servers getting better shifts simply based on seniority or ability to work the system. Suddenly management's and staff's interests would be completely aligned.

In some ways Beauregard's interest in creating a performance-based reward system recalls another entrepreneur from the previous decade. At the onset of the tech boom, Pierre Omidyar, a French-born Iranian American computer programmer, tried to purchase stock in a video game company shortly after it announced plans for an initial public offering. By the time his buy order went through, however, the stock had jumped 50 percent. Meanwhile insiders got in at the initial fifteen dollars per share. *That's not how a free market is supposed to work*, he thought. Musing over the ideal market mechanism, he came up with the concept of an auction, and the Web, he realized, was the perfect place to hold it. There could be complete transparency, equal access for all—insiders would have no special advantages—and the price of a good or service would be whatever the highest bidder was willing to pay. That business eventually became eBay.

In Beauregard and Grace's meetings, they asked, in essence, "If we build it, would you use it?" Would restaurants be interested in a platform that offers waitstaff a customer feedback loop in order to nudge better performance? Every one of the half-dozen restaurateurs they met with said yes. In fact, they wanted to know how long it would take for them to build the software. A year, they replied. Actually, it would take twice that long. The first challenge was that the restaurant industry's point-of-sale terminals ran on a balkanized mess of software products peddled by more than a dozen companies. Some were built on Microsoft.net, others in C # or Java. Before they could hunker down and start coding, Grace needed access to a restaurant's point-of-sale terminal so he could explore the back end, which would have to link up to anything he and Beauregard devised. It soon became clear that Grace would have to design the Rosetta Stone of point-of-sale software.

Then Beauregard approached another restaurateur, Steve Silverstein, CEO of Not Your Average Joe's, a chain of fifteen restaurants in

Massachusetts, Maryland, and Virginia that offers American casual fare like coconut shrimp, mustard-crusted chicken, and ahi tuna wontons. After listening to their spiel, Silverstein invited them to test MUSE at one of his restaurants. They chose the eatery in Beverly, Massachusetts, a suburb of Boston.

By this time Beauregard had plowed through his savings and was sixty thousand dollars in credit card debt, playing beat the clock with his monthly minimum payments. He set to raising what he calls "friends, family, fools money" for their venture, hitting up his father for a hundred thousand dollars and grabbing smallish sums from anyone, including Silverstein, who could chip in. By January 2010 Beauregard had amassed eight hundred thousand dollars, enough for Grace to quit his job to work on this full time, pay themselves salaries, and hire a few programmers. Still, it took two years to knit the 150,000 lines of code, which included regression analysis, nonlinear algorithms and exponential permutations, probability, and artificial intelligence, and tie it into the POS (point-of-sales) system at Not Your Average Joe's. About a dozen business flows had to go into creating a layer plan and a schedule, including availabilities, constraints, shift swapping, minimization of overtime, and pinpoint accuracy as far as when people could and couldn't clock in. The software also had to speak to the POS system and effectively rank people based on their performance.

While developing his digital masterpiece, Grace took a job as a Joe's waiter to better understanding the life of a server, and over the span of two months channeled his inner Margaret Mead. He undertook three six-hour training sessions in which he sampled food and tasted wine, shadowed servers, and took quizzes in addition to working lunches and dinners, and jotted down at every opportunity his impressions in a small notebook. It was a steep learning curve and left him with an appreciation for just how hard the staff worked. When they weren't taking care of customers, servers performed side work such as rolling up silverware in napkins and refilling ketchup containers, saltshakers, and pepper mills. After his first nontraining work session, Grace fell so far behind he had to stay almost an entire extra shift—partly because other servers dumped their side work on him.

That was the most overt hazing he got at Joe's, but Grace picked up how wary the other servers were of him, viewing him as the proverbial spy in their midst. Soon, though, they grew accustomed to him, and appreciated his willingness to instantly calculate tip percentages on the fly, and one young woman even asked for help with her math homework. Grace noted distinct archetypes working at the restaurant, from the ever-energetic college student to the directionless college dropout to the single-mom and service industry lifers. Timeliness, efficiency, and demeanor ranged across the spectrum. He quickly figured out that those who were the most consistent and relied on a tried-and-true go-to spiel achieved the highest sales.

In immersing himself he also captured data he would not have otherwise accessed. Grace carried a stopwatch in his apron (it was against company policy to use an iPhone on duty and difficult to click on and off anyway) to clock in when he was in front of a table and clock off when he wasn't. That way he could, during lunch and dinner shifts, measure what he later dubbed "the period of influence," the time a server spent interacting with customers.

This was more granular data than the restaurant chain's POS system was designed to dredge up. Grace reasoned he could capture the period of influence over a shift, and that would tell him how long he really spent in front customers. After timing himself over weeks, Grace calculated that he averaged seven minutes of direct contact with diners at lunch and ten minutes at dinner. Since customers typically spend less time in the restaurant at lunch than at dinner, that worked out to 12 percent of the total time at lunch and 10 percent for the evening's meal. So the natural question was what could a server say in the time he or she was in front of diners to influence their purchasing behavior?

"It boiled down to consistency, which translated nicely into probability, which governs all things living," Grace told me. When he applied his theory of constancy to his work his ability to upsell improved. All he had to do was draw on simple principles to waiting on customers: be enthusiastic, describe the menu in mouthwatering detail, ask the alcoholic/alpha/clearly heavy drinker if he wanted another round, address older diners as "folks," women as "ladies," visit tables frequently, keep glasses full, and above all smile. Now all he and Beauregard had to do was design software to forge this behavior in Not Your Average Joe's servers, who would benefit from the additional sales in the form of higher tips.

At their office, sifting through the mass of data Grace had been siphoning from Average Joe's POS system—he had installed data adapters in eight Average Joe's eateries so they would gain a baseline with which to compare their results—he and Beauregard sought clear missions they could assign servers. An easy one would be to instruct servers to sell six soups and salads in addition to lunch entrées, an additional dessert, or three dinner specials over the course of a shift. The soups and salads acted like appetizers, while an additional dessert often induces other diners to order their own desserts and coffee. A dinner special might come with a glass of wine, which, the data showed, often led to a diner leaving a more substantial tip (good for the server) and, in many cases, a second glass of wine (good for the restaurant). All of these boosted the final check and per-customer average and, when taken in aggregate, propelled profits.

In January 2011 Grace installed MUSE at the test restaurant in Beverly, Massachusetts. At first they had to work through the inevitable bugs, which they expected with such a complicated hunk of software, and finally unveiled it to the staff in March 2011. Initially there were inevitable grumbles of discontent. But the manager of the restaurant, Tom Weadock, took a shine to it because it automated scheduling, which typically took about eight hours a week and created innumerable headaches. Each server received missions—on Monday sell nine specials over a shift, on Tuesday twelve soup and salads, on Wednesday thirteen dinner entrées. They could see on a leaderboard their ranking for the week, average tip percentage and amounts, and the tally of money they brought into the restaurant.

Early on a couple of servers at the Beverly restaurant quit after they lost out on primo shifts, but the staff quickly adapted to the new system. Ryan Clark, a twenty-two-year-old red-haired waiter cum design student, remembers having a bad week; he just wasn't into the job. "I might have been burnt down," he says, "wasn't talking as much at tables," and it reflected in his ranking. So he rededicated himself and his ranking shot back up. "When you start a fresh week it's kind of like turning the page, starting a new chapter, and you're able to kind of rewrite the book."

Beauregard and Grace measured their results across the four quarters of 2011 and found that check averages increased by 2 percent to 3 percent, from $17 to $17.50. Over 60,000 transactions a week across the entire Average Joe's chain, and that translated into $1.5 million in additional revenue over margins of 40 percent. Servers, too, were earning more. While growth trended downward at other Joe's restaurants, sales in Beverly actually rose 192 percent over the year.

With success like this it wasn't surprising that Beauregard was able to raise $1.5 million in funding from Atlas Venture and Google Ventures, and now they've expanded the system across other Average Joe restaurants. And all because one restless night Beauregard wanted to right past wrongs, to level the playing field for his former self, a young waiter taken advantage of by older, more established servers.

As we lounge in his Boston-area office he tells me to think of MUSE as a means to maximize revenue on every shift. "Like a baseball lineup," he says. You want your power hitter batting fourth, not leading off. That's for someone who's fast and gets on base a lot. MUSE gets granular enough to tell you that you should start your grizzled veteran backup third baseman today and bat him sixth. The probability that he'll get two extra base hits is higher and he team will score. Six more runs per nine innings than if you start your regular third basemen because the team is facing a left-handed sinker-ball pitcher throwing into a seven-mile-per-hour wind at home during a day game on a day that the temperature hovers around eighty degrees.

"It optimizes the entire lineup from top to bottom," he says. "Think of it as *Moneyball* statistics on how to get better."

CHAPTER 12

THE BUG TESTER

After Ross Smith's promotion to team leader of the Windows Security Team at Microsoft, he scheduled one-on-one meetings with the eighty-five people under him. During these get-to-know-each-other sessions it dawned on Smith, a twenty-year software industry veteran who had worked a wide swath of jobs, that his new charges, all of them younger than he, took a distinctly different approach to work and life. They were "millennials," those seventy-eight million members of Generation Y born between 1980 and 2000 while he was a child of the 1960s. There was, as much as it pained him to admit, a generational divide.

Smith, in his late forties, is not your typical corporate manager. When I meet him on the Microsoft campus outside Seattle on an early spring day he's dressed in what for him constitutes office garb: shorts, ratty T-shirt, and flip-flops, despite the teeth-chattering weather—forty-two degrees and raining. That evening he plans to drive to his house in the hills and night ski, and he'll do that in shorts and a T-shirt, too. Several years earlier he had suffered an acute case of alopecia and ever since has had no hair—and not only on his head: no eyebrows, eyelashes, nor leg or arm hair either, and never feels cold, and with his florescent white skin he bears more than a passing resemblance to that famously friendly ghost. His first job out of Rider College in New Jersey was as a data processing coordinator for the county sheriff's office, which he did for four years until jumping to tech support for handheld devices for a couple of years.

In 1991 he started at Microsoft, where he provided product support, and has spent the past two-plus decades climbing the corporate ladder.

His eighty-five highly educated programmers—a third hold a master's degree or higher—are tasked with mind-numbing work, scrutinizing thousands of lines of code for security glitches, and the work ebbs and flows, Smith says, depending on where a product is in its development cycle. This yields substantial excess capacity. Worse, in these one-on-one meetings with him, many on his team reported feeling demoralized, underutilized, often underappreciated, with Carnegie Mellon and MIT computer graduates running basic, yawn-inducing tests such as inserting punch cards into a reader. While some of their peers were reaping fortunes exploiting Web 2.0 and building Facebook, Twitter, and a host of other glitzy start-ups, they were like Ivy League law grads assigned to traffic court.

When Smith started his career at Microsoft it was considered a "velvet sweatshop," a characterization reported in a widely read 1989 *Seattle Times* company profile detailing the lives of Microsofties and the eighty-hours-a-week "techaholism" that pervades its culture. These workforce issues, the story pointed out, were typical for "achievement-oriented, high-pressure Baby Boom professionals who during the '80s embraced work as their badge of identity but are now having to re-evaluate its impact on their personal lives, friendships and family, and life goals," calling it "a ticklish proposition for any fast-moving company: Keeping workers motivated, creative and energized while still offering them the chance for a balanced, self-nurturing existence."

The company prospered throughout the 1990s as Windows became the world's operating system, and in December 1999 its stock hit an all-time high of $119.94 a share. It has been dropping ever since. Apple, the company it almost drove out of business, has supplanted it as the most valuable tech company. As Kurt Eichenwald pointed out in *Vanity Fair*, one relatively new Apple product, the iPhone, is worth more than *all* of Microsoft. The company, which had been built on innovation, had stopped innovating. Products take eons to get to market, and when they do they are either too late or often not very good. Case in point: before I booked my air ticket to the West Coast, I felt compelled to phone Smith with a confession. Microsoft had removed all landline phones and required employees to use the company's Lync software, which runs phone calls through computers. Except every time I called Smith at Microsoft, the call would drop or the quality was miserable and I'd have to try again. And again. Microsoft personnel, I learned later, often just used their cell phones at work instead.

But I was more concerned with something else. "I use a Mac laptop and carry an iPad and iPhone," I told Smith. "Could this be a problem?"

After all, Bill Gates had banned his own kids from owning iPods, and Microsoft is notorious for its cutthroat behavior with competitors. Then there were all those critical stories I'd written about the company over the years. I was ruing the times I'd referred to Microsoft as "the dominatrix of the desktop."

"Nah, not at all," Smith replied. "It might have been a problem in the past, but the place has changed over the past ten years. This isn't the same Microsoft." He paused. "Um, you're not going to interview Steve Ballmer, are you?"—referring to Microsoft's famously blustery chief executive officer. Legend has it that Ballmer heaved a chair across a room amid an obscenity-laced tantrum after an executive broke the news he was joining Google.

I told him no.

"Yeah, yeah, then you'll be fine," he said.

Eichenwald traces Microsoft's demise to an obscure management practice known as "stack ranking." Premised on Jack Welch's vitality curve at GE, in which the lowest-performing employees (the bottom 10 percent) were driven from the company, Microsoft had each unit apportion a percentage of employees in one of five performance batches: top, good, average, below average, and poor. Instead of increasing the quality of Microsoft personnel, however, it had the exact opposite effect. "If you were on a team of ten people, you walked in the first day knowing that no matter how good everyone was, two people were going to get a great review, seven were going to get mediocre reviews, and one was going to get a terrible review," a former software developer told Eichenwald. "It leads to employees focusing on competing with each other rather than competing with other companies." Top programmers avoid working on the same teams, since it could harm their rankings. This in turn could affect their bonuses and promotions, because those at the bottom received no additional money or suffered the indignity of being fired. As a result, Eichenwald concluded, "Microsoft employees not only tried to do a good job but also worked hard to make sure their colleagues did not."

Nevertheless, Microsoft, almost forty years old and an entrenched member of the software establishment, still hired a lot of young engineers, and in addition to the gang warfare that characterized employment it was apparent to Smith the company was riven by a subtle culture war. As a Gen Xer Smith could have easily dismissed these corporate newbies as spoiled, selfish, self-involved hipster wannabes afflicted with a collective case of attention deficit disorder and suffused with a poor work ethic and grandiose belief that stoplights ought to turn from red to green on their command. If he had, he wouldn't have been alone. Eighty-five percent of hiring managers and human-resource executives polled by CareerBuilder.com described millennials as possessing a stronger sense of entitlement than older workers, expecting higher pay, flexible work schedules, promotions within a year, and more vacation or personal time. Workplace Solutions found that 68 percent of working Americans surveyed believed that Gen Y workers were less motivated to assume responsibilities and produce high-quality work than older workers. Talk to corporate recruiters and you'll hear many grouse about members of "Gen Whine": "They want to be CEO tomorrow," is one common refrain. But Smith also knew that today's underlings are tomorrow's bosses and eventually this generation would be running the show.

To understand millennials it's important to understand the environment from which they sprang, and while broad generalizations can be counterproductive there's consensus on several Gen Y characteristics. For one, they seem to have inherited their parents' quest for a work identity but without their parents' blind adherence to the job. The roots of this shift can be traced to the dissolution of the social contract that bound workers to companies, which are part technological and part cultural. Lifetime employment was common from the end of World War II until the 1970s. Then American corporations, battered by foreign competition and an economy mired in sluggish economic growth coupled with inflation and rising interest rates, laid off legions of workers. Seeing what happened to their parents, these Microsoft millennials—and those elsewhere—aren't likely to throw their lot in with one company (and why should they?). Yale professor Robert Hacker, author of *The Great Risk Shift*, calculated that income instability, which he defined as a 50 percent swing in income year to year, has tripled since the 1970s. Today's college-educated employees have as much income instability as those without high school degrees did in the 1970s. Now the formula is: no job security equals little company loyalty.

Another driver shaping Gen Y's relationship to life and work involves technology. These "digital natives" grew up with the Internet and embrace social networks. As Piotr Czerski, a Polish writer and commentator, declares in a popular manifesto titled "We, the Web Kids," Gen Y does not "surf" the Internet and to them it "is not a 'place' or 'virtual space.' The Internet to us is not something external to reality but a part of it: an invisible yet constantly present layer intertwined with the physical environment. We do not use the Internet, we live on the Internet and along it." Moreover the Web has been fused with their culture. "To us [it] is not a technology which we had to learn and which we managed to get a grip of. The Web is a process, happening continuously and continuously transforming before our eyes; with us and through us." Instead of memorizing names, dates, addresses, street names, and phone numbers, these inveterate Web users tap keywords into Google, rely on GPS to navigate cities, access smart phones to dial or text friends and colleagues, and because they have to filter so much information and make instantaneous decisions as to its reliability, they are also perhaps more skeptical. Simultaneously the tools of creation are accessible to all so anyone can blog, post photos, create videos—in short, share her words, thoughts, art, and actions with the world without barriers.

The emergence of social networks also contributes to the digital native "webanschauung," if you will. To Gen Yers, "society," Czerski writes, "is a network, not a hierarchy." With Twitter and Facebook, fans can chat with just about anyone, whether she's a rock musician, movie star, politician, or author. This Net generation prizes access to social networks and communication with friends and family on the job. Cisco's "Connected World Technology" report found that more than half of Gen Y employees surveyed ranked social media freedom over higher salaries when evaluating job offers, while 37 percent of those surveyed by Mom Corps said they would take a pay cut if it meant more flexibility (like the ability to set their own schedules and work from home). Meeting the demands of these younger workers could ultimately lead to the extinction of the traditional show-up-to-the-office workday.

Microsoft's Gen Y engineers are no different. Despite a steady and generous paycheck, many are unwilling to put down permanent roots at the empire Bill Gates built; a nationwide survey found that 60 percent of millennials expect to leave their current employers (contrast with baby boomers: 84 percent said they'd stick with their current employers until they retire). What's more, these Gen-Y Microsofties practically live online, conduct friendships and romance there, play games, work on side projects that interest them into the wee hours of the morning, and crave attention and notoriety for their accomplishments.

Multitaskers at heart and armed with smart phones, tablets, and laptops, they don't accept the traditional barriers separating work from the rest of their existence. Ever connected to their jobs through technology, no one—not them, not their bosses—is ever truly off the clock. When they go home or out to dinner or a club, they check e-mail and respond to text messages from the office and continue to work, as self-described "personal brand guru" Dan Schawbel notes, "because who they are personally and professionally have become one and the same."

Smith was faced with a dilemma: should his younger employees be forced to sublimate their millennial ways to fit in with Microsoft's corporate culture or should Microsoft bend to their wills? America's shifting demographics provided an answer. By 2016, Gen Yers will comprise about 40 percent of the American labor force and by 2025 that number should rise to 75 percent. At some companies like Ernst & Young, this group makes up 60 percent of the employee pool. A rising tide like this could put businesses underwater. It was clear to Smith that Microsoft—and by extension, he—had to address its workforce culture or face the consequences.

Smith wanted to see if game design could improve the quality, productivity, and job satisfaction of his crew, and concocted something he called the Code Review Game. It worked like this: four teams chose a section of code to attack. They received points based on the type of bugs they discovered. Different groups could come up with different strategies: one focused on code produced by error-prone developers, while another team waited until a flaw was identified and then hunted similar bugs, because the coder who contributed to the section would likely repeat the same mistake. The project went so well that the company has used such teams to vet at least six other major releases.

But this was only a small solution to the much larger problem of generational divide, and Microsoft wasn't the only one grappling with it. It's happening across the business landscape. Deloitte, the global accounting firm, concerned about high turnover among its youngest and newest employees, discovered that two-thirds of those who left the company took jobs doing something they could have done at Deloitte. High worker churn rates cost the firm $150,000 for each employee who left and whose position had to be refilled. In response the company created programs to help workers figure out their next career moves. Sun Microsystems embraced scheduling flexibility with a telecommuting program and now half of Sun's employees work outside the office. With a majority of workers in their twenties preferring to work for companies that embrace volunteerism, Salesforce.com set aside 1 percent of its profits to pay employees to volunteer 1 percent of their work time to community service. Estée Lauder provides training courses on Gen Y for managers on how to deal with millennials who don't share older colleagues' work habits or approach to the job.

To counter this trend, some businesses aim for more fun in the workplace. The corporate culture of online shoe seller Zappos reflects the whims of its comically happy CEO Tony Hsieh. His company employs a "chief happiness officer," and Hsieh once played an April Fool's gag in which Zappos claimed it was suing the Walt Disney Company for claiming that it was "the happiest place on earth." Google soothes its tightly knotted engineers with free massages and on its campus there's a yellow brick road, giant model dinosaur, volleyball courts, and regular roller hockey games. Twitter brags that it has "worked hard to create an environment that spawns productivity and happiness." Hyper-energy-drink maker Red Bull installed a slide in its London office. All of this emphasis on mixing play and work prompted the *Economist* to snark, "the cult of fun has spread like some disgusting haemorrhagic disease."

Microsoft, too, has also been swept by change, not all of it by intelligent design. While it still reaps billions from operating system software, it confronts a more malleable customer landscape. Its core business has been under assault as software continues to move beyond individual computers and to the cloud. So you're forgiven if "innovative" isn't the first word that comes to mind when you think of Microsoft.

Following Smith's *manager-a-mano* sessions with his team, he did what he always does when faced with a sticky work problem. He brainstormed with his brain trust, a small cadre of managers with whom Smith had climbed the ranks at Microsoft. One of them, Robert Musson, a man who reads data like others read *People*, recalled a research paper he'd come across that explored the relationship between trust in the workplace, job satisfaction, and pay. John Helliwell and Haifang Huang at the University of British Columbia calculated that for an employee a slight uptick in trust in management was equivalent to a 36 percent pay raise. The opposite was also true: a loss in trust led to a decline in job satisfaction equal to a 36 percent pay cut. The researchers found that those who worked on a variety of projects felt like they had earned a 21 percent pay boost while one requiring a high skill level was perceived as equivalent to a 19 percent salary hike.

All they had to do was increase trust among the workers and managers. It sounded so simple. But how do you foster it within a cutthroat organization like Microsoft? And where does trust come from?

Theory X and Theory Y

Within Microsoft's data-driven workplace, Ross Smith, Robert Musson, and a wicked-smart, soft-spoken software engineer named Harry Emil continued their quest for trust. They identified an inherent contradiction in their workplace. The idea of trust, which encourages managers to trust their employees, to experiment, innovate, and take risks, collided with Microsoft's need for what are called "predictable deliverables." It was the age-old conflict between management theories: Theory X and Theory Y. With Theory X, the boss assumes the worst—that workers are inherently lazy and will at the earliest opportunity slough off their duties and responsibilities. Theory Y is based on polar opposite assumptions: workers are innately ambitious and self-motivated. While Theory X might be applied to a factory in China where workers with brain- and hand-numbing efficiency assemble iPhones, Theory Y is usually more useful in organizations that must innovate to succeed. In general, Microsoft was a hybrid but in practice it was an adherent to Theory X. Smith wanted to become more Theory Y. For that to happen management had to trust workers and workers would have to reciprocate by trusting management.

Even defining something as squishy as trust, however, wasn't easy. It is, Smith says, a bit like freedom and air. You know when you don't have it, but don't give it much thought when you do. This made it hard to measure. He decided the first step would be to query his eighty-five-member team to identify specific behaviors that either enhanced or mitigated trust in the organization then create a simple online game to prioritize trust behaviors. The question was static: "Which trust factor is more important to you?" and players were faced with two choices. For example, "Tell the truth in a way people can verify" or "Do what you say you are going to do." Or "validate expectations" or "underpromise and overdeliver." Or "be understanding" or "establish a track record of results." There were dozens upon dozens of trust scenarios.

A user, after completing however many questions he wanted, could rate specific characteristics like "Say what you're going to do, then do what you say you're going to do" as either first choice, second, third, most likely to make an impact or most likely to backfire, et cetera. Then he could view the results. Over the years some of the top choices ended up being "a role model—have integrity," "be honest," "respect the dignity of every person and every role," and "listen before you speak. Understand, diagnose."

As a manager, Smith operated with the will of the crowd in mind, and he kept the lines of communication open, instituting a weekly pizza meeting, which became a forum for each employee to raise questions, brainstorm ideas, and build relationships. It helped forge a spirit of camaraderie. At least in this small corner of Microsoft, there now existed a kindler, gentler, more trusting work environment.

Meanwhile, Musson faced a more tangible challenge: how to get more people to "dog food" a new operating system in development. Before Microsoft can create a version of a new consumer-ready product, especially one as complicated as, say, Windows, thousands of people must "stress test" it internally. (It's called dog fooding because you are, in essence, eating your own dog food.) The more testers, the better. That's because everybody's computer is different and a Microsoft operating system has to support about a million different devices. More than a billion Windows users around the world means there are potentially a billion different configurations. Even if all Windows users bought the same Dell computer, they still customize them, and these combinations can cause serious trouble.

The software has to handle someone burning a CD while new e-mail messages download and he's surfing the Web. Or maybe he needs to print a research paper while copying and pasting data from an Excel file into a PDF. How do older devices—a ten-year-old mouse with an equally aged driver—behave with the system? Each action involves multiple software programs, all of which separately or combined have the potential to induce the operating system to spit up a digital hairball.

In the early stages of operating system development, stress testers simply run the program on their PCs overnight while a program fires commands at it; if the program freezes, there's a coding glitch, which must be identified and fixed. In later builds, users take the operating system for a test spin, using it like they would any other OS, or be asked to try specific combinations. The code is constantly updated, and there can be several builds over the course of a week, each of which must be tested.

But it's hard to gain cooperation. "I have to do my job, so why should I do yours?" becomes a popular, if not verbally expressed, refrain. Most everyone at Microsoft is busy and gains little by helping a colleague in another group or team. And no one wants to deal with the hassle of a frozen PC that the tech staff has to drag away and fix. Sure, Musson, Smith, and Emil could order underlings to stress test the software, but they knew that was exactly the wrong approach. Instead they analyzed the behaviors they believed would motivate people to cooperate.

Harry Emil had a manager he once worked under who stuck up a piece of paper on his door listing each team member and requiring them to sign their name when they completed specific tasks. The manager couched it like he didn't want to bother his team with a lot of unnecessary e-mail. "I'm not *narcing* on you guys," he would say, but in a way he was, and it was effective. The list functioned as an analog leaderboard, since no one wanted to be viewed as someone not pulling his weight, which would lead to subtle public humiliation.

Emil also recalled a workplace game he had helped create in early 2004 that had achieved similar goals, that is gently encourage Microsofties to perform tasks outside their job descriptions. At the time 80 percent of Microsoft personnel used Google as their search engine, but the company had spent a lot of money and devoted vast resources to developing its own, MSN. Management was embarrassed that a competitor's product was more popular in-house than the company's. There was talk of tweaking the corporate firewall to disable Google but Emil and others believed the best product should win. Microsoft simply had to make a better search engine.

This led Emil to suggest a simple game, which he took to calling a *Search Off*. He created a page that offered both engines side by side and when a user typed in a search query he received both sets of results to compare. That way people who wanted Google still got their Google results, but they were also exposed to MSN. Then Emil incorporated a function that enabled users to offer feedback on both sets. He wanted to know how often Google was better, which naturally made people look at the MSN results and wonder, "Are they as good as Google?" Usually, although not always, they were. He received messages from users like, "Hey, they both solved my problem: I searched for a certain book and they both brought me that book. But Google was better because it had the book higher in its results." Emil was pleased he had created a way to expose users to MSN without forcing anyone to use it. In the process, the game helped to clean up bugs (more than a hundred of them by the time he was done), things like when someone searched for a sports team but the top results pointed to a person with that last name.

He wondered if there were a method to further increase activity and decided to try a *Search Off* leaderboard listing the top twenty-five contributors. Every piece of feedback was worth a point. As soon as he turned it on the dynamics changed as people tried to leapfrog one another for the top spots. Within a week it took a minimum of a hundred clicks to get to number twenty-five on the leaderboard. After a while he noticed a falloff in new players, which he attributed to their inability to get on the leaderboard, because those who had been playing from the beginning had a head start. So he created a monthly leaderboard, which did the trick, then an interns-only leaderboard to trigger competition among them.

So when Emil and Musson's team began receiving nightly e-mails from a senior VP of Windows, urging them to find a hundred volunteers to stress test the new operating system in development, it made sense to capture the same game dynamics that had made the *Search Off* successful. But they couldn't simply use an identical comparison game. Instead the group looked at the behaviors they wanted to encourage: they needed people to install the operating system, vote, and run the stress test program. Three simple activities. They kicked around simple childhood games they could whip up: King of the Hill, Chutes and Ladders, tic-tac-toe, and memory games. They settled on Hangman, where they handed out letters to spell B-E-T-A-1 and announced to the entire Windows team that if a user installed the operating system, he'd get a "B." Run stress and that warranted an "E." Provide feedback, a

"T." If he ran stress for three builds in a row, that led to an "A" and a "1." A leaderboard would report on the action.

The game proved popular. People would run into one another in hallways and brag that they got their "B" and ask others if they had gotten theirs. Vice presidents and group managers also e-mailed Emil to complain. "I don't have a 'T.' I'm supposed to have one. What's up? Where is it?" Usually it was a product of human error—the player installed the new operating system on a different machine—or there was a bottleneck in the system. Over the span of three weeks more than two thousand people participated, far more than the minimum of a hundred they needed to exit this milestone.

The Windows Beta 2 team asked Emil and his colleagues to create another game to stress test the second iteration of the software. This time he had months to plan and chose to introduce a social aspect beyond plain vanilla letters, something that would be tangible in the physical world, not just points in the form of alphabetical letters a player could claim to have won. Emil ordered ten thousand Livestrong-like rubber wristbands in four colors and designed the Beta 2 game to award prizes based on escalating participation. Players received a bronze bracelet for overcoming the first hurdle, which was to download the operating system and run the stress test program. The following week they could win a gray wristband if they matched 100 percent of their participation from the prior week. A yellow band awaited those who ramped up their participation to 120 percent of the previous week, and a blue one for those who achieved a 150 percent rate of participation.

Initially, Emil planned to run the game for six weeks, but it proved so popular it went on for four months. Few wore them down the hall as jewelry as he thought they would. Instead they collected the wristbands, which they strung in their offices. He ran out of wristbands and had to order more.

And it led to Microsoft's most successful productivity game of all.

The Language Game

As director of tests for Windows International, James "Jim" Rodrigues was most concerned about three types of bugs in Microsoft operating software, which shipped in thirty-six languages and a hundred dialects (called "lips"). It could be that a bug caused the software to work improperly in the French version, but that's functional and was usually caught through standard test procedures. Another afflicted the user interface. A button could be offscreen or there was truncated text. Rodrigues didn't need to read and write French to find these obvious visual flaws. But the third kind of bug bothered him, and that had to do with the quality of the language translation. Rodrigues didn't have the expertise on his team to fix all of these. Yet if there was a bug reported in French—or Spanish, Hindi, German, and so on—he was responsible. Microsoft could hire translators but there was no way to check their work until complaints rolled in. He could ask those who worked overseas in the French subsidiary to give the operating system a through vetting, but Windows is a humongous hunk of software and it was unlikely they would find everything. Plus, as with the American staff, it was difficult to get people already working full time to take on bug testing.

Rodrigues was well aware of Ross Smith's game experiments at Microsoft; Smith even e-mailed an in-house newsletter around to engender interest. One day in Smith's office, Smith was showing Rodrigues a user interface he was building, fooling around with magazine covers and asking, "Do you like it or don't you like it?" It was a streamlined approach to a game, giving a player the absolute minimum action he would need to take to identify a bug. Rodrigues had a thought. He told Smith about the problems with the integrity of the languages within Microsoft's operating system user interface. "What if we could do screen shots of the UI for all the languages and ask native speakers, 'Do you like it or don't you like it?'" he said.

Smith thought it was an excellent idea. They talked it through and agreed it should be a simple, Web-based application. A user wouldn't have to install the latest software, which was a hassle. If a player had a spare five minutes, he could give a few opinions. On a twenty-minute break? Offer a bunch more.

They coded an automated system for grabbing screen shots of each page and set to work creating a game out of it. Instead of simple yes or no answers, he gave players markup pens in various colors. The player would review the text on a screen, use his mouse to circle it with a digital pen, and slide it into either the "Looks good" or the "Something wrong" bin. Then the next screen would pop up. But one challenge he and Smith quickly identified was the fact that language quality screen review was so easy for native speakers it wouldn't be interesting or enticing, especially when a player was faced with multiple screens. To counter this they created game levels comprised of twenty-five dialogs or screens. Each time a player rated a screen he got a point. If he did all twenty-five, he advanced to the next level and earned a different color pen, then presented with twenty-five more images. Various in-game leaderboards kept track of the action. That way French players could see how they stacked up against their colleagues.

Over several months they released the game in all thirty-six languages and were pleased with the level of participation. Some players ran through a thousand screens. The head of the Japanese subsidiary closed the office for a day and ordered every employee to play the game. Then Rodrigues posted leaderboards pitting language against language—Japanese versus Portuguese, for example. And this drove participation even more. Rodrigues realized the game tapped into foreign workers' sense of pride. Someone who worked for Microsoft in India or Brazil would hear it from friends and relatives if there were errors in the software. It made it seem that Microsoft didn't care enough about their country and its users to fix them. These workers felt an urgency to fix every typo or malapropism.

In the end all 36 languages were cleaned up and more than 4,500 Microsoft employees participated, viewing a total of 500,000 Windows 7 translations. The highest participation was China, with 130 players viewing 2,600 screens. The lowest was Estonia, with 3 people looking at 96 screens. Of the dialogs that were submitted for further review, 29 percent were accompanied by player comments, which involved further explanation, even though this was optional.

The game was such a success that Microsoft extended it across other products. There was a game that gave points to engineers who responded the quickest to bug notices, and Microsoft Research released a game called *Ribbon Hero* that had players learn how to use Excel and other Microsoft Office software. The Windows Security team came up with an Olympic-themed game, with "runners" attempting something brand-new to innovate in a way that could help the company. Each was judged as a team, on how well they performed their regular work as well as coming up with something new and unexpected.

Meanwhile, Ross Smith has become a workplace games guru, giving talks and authoring papers, influencing others to experiment.

While many of his cadres have adopted them in the workplace Smith has become the face of the movement within and outside Microsoft.

Over the past decade he has discovered that play leads to greater trust, and that encourages innovation. Collaborative play, such as his team-centric approach to bug testing, helps engender a climate of trust. Instead of his employees sitting in muffled coding silos, lost in their own little worlds, they're working toward common goals. Stronger players assist weaker ones, and each gravitates toward what he does best to benefit the entire team. These higher levels of trust then spawn greater experimentation and risk taking, which are usually in short supply in most institutional structures. That then results in greater creativity and ultimately more innovation.

His experiences, Smith says, have taught him that players are motivated by different things. Some are in it for the glory and shame of the leaderboard or just want to best their personal high scores. Others like the game for game's sake—to, say, crack a puzzle because they like puzzles, or participate because they enjoy the camaraderie of team play.

While productivity games can get "real work" done, like sifting through code to find bugs, adding one to an employee's "day job" doesn't work. It's not good, he's found, to have employees work toward amassing points, leapfrogging levels, climbing up leaderboards, or competing for prizes. That pits them against human resource systems and the paycheck they already receive. It's also a bad idea to offer prizes. Then players are likely to approach the game as merely a mechanism for racking up points, which degrades the game's ultimate purpose. Once, Bob Musson told me, they offered a mountain bike as a prize, and Musson found out a player had cheated by creating an automated program to play the game for him. But workplace games can function as a magnet to attract employees' core skills (those that most people have, such as an ability to type, speak a language, donate their computer's processing time, etc.) and improve "organizational citizenship behaviors." These contribute to a healthier workplace environment.

As for Smith, he established an enviable level of trust in the bug-testing group and continues this as head of product testing in the Skype division. Wherever he goes, he reports extremely low employee attrition rates, by far the lowest of any department in the company.

"That's what I'm most proud of," he says.

CONCLUSION

We've all heard that life is a game. But what if we are all, right now, actually living in one, designed by someone living deep into the future?

It's the kind of far-out idea debated in college dorms, often with the ritual passing of a bong, and constructed of equal parts *The Matrix* and *Star Trek*'s Holodeck. According to the theory, which an academic from Oxford and a scientist from NASA have put forth separately, there's an almost mathematical certainty that we're toiling inside an intricate simulation created by someone existing anywhere from thirty years to five million years or more into the future. In essence, we're just some future being's hobby, his or her version of *SimCity* or a massively multiplayer online role-playing game such as *World of Warcraft*. I suppose you could say we're living in sim.

Mind-bending, for sure, but is it any more far-fetched than the big bang theory, which holds that the entire universe started out as a speck of matter of incredible density smaller than a pore on your skin? Ten billion to fifteen billion years ago a massive explosion began stretching the fabric of space like a balloon, forming a hundred trillion galaxies in the universe and three hundred trillion stars in our galaxy. In the process it heralded the beginnings of time. Somewhat later the earth coalesced from hot gases and by sheer luck and happenstance ultimately created an environment from which life sprang.

If you buy that—and most scientists do—the notion that we exist in a game simulation seems downright plausible.

Nick Bostrom, a philosopher at Oxford University who's director of its Future of Humanity Institute, calls it the "simulation argument." Another adherent is astronomer Rich Terrile, director of the Center for Evolutionary Computation and Automated Design at NASA's Jet Propulsion Laboratory. These guys don't wear tinfoil hats, wander around city parks, and spout sci-fi-worthy conspiracy theories. Their views have been shaped by math, science, and human history.

In this book I explore how games and game design have been seeping into virtually every aspect of our lives and how they can unleash breakthrough thinking. Maybe, though, these games are actually seeping into our *game*. Instead of each of us controlling our bodies with our minds, our brains have been hooked up to one vast neural network and we're just role playing in a massively multiplayer fantasy game. After all, when you look at someone you're not really seeing that person. Your brain is simply interpreting light waves, converting them into data that it can interpret. You don't hear someone speak. Your mind processes sound waves that your ears pick up. When you grasp a cup of coffee, your brain interprets tactile sensations and when you sniff the steam, your brain converts that into information it can relate to (mmm, delicious coffee). As it is, we exist one step removed from reality. Our connection with the surrounding world is already simulated.

Bostrom bases his thesis on an assumption he calls "substrate-independence," which means that mental states are not solely attainable by humans and other animals. They can exist in other physical and/or digital phenomena. A conscious, intelligent, self-aware being could reside in an organic brain, silicon brain, or magnetic brain. I suppose you could say the product remains the same, only the packaging has changed. If he's right—and all indications are that he is, at least about artificial intelligence—a powerful enough computer running inordinately complex software could achieve a state of what we know as consciousness.

As for Terrile, he views consciousness as nothing more than the by-product of sophisticated architecture within the human brain. If computers' processing power follows the same exponential growth curve it has for the past hundred years—since the early days of manual tabulators—by 2030 (give or take) a computer could achieve an equivalent complexity to the human brain. According to Hans Moravec of Carnegie Mellon's Robotic Institute, a thousand-dollar computer in 1980 had the brainpower of a bacterium; by 1990 it was equal to a nematode worm; and by 2000 we were closing in on a lizard. Next up, a mouse, followed by a monkey, and then, if Moravec's calculations are correct, a human by 2030. Terrile seconds the motion, predicting that in the next ten to thirty years artificial consciousness will be embedded in machines. Even now, the fastest NASA supercomputers crunch data at twice the speed of the human brain. Plot that out on the exponential computer processing power curve and within the decade, he told *Vice*, we'll be able "to compute an entire human lifetime of 80 years—including every thought ever conceived during that lifetime—in the span of a month."

Wait, it gets better.

In his *Vice* interview he performed a back-of-the-napkin calculation involving the PlayStation, which Sony releases every six to seven years. Thirty years from now a Sony PlayStation should be able to compute ten thousand human lifetimes simultaneously and in real time, or about a human lifetime per hour. Between PlayStation 1, PS2, and PS3 there are about a hundred million devices in the world. If each held ten thousand humans, more people would reside in Sony PlayStations than maintain a corporeal existence on earth. And you thought decoding the entire human genome was an amazing feat.

Of course, you wouldn't know you were locked in a simulation. "If the simulators don't want us to find out, we probably never will," Bostrom wrote in a 2003 paper titled "The Simulation Argument: Why the Probability that You Are Living in a Matrix Is Quite High." What reasons might an advanced being have for conjuring these complex, albeit imperfect, simulated worlds? Bostrom doesn't know. Perhaps, he offers, this advanced hobbyist (or "posthuman" as the Oxford philosopher calls him/her/it) runs simulations for scientific purposes, say, studying his people's evolutionary history, designing virtual worlds peopled with virtual beings equipped with fully developed virtual nervous systems (read: us). Or maybe this posthuman just wants to see what happens if he puts Kim Jong-un in charge of a nuclear state.

He leaves it up to the individual to decode a motive for these grand theft human designers:

> If you think that there is a chance that the simulator of this world happens to be, say, a true-to-faith descendant of some contemporary Christian fundamentalist, you might conjecture that he or she has set up the simulation in such a way that the simulated beings will be rewarded or punished according to Christian moral criteria. An afterlife would, of course, be a real possibility for a simulated creature (who could either be continued in a different simulation after her death or even be "uploaded" into the simulator's universe and perhaps be provided with an artificial body there). Your fate in that afterlife could be made to depend on how you behaved in your present simulated incarnation.

Terrile finds inspiration in the idea that we may soon have the technological wherewithal to create our own synthesized universes. That would mean that we, who live in a simulated world, have created a simulated world, whose denizens wouldn't know they're the product of our collective computing imagination. Now, what if our master designers also lived inside a simulation? Same for those who designed their simulation. Potentially you could have levels and levels of sims, perhaps millions of them.

In that case, Terrile speculates, if there is a creator for our world, it is us, or at least an offshoot of us hailing from the distant future. In a sense, "we are both God and servants of God," he says. Even if we are "many orders of magnitude down in levels of simulation, somewhere along the line something escaped the primordial ooze to become us and to result in simulations that made us."

Now that's what I'd call the ultimate game design.

ACKNOWLEDGMENTS

I'm not a gamer, unless you count tennis, which you probably don't, so my writing a book about games and game design might seem odd. But that's one of the benefits of being a journalist. I'm afforded the opportunity to learn, which leaves me in a constant state of wonder. It's led me to publish books on topics as diverse as corporate espionage (*Spooked*), poorly designed cars that roll over and kill or maim thousands of people (*Tragic Indifference*, reissued as *Blood Highways*), businesses expressly divined to grow virally (*Viral Loop*), as well as novels that explore our tenuous connections between reality and virtual reality (*Virtually True*), and a murder mystery wrapped in a legal thriller (*Trial and Terror*).

It's a privilege to teach at the Arthur L. Carter Journalism Institute at New York University. It sports a world-class faculty and facility, which creates a stimulating intellectual environment that foments the exchange of ideas and attracts an eclectic, whip-smart student body. I'm indebted to Stephen Solomon, director of the Business and Economic Reporting (BER) program—easily the finest of its kind in the world—who often covered for me as my deadline loomed, as well as all my colleagues.

I owe a bottomless cup of thanks to Sarah Lacy, a force of nature who's the founder and CEO of *PandoDaily*. She allowed me the flexibility to finish this book while working as editor of the site. I'm also grateful to Paul Carr, founder of NSFW Corp., a peer-turned-friend, who introduced me to Sarah in the first place. Like many writers, most of my ideas spring from my own reporting and writing. This book grew out of a feature story I wrote for *Fast Company* and includes material from that, as well as various pieces of text I've posted elsewhere, including *PandoDaily*. I also appreciate the help I've received from the *Fast Company* crew over the years, including Noah Robischon, Tyler Gray, Anjali Mullany, Bob Safian, Rick Tetzelli, and many others.

While writing is largely a solitary pursuit every book is collaborative. Thanks to Courtney Young and the legendary Adrian Zackheim, who acquired the book for Portfolio. Brooke Carey is everything an author could want in an editor and helped me shape this maelstrom of ideas and half-baked theories into a book. Emily Angell then took the reins to bring it to market. Kate Lee did her usual fine job as agent, so I was sad (for me but happy for her) that she departed ICM to work as an editor at Medium. She left me in the capable hands of Kristine Dahl, who helped shepherd this book to publication.

I interviewed more than seventy people for this project, too many to list, but I feel obligated to express special appreciation to those who went the extra mile for me—letting me tap their brains for hours, sometimes days: Carnegie Mellon professors Jesse Schell and Luis von Ahn, whose fingerprints are all over this book; former DARPA director Regina Dugan and Jay Rogers of Local Motors; Quirky's Ben Kaufman, NYU research librarian Alexa Pearce, Avi Millman of Stray Boots, and Matthew Bernier from the Orthopaedic Foot and Ankle Center; the Foldit team, including Dr. David Baker, Seth Cooper, and Firas Khatib; Dr. Carla Pugh, who heads the University of Wisconsin Health Clinical Simulation Program; Susan Olson, who gave me a tour of the sim center; and Maimonides Medical Center chief of surgery Dr. Patrick Borgen; Joshua March of Conversocial, Philip Beauregard and Matthew Grace of Objective Logistics, and Ross Smith, the workplace games guru of Microsoft.

Paul Johnson of design firm Studioe9 engages me in thoughtful discussion on a variety of ethereal tech topics and has influenced how I see the world. Brendan Koerner is a talented writer who took time to share information on *Foldit* and other games that promote scientific research. Two listservs I'm on—Vor and BirdbyBird—are full of people doing great things and creating fascinating discussion threads. And a shout-out to my tennis buddies, who keep me sane by blasting forehands, backhands, and serves at me: Jon Furay, Sandy Miller, Jon Dahl, Mike Philips, Daniel Djan, and Jeff Amurao.

As challenging as any book is to a writer, it can be equally daunting for the people in his life. If life is a game, then I certainly leveled up to the top of the leaderboard when I married Charlotte. Remarkably generous of soul, she had to do without me for long stretches, as did my daughters, Lila and Sophie, who amaze me every day. (The cognitive teardown of *Angry Birds* is for you!) I'm also grateful to my extended family: Nana Lin, Nana Bacon, Auntie Me, Uncle B, Charlie, and Olivia, and everyone else who pitched in. Here's to the memory of Barbara and Arnold. I miss you.

Do many people read the acknowledgments? Consider this an "Easter egg." Visit penenberg.com and send me an e-mail telling me what you think of the book, or whatever else you want to talk about. I'll write back. You can also find me on Twitter: @penenberg.

ADAM L. PENENBERG
Brooklyn, New York
May 2013

NOTES

Introduction

1 *game designer and professor of digital media and interactive computing at the Georgia Institute of Technology:* Georgia Tech Digital Lounge, list of faculty: http://www.digitallounge.gatech.edu/faculty/?id=14.

1 Jetset, *which Bogost released through his company, Persuasive Games:* Persuasive Games Web site: http://www.persuasivegames.com/games/game.aspx?game=jetset.

1 *Simony* description: Ian Bogost Web site: http://www.bogost.com/games/simony.shtml.

1 *snippy Kinko's employees:* ibid. and "Game Lets Players Step into Toner-Stained Shoes of Kinko's Workers: In 'Disaffected!' you are an employee at the famous copy shop," Stephen Totilo, MTV.com, Jan. 13, 2006: http://www.mtv.com/news/articles/1520762/new-game-takes-on-fedex-kinkos.jhtml.

1 *tomato growers confronting* E. coli *outbreaks: Bacteria Salad*, released by Persuasive Games. Web site: http://www.persuasivegames.com/games/game.aspx?game=arcadewireecoli.

1 *dieters forced to manage their menus: Fatworld*, released by Persuasive Games, a "videogame about the politics of nutrition . . . Fit or Fat? Live or Die? You decide." Web site: http://www.persuasivegames.com/games/game.aspx?game=fatworld.

1 Oil God *seeks to explore ". . . unleashing war and disaster," reads the promotional copy that Bogost penned:* Released by Persuasive Games. Web site: http://www.persuasivegames.com/games/game.aspx?game=arcadewireoil.

2 *Bogost despises "gamification":* "Gamification Is Bullshit," Ian Bogost, *Atlantic*, Aug. 9, 2011, and cross-posted on his blog: http://www.bogost.com/blog/gamification_is_bullshit.shtml.

2 *Tropicana:* "Tropicana Juicy Rewards—Free Orange Juice And A Redemption Of Choice Today Only," *Mom Knows It All* (blog), May 26, 2010: http://www.valmg.com/index.php/2010/tropicana-juicy-rewards-free-orange-juice-and-a-redemption-of-choice-today-only.

2 *gamification as "exploitationware":* "Persuasive Games: Exploitationware," Ian Bogost, Gamasutra, May 3, 2011: http://www.gamasutra.com/view/feature/6366/persuasive_games_exploitationware.php.

2 *"grifter's game,"* etc.: "Gamification Is Bullshit," Ian Bogost, *Atlantic*, Aug. 9, 2011: http://www.theatlantic.com/technology/archive/2011/08/gamification-is-bullshit/243338.

2 *"the Wall Street hedge-fund guys of games":* "Zynga: For Being the $500 Million Alpha Dog of Social Gaming," *Fast Company* "50 Most Innovative Companies" issue, Mar. 2011: http://www.fastcompany.com/most-innovative-companies/2011/profile/zynga.php.

2 *"disrupt and change fundamental attitudes": Persuasive Games: The Expressive Power of Videogames*, Ian Bogost (Cambridge, MA: The MIT Press, 2007).

2 *"feared" this "behaviorist experiment with rats":* "Why Zynga ticks off the games industry," by Daniel Terdiman, CNET, Apr. 12, 2010: http://news.cnet.com/8301-13772_3-20002221-52.html.

3 *"friends aren't really friends; they are mere resources,"* etc.: "Cow Clicker: The Making of Obsession," Ian Bogost, bogost.com, July 21, 2010: http://www.bogost.com/blog/cow_clicker_1.shtml.

3 *"Social Games on Trial" seminar:* "Social Games on Trial: NYU Video Game Seminar IV," Ian Bogost, bogost.com: http://www.bogost.com/blog/social_games_on_trial.shtml.

3 *"It's a Facebook game about Facebook games,"* etc.: "Cow Clicker: A Facebook Game about Facebook Games," Ian Bogost, bogost.com, undated: http://www.bogost.com/games/cow_clicker.shtml.

3 *parody of game became a hit:* "The Curse of Cow Clicker: How a Cheeky Satire Became a Videogame Hit," Jason Tanz, *Wired*, Jan. 2012: http://www.wired.com/magazine/2011/12/ff_cowclicker/all.

4 *disturbed by the success of* Cow Clicker: ibid.

4 *introduced "mooney":* "Ian Bogost's Troubling Experiences With Cow Clicker," Leigh Alexander, Gamasutra, Oct. 6, 2012: http://www.gamasutra.com/view/news/121555/GDC_Online_Ian_Bogosts_Troubling_Experiences_With_Cow_Clicker.php.

4 *micropayment exchange rate:* "The Life-Changing $20 Rightward-Facing Cow," Leigh Alexander, Kotaku, Oct. 3, 2011: http://kotaku.com/5846080/the-life+changing-20-rightward+facing-cow.

4 *Steel Cow, Oil Cow, Bacon Cow, Mao Cow, and Bling Cow:* "Tipping cows down on the FarmVille," Caroline McCarthy, CNET, July 26, 2010: http://news.cnet.com/8301-13577_3-20011534-36.html; "The Curse of Cow Clicker: How a Cheeky Satire Became a Videogame Hit," Jason Tanz, *Wired*, Jan. 2012: http://www.wired.com/magazine/2011/12/ff_cowclicker/all.

4 *introduction of* Stargazer Cow and *drove 8,000 players (16 percent of his playing base) to quit the game in one day:* "Unsolicited Cow Clicker Analysis," Dakota Reese Brown, dakotareese.com: http://dakotareese.com/2010/09/unsolicited-cow-clicker-analysis.

4 Cow clicktivism, Oxfam, etc.: "Cow Clicktivism: Click a cow, change the world," Ian Bogost, bogost.com, Mar. 3, 2011: http://www.bogost.com/blog/cow_clicktivism.shtml; "Donate a Cow: Charity Gifts for a Family in Need," Oxfam America "Unwrapped": http://www.oxfamamericaunwrapped.com/donate-cow; "The Curse of Cow Clicker: How a Cheeky Satire Became a Videogame Hit," Jason Tanz, *Wired*, Jan. 2012: http://www.wired.com/magazine/2011/12/ff_cowclicker/all.

4 *"distilled social games to their essence,"* etc.: "Cowclickification: Anything you can click you can cow click!" Ian Bogost, bogost.com, Jan. 20, 2011: http://www.bogost.com/blog/cowclickification.shtml.

4 *Golden Cowbell:* "Ian Bogost: the sarcastic game dev and academic who gave us Cow Clicker," Cory Doctorow, *BoingBoing*, Feb. 2, 2012: http://boingboing.net/2012/02/02/ian-bogost-the-sarcastic-game.html.

5 *T-shirts, hoodies, commemorative mugs:* "The Life-Changing $20 Rightward-Facing Cow," Leigh Alexander, Kotaku, Oct. 3, 2011: http://kotaku.com/5846080/the-life+changing-20-rightward+facing-cow.

5 *entered a "no-win spiral," "mad scientist,"* etc.: ibid.

5 *"Just like playing one, running a game":* "Cow Clicker: The Making of Obsession," Ian Bogost, bogost.com, July 21, 2010: http://www.bogost.com/blog/cow_clicker_1.shtml.

5 "cowclickification," etc.: "Cowclickification: Anything you can click you can cow click!" Ian Bogost, bogost.com, Jan. 20, 2011: http://www.bogost.com/blog/cowclickification.shtml.

5 Cow Clicker Blitz: "Facebook Game Satire Continues With 'Cow Clicker Blitz,'" Owen Good, Kotaku, Jan. 20, 2011: http://kotaku.com/5739269/facebook-game-satire-continues-with-cow-clicker-blitz.

5 *Moogle:* http://moogle.cowclicker.com.

5 *"Cow Clicker Moobile":* "Cowclickification: Anything you can click you can cow click!" Ian Bogost, bogost.com, Jan. 20, 2011: http://www.bogost.com/blog/cowclickification.shtml.

5 *"The Stockyard":* "Cow Clicker on Facebook": http://apps.facebook.com/cowclicker/cowclickification.

5 *let players pay $1:* "The Curse of Cow Clicker: How a Cheeky Satire Became a Videogame Hit," Jason Tanz, *Wired*, Jan. 2012: http://www.wired.com/magazine/2011/12/ff_cowclicker/all.

5 *Cowpocalypse:* "Cowpocalypse Now": "The Cows Have Been Raptured," Ian Bogost. bogost.com, Sept. 8, 2011: http://www.bogost.com/blog/cowpocalypse_now.shtml.

6 *"reached its maximum level of minimalism":* "Cowpocalypse Now": "The Cows Have Been Raptured," Ian Bogost. bogost.com, Sept. 8, 2011: http://www.bogost.com/blog/cowpocalypse_now.shtml.

6 *his greatest success or a colossal failure:* "The Curse of Cow Clicker: How a Cheeky Satire Became a Videogame Hit," Jason Tanz, *Wired*, Jan. 2012: http://www.wired.com/magazine/2011/12/ff_cowclicker/all.

6 *Target maintains a running average:* "Target's Cashier Game: Is It Really a Game?" *Impact Simulations* blog, Nov. 29, 2011: http://www.impact simulations.com/?p=263.

6 *In some urinals men may see a fly:* http://www.urinalfly.com.

7 *At Google, engineers have been able to spend an in-house currency:* "Google's Lunchtime Betting Game," Noam Cohen, *New York Times*, Jan. 7, 2008: http://www.nytimes.com/2008/01/07/technology/07link.html?ref=business&_r=0.

7 *savings can be donated to a charity:* "Gamification Facts and Figures," Mario Herger, Enterprise-Gamification.com, Oct. 24, 2011: http://enterprise-gamification.com/index.php/en/facts.

7 *Microsoft released a game,* Ribbon Hero*:* Download site: http://www.ribbonhero.com.

7 *Canon's repair techies:* "Games: Improving the Workplace," Electronic Software Association fact sheet: http://www.theesa.com/games-improving-what-matters/workplace.asp.

7 *Cisco has developed a "sim" called myPlanNet:* Cisco fact sheet: http://www.cisco.com/web/solutions/sp/myplannet/index.html?POSITION=vanity+&COUNTRY_SITE=us&CAMPAIGN=mPN&CREATIVE=onsite&REFERRING_SITE=Vanity+URL.

7 *IBM created a game that has players run whole cities:* IBM Innov8 download site: http://www-01.ibm.com/software/solutions/soa/innov8/full.html.

7 *L'Oréal created games for recruitment:* "L'Oréal hopes recruitment game will attract top graduates," Anna Times, *The Guardian*, Jun 11, 2010: http://www.guardian.co.uk/money/2010/jun/12/loreal-recruitment-game-top-graduates.

7 *Sun Microsystems has games for employee training:* "Training Games," Dave Zielinksi, Society for Human Resources Management, July 11, 2011: http://www.weknownext.com/trends/training-games.

7 *Lexus safety tests vehicles in what it brags is the world's most sophisticated driving simulator:* "Lexus unveils 'world's most advanced' driving simulator," Ben Coxworth, *Gizmag*, Oct. 12, 2010: http://www.gizmag.com/lexus-unveils-driving-simulator/16630.

7 *FedEx and airlines deploy game simulations to train pilots:* "FedEx Trains Pilots with High-Tech Simulators," Jane Roberts, *The Commercial Appeal*, posted on RedOrbit, Feb. 1, 2006: http://www.redorbit.com/news/technology/378759/fedex_trains_pilots_with_hightech_simulators.

7 *UPS has its own version for new drivers:* "UPS Thinks Outside the Box on Driver Training," Jennifer Levitz, *Wall Street Journal*, Apr. 6, 2010: http://online.wsj.com/article/SB20001424052702303912104575164573823418844.html.

8 *trace the term "gamification" to 2002:* "Does Gamification Really Work," Noelle Tasarra-Twigg, TechBeat, Dec. 16, 2012: http://techbeat.com/2012/12/does-gamification-really-work.

8 *70 percent of major employers use interactive software and games for training:* Entertainment Software Association fact sheet: http://www.theesa.com/newsroom/release_detail.asp?releaseID=24.

8 *by 2014, 70 percent of two thousand global organizations will depend on gamified applications:* "Gartner Predicts Over 70 Percent of Global 2000 Organisations Will Have at Least One Gamified Application by 2014," Gartner press release: http://www.gartner.com/newsroom/id/1844115.

8 *Badgeville, based in Redwood City and backed by forty million dollars in venture capital:* "Badgeville Secures $40 Million Series B Investment, Following Early Round Recognition by Felix Investments," press release, Jan. 17, 2012: http://www.sfgate.com/business/article/Badgeville-Secures-40-Million-Series-B-2576668.php#ixzz2SMFiMlt0.

8 Wells Fargo, Chevron, GE, Deloitte, Coursera, etc., using Badgeville: Badgeville and Ant's Eye View are Bringing Gamification to the Fortune 500, press release, Mar. 20, 2012: http://badgeville.com/?q=news/announcements/badgeville-and-ant%E2%80%99s-eye-view-are-bringing-gamification-fortune-500 and interview with Kris Duggan, CEO of Badgeville.

8 *Samsung layered Badgeville over its Samsung Nation:* "You've Won a Badge (and Now We Know All About You)," Natasha Singer, *New York Times*, Feb. 4, 2012: http://www.nytimes.com/2012/02/05/business/employers-and-brands-use-gaming-to-gauge-engagement.html?_r=0.

8 *"I think of gamification as music":* Interview with Kris Duggan, CEO, Badgeville.

8 *Popchips' sales increased 40 percent:* "Businesses Use Gaming Principles in Marketing," Mike Snider, *USA Today*, Aug. 3, 2012: http://usatoday30.usatoday.com/money/smallbusiness/story/2012-07-29/efficient-small-business-using-game-technology/56545082/1.

8 *Bell Media increased:* "Bell Media Teams with Badgeville to Gamify Fan Loyalty with 'MuchCloser,'" Badgeville case study: http://badgeville.com/content/case-study-bell-media.

8 *NextJump tasks games:* "Fun and games at work lead to higher productivity at Next Jump," Katie Gilbert, GamerFitNation, Jan. 14, 2013: http://gamerfitnation.com/2013/01/fun-and-games-at-work-lead-to-higher-productivity-at-next-jump.

8 *AETNA uses Mindbloom's* Life Game*:* "Aetna and Mindbloom Gamify Wellness to Help Drive Healthy Habits," Aetna press release, Apr. 11, 2012: http://newshub.aetna.com/press-release/member-and-consumer-health/aetna-and-mindbloom-gamify-wellness-help-drive-healthy-habi.

9 *SAP created a game:* Interview with Mario Herger, senior innovation strategist at SAP.

9 *RecycleBank and OpowerL increased recycling:* "21 Companies Use Gamification to Get Better Business Results," Rob Petersen, BarnRaisers company blog, Mar. 30, 2013: http://barnraisersllc.com/2013/03/companies-use-gamification-get-better-business-results.

9 *marines adopted* Doom*:* "Doom Goes to War," Rob Riddel, *Wired*, Apr. 1997: http://www.wired.com/wired/archive/5.04/ff_doom.html.

9 *army budgeted fifty million dollars to develop gaming systems:* "Not playing around: Army to invest $50M in combat training games," Seth Robson, *Stars and Stripes*, Nov. 23, 2008: http://www.stripes.com/news/not-playing-around-army-to-invest-50m-in-combat-training-games-1.85595.

9 *Lockheed Martin manufactured* Virtual Combat Convoy Trainer*:* "Virtual Reality Lifesaver—the VCCT," Lockheed Martin corporate Web site: http://www.lockheedmartin.com/us/100years/stories/vcct.html.

9 *$146 million government contract to develop a war-game training system:* "Lockheed's $146M Army training deal latest to survive sequester," Richard Burnett, *Orlando Sentinel*, Apr. 3, 2013: http://articles.orlandosentinel.com/2013-04-03/technology/os-lockheed-army-war-game-deal-20130403_1_training-system-army-contract-combat.

9 America's Army: Download site: http://www.americasarmy.com.

9 *One study concluded that the game has done more to influence recruits:* "Changing the Game: How Video Games Are Transforming the Future of Business," David Edery and Ethan Mollick, FT Press, Oct. 2008, 141.

10 *Defense Intelligence Agency (DIA) trains spies:* "U.S. Spies Use Custom Videogames to Learn How to Think," Michael Peck, Wired.com, Apr. 24, 2008: http://www.wired.com/politics/security/news/2008/04/spy_games?currentPage=all.

10 *CIA has commissioned the creation of video games:* "CIA Pursues Video Game," *Washington Times*, Sept. 29, 2003: http://www.washingtontimes.com/news/2003/sep/29/20030929-123116-1145r/?page=all#pagebreak.

10 *FBI uses Microsoft's Xbox in the classroom:* Federal Bureau of Investigation Web site: http://www.fbi.gov/news/videos/simulation-team-video.

10 *97 percent of twelve-to-seventeen-year-olds play computer games:* Entertainment Software Association fact sheet, which reports that the average gamer is thirty-five and has been at it a dozen years, and 40 percent of them are women: http://www.theesa.com/facts/index.asp.

10 *One survey found that 35 percent of C-suite executives play video games:* "Survey: Tens of Millions of 'White Collar' Workers Play 'Casual' Video Games—One in Four Play at Work, and Senior Execs Play Even More," Popcap press release: http://www.prnewswire.com/news-releases-test/survey-tens-of-millions-of-white-collar-workers-play-casual-video-games—one-in-four-play-at-work-and-senior-execs-play-even-more-57748872.html.

10 *Before turning twenty-one, the average American has spent two thousand to three thousand hours reading books—and more than three times that playing computer and video games: Reality Is Broken: Why Games Make Us Better and How They Can Change the World*, Jane McGonigal (New York: The Penguin Press, 2011).

10 *350 million people spend a combined three billion hours per week:* ibid.

10 *PricewaterhouseCoopers estimates:* "Gaming expected to be a $68 billion business by 2012," Frank Caron, *Ars Technica*, June 18, 2008: http://arstechnica.com/gaming/2008/06/gaming-expected-to-be-a-68-billion-business-by-2012.

11 World of Warcraft *boasted at its peak twelve million registered:* "World of Warcraft Subscriber Base Reaches 12 Million Worldwide," Blizzard Entertainment press release, Oct. 7, 2012: http://us.blizzard.com/en-us/company/press/pressreleases.html?id=2847881.

11 *fifty billion hours of playing time—the equivalent of 5.93 million years: Reality Is Broken: Why Games Make Us Better and How They Can Change the World*, Jane McGonigal (New York: The Penguin Press, 2011).

11 *"We've spent as much time playing":* ibid.

11 *"Nearly every company in the world gives lip service":* "The Happiness Dividend," Shawn Anchor, *Harvard Business Review* blog, June 23, 2011: http://blogs.hbr.org/cs/2011/06/the_happiness_dividend.html.

11 *found in a 2010 survey that only 45 percent of American workers:* "I Can't Get No . . . Job Satisfaction, That Is," Conference Board annual job satisfaction survey, John M. Gibbons, Conference Board Web site: http://www.conference-board.org/publications/publicationdetail.cfm?publicationid=1727.

11 *61 percent of workers reported being happy:* ibid.

12 *32 percent of workers were seriously considering leaving their jobs:* "Mercer's What's Working Survey Shows Declining Employee Loyalty Worldwide," Mercer press release, Oct. 27, 2011: http://www.mercer.com/press-releases/1430455.

12 *A Gallup poll that same year:* "Majority of American Workers Not Engaged in Their Jobs," Nikki Blacksmith and Jim Harter, Gallup Web site, Oct. 28, 2011: http://www.gallup.com/poll/150383/majority-american-workers-not-engaged-jobs.aspx.

14 *"Game mechanics cannot solve fundamental business problems": Gamification by Design: Implementing Game Mechanics in Web and Mobile Apps*, Gabe Zichermann and Christopher Cunningham (Cambridge, MA: O'Reilly Media, 2011), 1.

PART 1: GAMEFUL DESIGN

16 *Tom's aunt orders him to whitewash: Tom Sawyer*, Mark Twain, 1876, chapter 2. Excerpt: http://www.pbs.org/marktwain/learnmore/writings_tom.html.

17 *gameful design "helps you do what you want to do":* "Game Design (Part 1)," Chelsea Howe, *Game Design Aspect* blog, Sept. 2, 2012: http://gamedesignaspect.blogspot.com/2012/09/gameful-design-part-i.html.

17 *"No one is telling you to play"*, etc.: Interview with Chelsea Howe.

Chapter 1: This Is Your Brain on Games

19 *speech by game designer Jesse Schell:* 2010 DICE conference: Transcript and video available here: http://www.realtimetranscription.com/showcase/DICE2010/JesseSchell/index.php.

19 *his work at Disney Imagineering* and all other Jesse quotes and material in this chapter: Interview with Jesse Schell.

19 *"There are all these ways that games":* From Jesse Schell's DICE 2010 speech.

20 *"the most mind-blowing thing":* "Video: Reality TV, the iPhone & the Future of Technology—Why It's All a Game," Om Malik, Gigaom, Feb. 22, 2010: http://gigaom.com/2010/02/22/video-reality-tv-iphone-the-future-of-technology-why-its-all-a-game.

21 *trigger the release of dopamine:* "Video Games Can Activate the Brain's Pleasure Circuits," David J. Linden, *Psychology Today*, Oct. 25, 2011: http://www.psychologytoday.com/blog/the-compass-pleasure/201110/video-games-can-activate-the-brains-pleasure-circuits-0.

22 *video games uncork almost double the levels experienced by humans at rest:* "Negative Potential of Video Games," Russell A. Sabella, PhD, Education.com, 2008: http://www.education.com/reference/article/negative-potential-video-games.

22 *"threshold effects"* and *drives compulsive gamblers and cocaine addicts:* Interview with Professor Paul Zak, neuroeconomist, Claremont College.

22 *"flow": Flow: The Psychology of Optimal Experience*, Mihaly Csikszentmihalyi (New York: Harper Perennial, 2008).

22 *In 2003, two researchers at the University of Southern California:* "This is Your Brain on Video Games: Gaming sharpens thinking, social skills, and perception," Victoria Schlesinger, Steven Johnson, and Gary Panter, *Discover*, July 9, 2007: http://discovermagazine.com/2007/brain/video-games#.UYWjHJXA20t.

23 *"Our pleasure center consists not of some set of mechanisms": Kluge: The Haphazard Evolution of the Human Mind*, Gary Marcus (New York: Mariner Books, 2009).

24 University of Leicester, England, study on music and wine: "In-store music affects product choice," Adrian C. North, David J. Hargreaves, and Jennifer McKendrick, *Nature*, Nov. 13, 1997: http://www.nature.com/nature/journal/v390/n6656/abs/390132a0.html; and University of Leicester press release: http://www.le.ac.uk/press/ebulletin/news/havingtherighttaste.html.

24 *slow music resulted in a 38.2 percent increase in sales: Music in the Human Experience: An Introduction to Music Psychology*, Donald Hodges and David Conrad Sebald (New York: Routledge, 2010).

24 *walked 30 percent more slowly and spent 12 percent more than when there was no music:* ibid.

24 *slow music causes restaurant patrons to stay longer and order more food while fast music lessens the length of time it takes to drink a can of soda:* ibid.

25 *to unveil Mynd:* "Thinking Cap: Mynd is the First Dry, iPhone-Compatible, Portable Brain Scanner," David Zax, fastcompany.com, Mar. 21, 2011: http://www.fastcompany.com/1741403/thinking-cap-mynd-first-dry-iphone-compatible-portable-brain-scanner.

25 *"Good news," he cracks. "You're alive,"* and other A. K. Pradeep material: Interviews with A. K. Pradeep.

27 *"Video games change your brain":* "When Gaming Is Good for You," Robert Lee Holtz, *Wall Street Journal*, Mar. 5, 2012: http://online.wsj.com/article/SB10001424052970203458604577263273943183932.html.

27 *playing the piano, learning to read, and wandering London's streets:* ibid.

27 *Combat veterans who play violent games sleep better and suffer fewer nightmares:* "Video Gamers Can Control Dreams, Study Suggests," Jeremy Hsu, *Live Science*, May 25, 2010: http://www.livescience.com/6521-video-gamers-control-dreams-study-suggests.html.

27 *playing video games, even for just a short time, improves a player's visual attention:* "Playing a First-person Shooter Video Game Induces Neuroplastic Change," Sijing Wu, Cho Kin Cheng, Jing Feng, Lisa D'Angelo, Claude Alain, and Ian Spence, *Journal of Cognitive Neuroscience*, June 2012, vol. 24, No. 6, pp. 1286-1293: http://www.mitpressjournals.org/doi/abs/10.1162/jocn_a_00192.

27 *players of action-packed games make decisions 25 percent faster:* "'Call of Duty' Video Game Trains Brains for Fast, Accurate Decision-Making," Ellen Gibson, Bloomberg, Sept. 13, 2010: http://www.bloomberg.com/news/2010-09-13/-call-of-duty-video-game-trains-brains-for-fast-accurate-decision-making.html.

27 *the more the kids played video games, the higher they scored on a test:* "When Gaming Is Good for You," Robert Lee Holtz, *Wall Street Journal*, Mar. 5, 2012: http://online.wsj.com/article/SB10001424052970203458604577263273943183932.html.

27 *surgeons who play games three hours a week commit 37 percent fewer errors:* "Surgeons may err less by playing video games," Verena Dobnik, Associated Press, Apr. 7, 2004: http://www.nbcnews.com/id/4685909ns/technology_and_science-games/t/surgeons-may-err-less-playing-video-games/#.UYWmHZXA20s.

28 *performed gallbladder surgery 29 percent faster:* "Virtual Reality Training Improves Operating Room Performance: Results of a Randomized, Double-Blinded Study," Neal E. Seymour, Anthony G. Gallagher,

Sanziana A. Roman, Michael K. O'Brien, Vipin K. Bansal, Dana K. Andersen, and Richard M. Satava, *Annals of Surgery*, Oct. 2002, vol. 236(4), 458–464: http://www.ncbi.nlm.nih.gov/pmc/articles/PMC1422600.

28 *reshaped a Wii golf club into a laparoscopic probe: I Live in the Future & Here's How It Works: Why Your World, Work & Brain Are Being Creatively Disrupted*, Nick Bilton (New York: Crown Business, 2011), 150.

28 Definitions of game: Merriam-Webster dictionary: http://www.merriam-webster.com/dictionary/game.

28 *"A game is a system in which players engage in an artificial conflict": Rules of Play: Game Design Fundamentals*, Katie Salen and Eric Zimmerman (Cambridge, MA: The MIT Press, 2003), 80.

29 *"A game is a closed, formal system that engages players in structured conflict": The Art of Game Design: A Book of Lenses*, Jesse Schell (New York: CRC Press, 2008), 33.

31 *downloaded almost two billion times:* "Angry Birds hits 1.7bn Downloads As Its Games Become Cartoon Channels," Stuart Dredge, *The Guardian*, Mar. 11, 2013: http://www.guardian.co.uk/technology/appsblog/2013/mar/11/angry-birds-toons.

31 *game was being played two hundred million minutes a day, or 1.2 billion hours a year:* "I Have Found the Cognitive Surplus, and It Hates Pigs," Joshua Benton, Nieman Journalism Lab, Dec. 29, 2010: http://www.niemanlab.org/2010/12/i-have-found-the-cognitive-surplus-and-it-hates-pigs.

31 *ten million* Angry Birds*–themed toys:* "Angry Birds Aim for World Domination," FoxNews, Oct. 19, 2011: http://www.foxnews.com/tech/2011/10/19/angry-birds-aim-for-world-domination.

31 *Angelina Jolie, Justin Bieber,* Mad Men*'s Jon Hamm,* Satanic Verses *author Salman Rushdie, and British prime minister David Cameron:* Jolie: *National Enquirer*, Apr. 4, 2011; Justin Bieber tweet: https://twitter.com/justinbieber/status/27604513287; "Angry Birds pointers? Ask Jon Hamm," Matthew Shaer, *Christian Science Monitor*, Sept. 27, 2010: http://www.csmonitor.com/Innovation/Horizons/2010/0927/Angry-Birds-pointers-Ask-Jon-Hamm; Rushdie: "Why We Can't Stop Playing," Nick Wingfield, *Wall Street Journal*, Nov. 30, 2010: http://online.wsj.com/article/SB10001424052748703945904575644940111605862.html; "David Cameron admits to Angry Birds addiction," School Report, BBC, Mar. 9, 2012: http://www.bbc.co.uk/schoolreport/17315004.

31 *playing casual games can boost a player's mood:* "Study: Casual video games demonstrate ability to reduce depression and anxiety," East Carolina University press release, Feb. 16, 2011: http://www.ecu.edu/cs-admin/news/newsstory.cfm?ID=1906.

32 *provided a cognitive breakdown of the game's:* "Why Angry Birds is so successful and popular: a cognitive teardown of the user experience," MauroNewMedia company blog, Feb. 6, 2011: http://www.mauro

newmedia.com/blog/why-angry-birds-is-so-successful-a-cognitive-teardown-of-the-user-experience.

34 *games provide feedback loops:* "What Are Game Mechanics," Daniel Cook, *Lost Garden* personal blog (collection of essays on game design theory), Oct. 23, 2006: http://www.lostgarden.com/2006/10/what-are-game-mechanics.html.

35 *"fractal elegance":* Interview with Chelsea Howe.

36 *cheat sheet of game mechanics:* "SCVNGR's Secret Game Mechanics Playdeck," Erick Schonfeld, *TechCrunch*, Aug. 25, 2010: http://techcrunch.com/2010/08/25/scvngr-game-mechanics.

37 LinkedIn status bar: "The Psychology of Gamification," Clarissa Sajbl, *LinkDex* blog, Oct. 8, 2012: http://www.linkdex.com/blog/the-psychology-of-gamification.

37 *Starbucks has a rewards program:* "What Is Gamification and Real World Examples of It," Ada Chen, *@adachen* blog, Oct. 4, 2010: http://adachen.com/2010/10/04/what-is-gamification-and-real-world-examples-of-it and "My Starbucks Rewards," Starbucks Web site: http://www.starbucks.com/card/rewards.

38 *get fewer colds and flus:* "Social ties and susceptibility to the common cold," S. Cohen, W. J. Doyle, D. P. Skoner, B. S. Rabin, and J. M. Gwaltney, Jr., *Journal of the American Medical Association*, June 25, 1997: http://www.ncbi.nlm.nih.gov/pubmed/9200634.

38 *A decade-long Australian study*: "What Are Friends For? A Longer Life," Tara Parker-Pope, *New York Times*, Apr. 20, 2009: http://www.nytimes.com/2009/04/21/health/21well.html and "Good Friends Are Good for You," Tom Valeo, WebMD: http://www.webmd.com/balance/features/good-friends-are-good-for-you.

38 *scanned the brains of fiction readers:* "Reading Stories Activates Neural Representations of Visual and Motor Experiences," Nicole K. Speer, Jeremy R. Reynolds, Khena M. Swallow, and Jeffrey M. Zacks, *Psychological Science*, Aug. 2009: http://phys.org/news152210728.html.

38 *the Internet, in particular social networks, engender trust:* "Social networking sites and our lives," Keith Hampton, Lauren Sessions Goulet, Lee Rainie, and Kristen Purcell, Pew Foundation Report, Jun 16, 2011: http://www.pewinternet.org/Reports/2011/Technology-and-social-networks/Summary.aspx.

39 Paul J. Zak material: Interviews with Paul Zak.

42 *it has been "overhyped":* Interview with Dan Ariely.

42 *rant with the hashtag #schmoxytocin:* Storify of Ed Yong's tweets on Paul Zak and oxytocin, Rachel Feltman: http://storify.com/RFelt/schmoxytocin-with-ed-yong.

Chapter 2: Mass Organizer

46 Luis von Ahn material: Interviews with Luis von Ahn.

46 von Ahn PhD dissertation: "Human Computation," Luis von Ahn, Dec. 7, 2005, School of Computer Science, Carnegie Mellon University: http://reports-archive.adm.cs.cmu.edu/anon/2005/CMU-CS-05-193.pdf.

47 *took tens of thousands of men and more than twenty years to build:* "Who Built the Pyramids?" PBS *Nova*, Feb. 4, 1997: http://www.pbs.org/wgbh/nova/ancient/who-built-the-pyramids.html.

47 *laborers digging the Panama Canal clocked twenty million hours:* SEABEE combat handbook, Naval Education and Training Program Management Support Activity (U.S.), 1989.

47 *Empire State Building tallied seven million:* Empire State Building Trivia, NPR, Dec. 30, 2002: http://www.npr.org/programs/morning/features/patc/empirestate.

47 *Burj Khalifa:* "Electric Avenue: Mother nature lights up the world's tallest building in down town Dubai," *Daily Mail*, Apr. 12, 2011: http://www.dailymail.co.uk/news/article-1375724/Electric-Avenue-Mother-nature-lights-worlds-tallest-building-town-Dubai.html.

47 *Von Ahn, a former MacArthur "genius" grant winner:* "Brilliant Young Scientist Luis von Ahn Earns $500,000 MacArthur Foundation 'Genius Grant,'" Carnegie Mellon press release: Sept. 18, 2006: http://www.cmu.edu/cmnews/extra/060918_ahn.html.

48 *Within a week it had logged two million page views:* Interviews with HotorNot founders James Hong and Jim Young.

54 *"They were like completely depleted":* Interview with Jose Fuentes.

Chapter 3: The Red Balloon Game

55 Regina Dugan material: Interview with Regina Dugan.

55 *Bell-Boeing V-22 Osprey helicopter program cost taxpayers more than $20 billion: The Dream Machine: The Untold History of the Notorious V-22 Osprey*, Richard Whittle (New York: Simon & Schuster, 2010), 370.

56 *USS* George H. W. Bush *warship ran $6.2 billion:* "Naval ship faces chronic toilet outages at sea," Jason Ukman, *Washington Post*, Nov. 16, 2011: http://www.washingtonpost.com/blogs/checkpoint-washington/post/naval-ship-faces-chronic-toilet-outages-at-sea/2011/11/15/gIQALCZ3QN_blog.html.

56 *It took the air force twenty-five years to launch a space-based infrared system, a satellite first conceived in 1986:* Interview with DARPA program manager Rob McHenry.

56 *General Accounting Office (GAO) reported almost three hundred billion dollars in cost overruns between 2001 and 2008: Defense Acquisitions:*

Assessment of Selected Weapon Program, General Accounting Office, Mar. 2008: http://www.gao.gov/new.items/d08467sp.pdf.

56 *2054. That's the year DARPA estimates the cost of a single, state-of-the-art aircraft could equal the entire Department of Defense budget:* Interview with DARPA Deputy Director Kaigham Gabriel.

56 *Hollywood has had hundred-million-dollar movies* (Pluto Nash, Cutthroat Island): "This decade's biggest movie failure: Eddie Murphy's *Pluto Nash*," Internet Movie Database, Nov. 30, 2009: http://www.imdb.com/title/tt0180052/news?year=2009 and "The vanity that led to a $100m bonfire," Daniel Jeffreys, *The Independent*, Apr. 10, 1996: http://www.independent.co.uk/news/the-vanity-that-led-to-a-100m-bonfire-1304053.html.

56 *R. J. Reynolds poured $325 million into developing smokeless cigarettes:* "The 20 Worst Product Failures," Zac Frank and Tania Khadder, SalesHQ: http://saleshq.monster.com/news/articles/2655-the-20-worst-product-failures.

56 *$10 billion to develop and ship Microsoft Vista:* "Why Vista might be the last of its kind," Dean Takahashi, *San Jose Mercury News*, Dec. 4, 2006: http://seattletimes.com/html/businesstechnology/2003460386_btview04.html.

56 Time *named one of the "10 Biggest Tech Failures of the Last Decade": Time*, May 14, 2009: http://www.time.com/time/specials/packages/article/0,28804,1898610_1898625_1898627,00.html.

57 DARPA inventions and research; DARPA History: http://www.darpa.mil/About/History/First_50_Years.aspx.

57 *"DARPA Loses Hypersonic Vehicle, Goes from $320M to Zero in 2,700 Seconds":* Michelle Macaluso, FoxNews.com, Aug. 11, 2011: http://www.foxnews.com/tech/2011/08/11/darpa-readies-hypersonic-aircraft-for-mach-20-launch-test.

58 *timing coincided with the fortieth anniversary of ARPANet:* "DARPA Celebrates Internet Anniversary with Bizarre Balloon Challenge," Jeremy Hsu, PopSci, Oct. 30, 2009: http://www.popsci.com/technology/article/2009-10/darpa-celebrates-internet-anniversary-bizarre-balloon-challenge.

58 *On Dec. 5, 1969, DARPA linked the first four nodes of a network:* "Connecting with an Internet Pioneer, 40 Years Later," Larry Greenemeier, *Scientific American*, Dec. 4, 2009: http://www.scientificamerican.com/article.cfm?id=internet-pioneer-cerf.

59 *winner would collect a forty-thousand-dollar prize:* "DARPA announces a $40,000 red-balloon Network Challenge," Homeland Security News Wire, Oct. 30, 2009: http://www.homelandsecuritynewswire.com/darpa-announces-40000-red-balloon-network-challenge.

59 *the continental United States cover 3.1 million square miles:* "Intermap Completes USA Collection," Matt Ball, *Spatial Sustain* blog, Mar. 23, 2009: http://www.sensysmag.com/spatialsustain/intermap-completes-usa-collection.html.

59 *The nation has some 4 million miles of paved roads:* American Road & Transportation Builders Assoc. FAQs: http://www.artba.org/about/faqs-transportation-general-public/faqs/#9.

60 *Twitter reported 18 million users who logged in at least once a month*: "18 Million Twitter Users by End of 2009," Adam Ostrow, *Mashable*, Sept. 14, 2009: http://mashable.com/2009/09/14/twitter-2009-stats.

60 *Facebook had 120 million members living in the United States:* ibid.

60 *competition for robotic driverless cars through a 150-mile course:* http://driverlessworld.com/2011/06/a-brief-history-of-driverless-vehicles.

60 *A team from Carnegie Mellon nabbed the $2 million first prize:* ibid.

60 *three engineers from California, Ohio, and Texas $1 million for their design of a military tank that can swim:* "This Is the Million-Dollar Design for Darpa's Crowdsourced Swimming Tank," Spender Ackerman, Wired's Danger Room, Apr. 22, 2013: http://www.wired.com/dangerroom/2013/04/darpa-fang-winner.

60 *4,367 entrants signed up in the five weeks between the initial announcement and the day of the contest:* DARPA Network Challenge Project Report, Feb. 16, 2010: http://www.hsdl.org/?view&did=17522.

60 *"Army of Eyes":* "Pentagon offers $40K in red balloon challenge," ABC News, Dec. 5, 2009: http://abclocal.go.com/wtvd/story?section=news/national_world&id=7155229.

60 *i-Neighbors*: http://www.i-neighbors.org/redballoon.php.

60 *"Open Red Balloon Project":* "MIT Harnesses Online Crowds to Beat Darpa Balloon Challenge in Just 9 Hours," Jeremy Hsu, *Popular Science*, Dec. 7, 2009: http://www.popsci.com/technology/article/2009-12/how-mit-mobilized-social-networks-win-nationwide-hunt-10-red-balloons.

61 *George Hotz, a twenty-year-old hacker from New Jersey who gained notoriety for being the first to jailbreak an iPhone and hack the Sony PlayStation:* "Machine Politics: The man who started the hacker wars," David Kushner, *The New Yorker*, May 7, 2012: http://www.newyorker.com/reporting/2012/05/07/120507fa_fact_kushner.

61 *tweeted to his thirty-five thousand Twitter:* "Solve the world's hardest jigsaw puzzle. Pin the coordinates on the balloons," TMC News, Dec. 2, 2011: http://www.tmcnet.com/usubmit/2011/12/02/5969138.htm.

61 *Jon Cannell, a Web designer from Port Charlotte, Florida, announced:* "Grass Roots Red Balloon Challenge Team Formed," press release, Dec. 2, 2009: http://www.pressreleasepoint.com/grass-roots-red-balloon-challenge-team-formed.

61 *Larry Moss, a professional artist who designed balloon sculptures, promised:* "Pentagon offers $40K in red balloon challenge," ABC News, Dec. 5, 2009: http://abclocal.go.com/wtvd/story?section=news/national_world&id=7155229.

61 *opted for an altruism-based incentive mechanism:* Georgia Tech Institute of Technology case study: "I Spy A Red Balloon: Georgia Tech Team Wins Key Insights—and a Second-Place Finish—in DARPA Network Challenge," case study: http://www.gtri.gatech.edu/casestudy/red-balloon-darpa-challenge.

61 *team of students and professors from Harvard Business School, pursued a quasi altruism-based incentive model:* DARPA Network Challenge Project Report, Feb. 16, 2010: http://www.hsdl.org/?view&did=17522.

61 *Leading a group from MIT:* "MIT floats ideas in DARPA balloon challenge (Q&A with Riley Crane)," Lance Whitney, CNET, Dec. 8, 2009: http://news.cnet.com/8301-1023_3-10411211-93.html.

62 *"We're giving $2000 per balloon":* "Geeks Tweak Balloon Seek Technique," Andrew McAfee, personal blog, Dec. 7, 2009: http://andrewmcafee.org/2009/12/geeks-tweak-balloon-seek-technique.

62 *joined his agency colleagues at San Francisco's Union Square:* "DARPA Tasks Social Networkers to Find Balloons," interview with Dr. Peter Lee, NPR, Dec. 15, 2009: http://www.npr.org/templates/story/story.php?storyId=121452513.

63 *In Royal Oaks, Michigan, someone positioned a decoy balloon complete with an imposter DARPA official:* DARPA Network Challenge Project Report, Feb. 16, 2010: http://www.hsdl.org/?view&did=17522.

63 *10 Red Balloons, announced that it had spotted a balloon even before the contest kicked off:* MIT Team Wins Darpa's Balloon-Spotting Contest, Matthew Rivera, *Wall Street Journal*, Dec. 7, 2009: http://blogs.wsj.com/digits/2009/12/07/mit-team-wins-darpas-balloon-spotting-contest.

63 *Lee, whose office managed the competition, told NPR:* "DARPA Tasks Social Networkers to Find Balloons," interview with Dr. Peter Lee, NPR, Dec. 15, 2009: http://www.npr.org/templates/story/story.php?storyId=121452513.

63 *To determine the legitimacy of balloon sightings:* Interview with Regina Dugan; and "Time Critical Social Mobilization: The DARPA Network Challenge Winning Strategy," Galen Pickard, Iyad Rahwan, Wei Pan, Manuel Cebrian, Riley Crane, Anmol Madan, and Alex (Sandy) Pentland (research paper): https://people.cs.umass.edu/~wallach/workshops/nips2010css/papers/pickard.pdf.

64 *"real nail-biter":* "DARPA Tasks Social Networkers to Find Balloons," NPR, Dec. 15, 2009: http://www.npr.org/templates/story/story.php?storyId=121452513.

64 Rob McHenry submarine game material: Interview with Rob McHenry.

65 *"One of the things":* Interview with DARPA Deputy Director Kaigham Gabriel.

65 Dangerous Waters, *a naval warfare simulation released on Microsoft Windows in 2005:* "S.C.S. Dangerous Waters-PC-Review," jkdmedia,

GameZone, Mar. 30, 2005: http://www.gamezone.com/reviews/2005/03/30/s_c_s_dangerous_waters_pc_review.

Chapter 4: The Wisdom of Cars

68 Phone conversation between Regina Dugan and Jay Rogers: Interviews with Regina Dugan and Jay Rogers.

69 Ralph Burton Rogers and Indian Motors: "Ralph Rogers, 87, Philanthropist Who Led and Defended PBS," Bill Carter, *New York Times*, Nov. 6, 1997: http://www.nytimes.com/1997/11/06/arts/ralph-rogers-87-philantropist-who-led-and-defended-pbs.html; *Motorcycle: The Definitive Visual History* (New York: DK Publishing, 2012); "The Man Who Killed Indian: Or Was Ralph Rogers Simply Ahead of His Time?" Ed Youngblood (curator for "The Century of Indian" exhibit at AMA's Motorcycle Hall of Fame), *Cycle World Magazine*, Jan.–July 2001; "Everything You Need to Know About Indian Motorcycles," Parker Kennedy, posted on HubPages: http://parkerk393.hubpages.com/hub/Everything-You-Need-to-Know-About-Indian-Motorcycles and interview with Jay Rogers.

70 Local Motors material: Interviews with Jay Rogers and Local Motors staff, including Damien Declercq, Alexis Fichter, Aurel Francois, Adam Keiser, Mike Pisani, Nyko Peyer, David Rhia, Tim Thomas, and Wade Williams.

73 *Ford Edsel, a $350-million dud:* "50 years ago today Ford pulled the plug on the ill-conceived Edsel," Fred Meier, *USA Today*, Nov. 19, 2009: http://content.usatoday.com/communities/driveon/post/2009/11/50-years-ago-today-ford-pulled-the-plug-on-the-ill-conceived-edsel/1#.UYZaVILvbjU.

73 *Ford squandered six billion dollars on a "world car":* "Ford's $6 Billion Baby," Alex Taylor III, *Fortune*, June 28, 1993: http://money.cnn.com/magazines/fortune/fortune_archive/1993/06/28/78013.

73 *Threadless:* "The Customer is the Company: Threadless churns out dozens of new items a month—with no advertising, no professional designers, no sales force and no retail distribution. And it's never produced a flop," Max Chafkin, *Inc.*, June 1, 2008: http://www.inc.com/magazine/20080601/the-customer-is-the-company.html and "How Jake Nickell Built His Threadless Empire," Marcia Froelke Cobrn, *Chicago Magazine*, Jul 2012: http://www.chicagomag.com/Chicago-Magazine/July-2012/How-Jake-Nickell-Built-His-Threadless-Empire.

74 Bell Labs material: *The Idea Factory: Bell Labs and the Great Age of American Innovation*, Jon Gertner (New York: The Penguin Press, 2012).

75 Neal Gabler and globalized understanding of innovation: ibid.

75 *open-source collective of programmers coded Mozilla's Firefox:* "History of the Mozilla Project," Mozilla "about" on home page: http://www.mozilla.org/en-US/about/history.

75 *Netflix handed out one million dollars in prize money to BellKor's Pragmatic Chaos:* "BellKor's Pragmatic Chaos Wins $1 Million Netflix Prize by Mere Minutes," Eliot Van Buskirk, *Wired*, Sept. 21, 2009: http://www.wired.com/business/2009/09/bellkors-pragmatic-chaos-wins-1-million-netflix-prize.

75 *the* Guardian *crowdsourced the expense reports:* "MPs' expenses," curated page on *Guardian* homepage: http://www.guardian.co.uk/politics/mps-expenses.

75 *trove of Sarah Palin e-mails:* "WaPo, NYT to crowdsource Palin e-mails," Keach Hagey, *Politico*, June 9, 2011: http://www.politico.com/blogs/onmedia/0611/WaPo_to_crowdsource_Palin_e-mails.html; "Help Us Review the Sarah Palin E-Mail Records," Derek Willis, *New York Times*, June 9, 2011: http://thecaucus.blogs.nytimes.com/2011/06/09/help-us-investigate-the-sarah-palin-e-mail-records; "Read the Palin e-mails," Ryan Kellett, *Washington Post*, June 9, 2011: http://www.washingtonpost.com/blogs/the-fix/post/help-analyze-the-palin-e-mails/2011/06/08/AGZAaHNH_blog.html.

76 *deciphering financial statements:* "The Bain Files: Inside Mitt Romney's Tax-Dodging Cayman Schemes," John Cook, *Gawker*, Aug. 23, 2012: http://gawker.com/5936394/the-bain-files-inside-mitt-romneys-tax+dodging-cayman-schemes.

76 *FBI crowdsourced cryptography in a murder investigation:* "Breaking Codes to Stop Crime, Part 1," Federal Bureau of Investigation Web site, Mar. 21, 2011: http://www.fbi.gov/news/stories/2011/march/cryptanalysis_032111; and "Help Solve an Open Murder Case, Part 2," Federal Bureau of Investigation Web site, Mar. 29, 2011: http://www.fbi.gov/news/stories/2011/march/cryptanalysis_032911.

76 *"No matter who you are, most of the smartest people work for someone else": The Network Is Your Customer: Five Strategies to Thrive in a Digital World*, David Rogers (New Haven: Yale University Press, 2012).

76 *set up shop in a three-thousand-square foot microfactory in an industrial park in Wareham, Massachusetts:* Interview with Jay Rogers and "In the Next Industrial Revolution, Atoms Are the New Bits," Chris Anderson, *Wired*, Jan. 25, 2010: http://www.wired.com/magazine/2010/01/ff_newrevolution/all.

77 *Sangho Kim, a thirty-year-old graphic arts student at the Art Center College of Design in Pasadena, California, had modeled his illustrations:* ibid. and "Design in the Age of Open Source Design," Art Center College of Design press release, Jan. 29, 2010: http://blogs.artcenter.edu/dottedline/tag/sangho-kim.

77 *forged from parts cobbled together from Chevy, BMW, and a host of other automotive companies:* Interview with Local Motors engineer David Rhia.

77 Popular Mechanics *took it for a spin:* "Local Motors Rally Fighter Test Drive," Ezra Dyer, *Popular Mechanics*, Dec. 20, 2010: http://www

.popularmechanics.com/cars/reviews/preview/local-motors-rally-fighter-off-road-test-drive.

77 *the "coolest looking car ever":* "Local Motors Rally Fighter: The First-Ever Creative Commons Car," Ray Wert, *Jalopnik*, Nov. 6, 2009: http://jalopnik.com/5398864/local-motors-rally-fighter-the-first+ever-creative-commons-car.

77 *"the most badass car you've never heard of":* "Rally Fighter: The Most Badass Car You've Never Heard Of," Max Johnson, *Car Throttle*, Mar. 2013: http://www.carthrottle.com/rally-fighter-the-most-badass-car-youve-never-heard-about.

78 *Lean Startup methodology: The Lean Startup: How Today's Entrepreneurs Use Continuous Innovation to Create Radically Successful Businesses*, Eric Ries (New York: Crown, 2011).

79 *awarded a $639,000 contract:* "How The First Crowdsourced Military Vehicle Can Remake the Future of Defense Manufacturing," Rebecca Boyle, *Popular Science*, June 30, 2011: http://www.popsci.com/cars/article/2011-06/how-first-crowdsourced-military-car-can-remake-future-defense-manufacturing.

79 *"Experimental Crowd-derived Combat-support Vehicle":* "DARPA XC2V Design Challenge Explores Advantages of Crowd-Sourced Design," DARPA press release, Mar. 15, 2011: http://www.darpa.mil/NewsEvents/Releases/2011/2011/03/15_DARPA_XC2V_Design_Challenge_Explores_Advantages_of_Crowd-Sourced_Design.aspx.

79 *a total of ten thousand dollars in prize money:* "Local Motors announces Flypmode concept wins DARPA XC2V competition," by Jeff Glucker, *Autoblog*, Mar. 22, 2011: http://www.autoblog.com/2011/03/22/local-motors-announces-flypmode-concept-wins-darpa-xc2v-competit.

79 Victor Garcia material: Interview with Victor Garcia. His drawings are available here: https://forge.localmotors.com/pages/project.php?cg=7564&tab=project-home.

80 *The seats came from MasterCraft* and other components: Interviews with Jay Rogers, David Rhia, and Victor Garcia.

80 *"It was a lot of work":* Interview with David Rhia. Time-lapse video of the building of the XC2V at Local Motors factory in Chandler, Arizona: http://www.youtube.com/watch?v=FQ_LwpfU8oE.

80 *XC2V was unveiled in June 2011 at Carnegie Mellon University's National Robotics Center:* "The First Crowd-Sourced Military Vehicle is Unwrapped," Osha Gray Davidson, Forbes.com, June 24, 2011: http://www.forbes.com/sites/oshadavidson/2011/06/24/the-first-crowd-sourced-military-vehicle-is-unwrapped.

80 *"out to theater faster":* "Remarks by the President at Carnegie Mellon University's National Robotics Engineering Center," White House transcript, June 24, 2011: http://www.whitehouse.gov/the-press-office/2011/06/24/remarks-president-carnegie-mellon-universitys-national-robotics-engineer.

81 Impressions of riding in the XC2V: Interviews with Victor Garcia and DARPA Deputy Director Kaigham Gabriel.
81 *"It's one thing to look at drawings":* Interview with Victor Garcia.
81 Past challenges on Local Motors' The Forge, including BMW, Peterbilt, Reebok, etc.: https://forge.localmotors.com/pages/competition.php#past.

Chapter 5: Anyone Can Be an Inventor

82 Ben Kaufman and Quirky material: Interviews with Ben Kaufman and Quirky inventors Jake Zien (Pivot Power), Bill Ward (Broom Groomer), and Judi Sigler (MugStir).
82 Thursday night product discussion: Author attended event.
82 *Pivot Power:* Quirky product page: http://www.quirky.com/products/44.
83 *MugStir:* Quirky product page: http://www.quirky.com/products/28.
83 *Broom Groomer:* Quirky product page: http://www.quirky.com/products/36.
83 *Cordies:* Quirky product page: http://www.quirky.com/products/11.
83 *Pluck:* Quirky product page: http://www.quirky.com/products/426.
83 *Digits:* Quirky product page: http://www.quirky.com/products/37.
86 *Trada, a crowdsourced paid search marketplace that did gamify:* "Trada Reinvents Game Mechanics for Crowdsourcing Businesses," Rachel Cihlar, *The Trada* Blog, Dec. 1, 2010: http://www.trada.com/blog/trada-reinvents-game-mechanics-for-crowdsourcing-businesses.
88 *Mophie won a Best in Show award at MacWorld for his Relo series:* "2006 Best of Show Awards: Who Won, and Why," Jeremy Horwitz, iLounge, Jan. 11, 2006: http://www.ilounge.com/index.php/articles/comments/2006-best-of-show-awards-who-won-and-why.
90 *the idea for a telescoping surge protector* and all material on Pivot Power: Interview with Jake Zien.
91 *earned more than $350,000:* Jake Zien Quirky community profile: http://www.quirky.com/users/26599.
91 *She first heard about Quirky* and all material on MugStir: Interview with Judi Sigler.
92 *Altogether Sigler has made about five thousand dollars:* Judi Sigler Quirky community profile: http://www.quirky.com/users/13394.
93 *whose idea came to him while he was sweeping his garage* and all material on Bill Ward: Interview with Bill Ward.
95 *Ward has collected a little more than $18,000:* Bill Ward Quirky community profile: http://www.quirky.com/users/16810.
95 *Ben Kaufman's appearance on* The Tonight Show with Jay Leno: (video) http://www.nbc.com/the-tonight-show/as-seen-on-the-show/quirky.
95 *compact fruit spritzer:* http://www.quirky.com/products/187.
95 *egg deyolker:* http://www.quirky.com/products/426.

95 *motorcycle helmet that displays turn lights and brake signals:* "Signal": http://www.quirky.com/products/249-Signal-led-brake-light-helmet.

95 *Fruity Tush:* http://www.quirky.com/users/205138/feed.

PART 2: SERIOUS PLAY

98 Michael Fergusson and Ayogo material: Interview with Michael Fergusson.

98 *HealthSeeker:* Ayogo case study: http://ayogo.com/blog/case-study-health seeker.

99 *Lea Bakalyar, a stay-at-home mom:* E-mail interview with Lea Bakalyar.

99 *Tanya Ortiz, a homemaker from Queens:* E-mail interview with Tanya Ortiz.

99 The Great Race: *Ayogo* blog: http://ayogo.com/blog/the-great-race.

99 *I ❤ Jellyfish:* Ayogo site: http://ayogo.com/blog/i-heart-jellyfish.

100 *Lockheed Martin reports that in 2012 it trained twenty-two thousand military commanders and support staff with* Warfighters' Simulation *(or* WarSim*) in a fourteen-war game exercise:* "Lockheed Martin to Provide U.S. Army with Simulation-Based Command and Battle Staff Training System," Lockheed Martin press release, Apr. 3, 2013: http://www.lockheedmartin.com/us/news/press-releases/2013/april/lockheed-martin-to-provide-u-s-army-with-simulation-based-comma.html.

100 Peacemaker: *Peacemaker* Web site: http://www.peacemakergame.com/game.php.

100 *humanitarian game called* Food Force: "Online Game 'Food Force' Puts Players on Front Lines of Hunger," World Food Programme site: http://www.wfp.org/stories/online-game-food-force-puts-players-front-lines-hunger.

100 Democracy: *Democracy:* "The ultimate political strategy game." Positech Web site: http://www.positech.co.uk/democracy.

100 *Innov8:* "Play the Innov8 game to learn business process management," IBM press release: http://www.ibm.com/developerworks/webservices/library/ws-bpm-innov8.

101 *"Fun is functional":* Interview with Michael Fergusson.

Chapter 6: That's Edutainment!

103 *Business and Economic Reporting program at New York University:* BER Web site: http://journalism.nyu.edu/graduate/courses-of-study/business-and-economic-reporting.

104 *"The problem is that our schools":* Interview with Paul Gee.

104 *Quest to Learn, a public school for sixth to twelfth graders in Manhattan:* "Learning by Playing: Video Games in the Classroom," Sara Corbett,

New York Times Magazine, Sept. 15, 2010: http://journalism.nyu.edu/graduate/courses-of-study/business-and-economic-reporting.

104 *2006 Summit on Educational Games by the Federation of American Scientists:* "Harnessing the Power of Videogames for Learning" (report), "Summit on Educational Games," Federation of American Scientists: http://www.fas.org/gamesummit/Resources/Summit%20on%20Educational%20Games.pdf.

106 *Stray Boots:* http://www.strayboots.com.

107 *Avi Millman, the twenty-eight-year-old cofounder:* Interview with Ari Millman.

107 *views traditional methods of teaching:* Sebastian Thrun: "Grave Times Require Radical Thinkers," video interview by Sarah Lacy, *PandoDaily*, Apr. 30, 2013: http://pandodaily.com/2013/04/30/sebastian-thrun-grave-times-require-radical-thinkers.

107 GameDesk and *"classroom of the future":* Interview with Lucien Vattel and "Gamedesk's 'Classroom of the Future.' Why is it so hard to reinvent K-12 education?" David Holmes, *PandoDaily*, Apr. 29, 2013: http://pandodaily.com/2013/04/29/gamedesks-classroom-of-the-future-why-is-it-so-hard-to-reinvent-k-12-education.

108 Aero: GameDesk Web site: http://www.gamedesk.org/projects/aero.

108 MathMaker, *underwritten by Motorola:* "MathMaker: Teaching Math Through Game Design and Development," Lucien Vattel and Michelle Risconscente, study (undated) posted on GameDesk Web site: http://gamedesk.org/reports/MATHMAKER_REPORT.pdf.

108 *"The best way to learn":* Interview with Lucein Vattel.

108 *has created courses that double as multiplayer games:* "Multiplayer Game Design" syllabus, by Lee Sheldon: http://gamingtheclassroom.wordpress.com/syllabus.

109 *Sheldon shares examples of teachers in other disciplines: The Multiplayer Classroom: Designing Coursework as a Game*, by Lee Sheldon, Course Technology, June 2011.

109 *"Who said education is supposed to be fun"* and *"If you follow human desire":* Interview with Alexander Galloway.

Chapter 7: Wii-hab

114 Mary Clark material: Interview with Mary Clark.

114 *performing between seven hundred and eight hundred* and diagnosis of Clark's Achilles: Interview with Dr. Steven Neufeld.

115 *fibers called proprioception* and anatomical explanations: ibid.

115 *physical therapists at the Foot and Ankle Center have been supplementing rehabilitation:* Interview with Matthew Bernier.

116 *Wakemed: Today Show* segment, Mar. 14, 2012: http://www.today.com/video/today/23629747#23629747; and "Wii speeds up the rehab process,"

Joe Miller, *USA Today*, July 24, 2007: http://usatoday30.usatoday.com/tech/gaming/2007-07-24-wii-therapy_N.htm.

116 *Hines Veterans Affairs Hospital:* "Doctors get patients to go to 'Wiihab,'" Lindsey Tanner, Associated Press, Feb. 8, 2008: http://abcnews.go.com/Technology/story?id=4267163&page=1#.UYalHYLvbjU.

116 *Walter Reed Army Medical Center:* "Wii Habilitation at Walter Reed," Carrie McLeroy, *Soldiers*, Vol. 63, No. 9, Aug. 2008: Excerpt: http://www.wired.com/dangerroom/2008/08/wounded-gis-new/and full text: http://www.thefreelibrary.com/Wii+habilitation+at+Walter+Reed.-a0190244968.

116 *"When the body is hurt, it tries to stop movement":* ibid.

116 *"I might notice the pain"*: ibid.

116 *improvement in eleven stroke victims:* "Wii Video Games May Help Stroke Patients Improve Motor Function," *ScienceDaily*, Feb. 26, 2010: http://www.sciencedaily.com/releases/2010/02/100225164849.htm.

116 *thirteen-year-old boy with spastic diplegic cerebral palsy:* "Use of a low-cost, commercially available gaming console (Wii) for rehabilitation of an adolescent with cerebral palsy," J. E. Deutsch, M. Borbely, J. Filler, K. Huhn, Guarrera-Bowlby, *Physical Therapy: Journal of the American Physical Therapy Association*, Aug. 8, 2008: http://www.physther.org/content/88/10/1196.full.pdf.

117 *treat symptoms of Parkinson's:* "The Nintendo Wii and PD," research paper by Dr. Nathan Ben Herz, Medical College of Georgia, presented at Games for Health Conference, Dec. 2009: http://www.parkinson.org/NationalParkinsonFoundation/files/cd/cdf0b319-a28b-4082-bf07-64888dbd2c90.pdf.

117 *study on eleven elderly patients:* "Phys Ed: Why Wii Fit Is Best for Grandparents," Gretchen Reynolds, *New York Times*, Dec. 1, 2010: http://well.blogs.nytimes.com/2010/12/01/phys-ed-why-wii-fit-is-best-for-grandparents/ and "Wii-habilitation 'could prevent elderly from falls,'" by Anouk Lorie, CNN, Feb. 11, 2009: http://www.cnn.com/2009/HEALTH/02/11/wii.fit.elderly.

117 *with the help of a $379,741 grant:* "Researcher Uses Nintendo Wii to Address Cancer-Related Fatigue," Michigan State University press release, July 16, 2012: http://msutoday.msu.edu/news/2012/researcher-uses-nintendo-wii-to-address-cancer-related-fatigue.

117 *introduced the Wii:* Interview with Matthew Bernier.

Chapter 8: Blinded Me with Science

120 *"biological workhorses" that "carry out vital functions":* "The importance of protein folding," Joachim Pietzsch, Horizon Symposia, http://www.nature.com/horizon/proteinfolding/background/importance.html.

120 *determined by how it folds into shape:* "Scientists unlock secrets of protein folding," *PhysOrg*, Sept. 17, 2007: http://phys.org/news109269396.html.

form a Tetris-*like puzzle:* "When Scientists Fail, It's Time to Call In the Gamers," NPR, Oct. 2, 2011: http://www.npr.org/2011/10/02/140979241/when-scientists-fail-its-time-to-call-in-the-gamers.

121 *created Rosetta@home:* David Baker's Rosetta@home Journal: http://boinc.bakerlab.org/rosetta/forum_thread.php?id=1177 and "The Shape of Protein Structures to Come: Modeling Effort Uses Mass Computing Power to Make Breakthrough," Ewen Callaway, *Nature*, Oct. 16, 2007: http://www.nature.com/news/2007/071016/full/449765a.html.

121 *distributed computing power wasn't enough to handle more complex protein shapes:* Interview with Firas Khatib.

121 *eighty-six thousand PCs:* "Gamers Unravel the Secret Life of Protein," John Bohannon, *Wired*, Apr. 20, 2009: http://www.wired.com/medtech/genetics/magazine/17-05/ff_protein?currentPage=all.
Atomix: Old-Games.com: http://www.old-games.com/download/3508/atomix.

121 *how Google operates:* "Inside the Internet: Google Allows First Ever Look at the Eight Vast Data Centres That Power the Online World," Mark Prigg, *Daily Mail*, Oct. 17, 2012: http://www.dailymail.co.uk/sciencetech/article-2219188/Inside-Google-pictures-gives-look-8-vast-data-centres.html#ixzz2SSAhPccA.

122 *crack a fifty-six-bit encryption algorithm:* "Users take crack at 56-bit crypto," CNET News.com Staff, CNET, Apr. 8, 1997: http://news.cnet.com/2100-1023-278658.html.

122 *distributed.net:* "Distributed Team Cracks Hidden Message in RSA's 56-Bit RC5 Secret-Key Challenge," RSA press release, Oct. 22, 1997: http://www.rsa.com/press_release.aspx?id=716.

122 *"some things are better left unread":* "Codebusters Crack Encryption Key," Andy Patrizio, *Wired*, Oct. 7, 2002: http://www.wired.com/science/discoveries/news/2002/10/55584.

123 *Hanny van Arkel discovered a mysterious blob:* "Mystery Green Blob in Space Captured by Hubble," Seth Borenstein, Associated Press, Jan. 18, 2013: http://www.huffingtonpost.com/2011/01/11/hannys-voorwerp-green-blob-hubble_n_807298.html.

123 *piece together documents that had been shredded into ten thousand pieces:* "A Winner in DARPA'S Shredder Challenge competition," Homeland Security News Wire, Dec. 6, 2011: http://www.homelandsecuritynewswire.com/dr20111206-a-winner-in-darpa-s-shredder-challenge-competition.

123 *over lunch with Zoran Popović:* "Gamers Unravel the Secret Life of Protein," John Bohannon, *Wired*, April 20, 2009: http://www.wired.com/medtech/genetics/magazine/17-05/ff_protein?currentPage=all.

124 Foldit material: Interviews with Seth Cooper and Firas Khatib, University of Washington; Cooper's dissertation: "A Framework for Scientific Discovery through Video Games," Seth Cooper, 2010: http://grail.cs

.washington.edu/theses/Cooper2011PhD.pdf; "Foldit: The Protein Folding Game: Predicting Protein Structures with a Multiplayer Online Game," Seth Cooper, Firas Khatib, Adrien Treuille, Janos Barbero, Jeehyung Lee, Michael Beenen, Andrew Leaver-Fay, David Baker, Zoran Popović, and Foldit players; "Algorithm discovery by protein folding game players," Firas Khatiba, Seth Cooper, Michael D. Tykaa, Kefan Xub, Ilya Makedonb, Zoran Popovićb, David Baker, and Foldit Players, Proceedings of the National Academy of Sciences, Oct. 2011: http://www.pnas.org/content/108/47/18949.full; "New Videogame Lets Amateur Researchers Mess With RNA," Brendan I. Koerner, Wired, July 5, 2012: http://www.wired.com/wiredscience/2012/07/ff_rnagame/all.

124 *"I never forgot how much joy":* Interview with Seth Cooper.

124 [Treuille] *had always been fascinated by games* and *suggested they view their game as more of a toy:* NOVA Profile of Adrien Treuille, PBS, Nov. 14, 2012: http://www.pbs.org/wgbh/nova/tech/adrien-treuille.html and "Why video games are key to modern science," by John D. Sutter, CNN, Nov. 2, 2011: http://www.cnn.com/2011/10/23/tech/innovation/foldit-game-science-poptech.

125 *the essence of scientific discovery, which has no predictable end:* Interview with Firas Khatib.

125 *organized the game around a standard competition:* Interview with Seth Cooper.

125 *taxed the system's memory:* ibid.

126 *Popović created an interface that rendered these proteins as playful animated loops and spirals:* "Gamers Unravel the Secret Life of Protein," John Bohannon, *Wired*, April 20, 2009: http://www.wired.com/medtech/genetics/magazine/17-05/ff_protein?currentPage=all.

127 The Economist *wrote about it:* "Game not over: Gamers pit their wits against nature's puzzles," *Economist*, Aug. 5, 2010: http://www.economist.com/node/16740629.

127 *"Unlike scientists, they have the freedom":* Interview with Firas Khatib.

128 *were very good about detecting a hydrophobic amino acid:* John Timmer, Ars Technica.

128 *trove of user data helped researchers:* Interview with Firas Khatib.

129 *Mason-Pfizer Monkey Virus Retroviral Protease:* "Crystal Structure of a Monomeric Retroviral Protease Solved by Protein Folding Game Players," Firas Khatib, Frank DiMaio, Foldit Contenders Group, Foldit Void Crushers Group, Seth Cooper, Maciej Kazmierczyk, Miroslaw Gilski, Szymon Krzywda, Helena Zabranska, Iva Pichova, James Thompson, Zoran Popović, Mariusz Jaskolski, and David Baker, *Nature Structural and Molecular Biology*, Sept. 18, 2011: http://homes.cs.washington.edu/~zoran/NSMBfoldit-2011.pdf.

129 Contenders material: E-mail interviews with Contenders players spvincent, grabhorn, and Michele Minett (mimi).

130 *"The Folded monomer of protease from Mason-Pfizer monkey virus is currently unsolved by protein crystallographers":* 390: Unsolved monkey virus protein, foldit Web site: http://fold.it/portal/node/989012.
130 *"a remarkably ugly shaped protein":* Interview with Michele Minett (mimi).
131 *Khatib and his biochemist colleagues analyzed the data:* Interview with Firas Khatib.
131 *The researchers in Poland were thrilled:* Interview with Seth Cooper.
131 *All this was made possible because players inserted thirteen amino acids:* ibid.

Chapter 9: Med-Sims

133 Carla Pugh material: Interview with Carla Pugh.
137 *historian Carol Blum reports: Strength in Numbers: Population, Reproduction, and Power in Eighteenth-Century France,* Carol Blum (Baltimore: Johns Hopkins University Press, 2002).
138 *estimates that as many as ten thousand women* and other Du Coudray material: *The King's Midwife: A History and Mystery of Madame du Coudray,* Nina Rattner Gelbart (Berkeley: University of California Press, 1999).
139 Pelvic exam material: Interview with Carla Pugh and "Evaluating Simulators for Medical Training: The Case of the Pelvic Exam Model," Carla Pugh, Mar. 2001, Stanford University dissertation.
140 *Surveys dating from 1912 found that 90 percent of flight accidents came down to inadequate pilot training: Fundamentals of Aerospace Medicine,* edited by Jeffrey R. Davis, MD, Robert Johnson, and Jan Stepanek, MD (New York: Lippincott Williams & Wilkins, 2008), 4.
140 *more than half a million Allied pilots trained on Link simulators:* "The Link Flight Trainer: A Historic Mechanical Engineering Landmark, American Society of Mechanical Engineers (ASME) International, June 10, 2000: http://files.asme.org/asmeorg/Communities/History/Landmarks/5585.pdf.
141 *Two medical students:* Interview with Carla Pugh.
142 *"Everywhere I go, anything I see, touch, and feel is fair game for building a human being or a part":* ibid.
143 Dr. Patrick Borgen material: Interview with Dr. Patrick Borgen.
143 Operating room: Author was eyewitness.
149 *"real, actual 3-D space, not a 2-D space virtually created":* Interview with Dr. Jacob Greenberg.
150 Nurse Susan Olson material: Interview/tour with Susan Olson, RN.
152 *Stan D. Ardman:* "Is It a Standard Man, or Stan D. Ardman?" David Kinney, Associated Press, Aug. 1, 1999: http://articles.latimes.com/1999/aug/01/news/mn-61471; "The Perfect Patient," Mary Ellen Egan, *Forbes,* June 21, 2004: http://www.forbes.com/forbes/2004/0621/210.html; "The Science of Experience," by John Cloud, *Time,* Feb. 28, 2008: http://www.time.com/time/magazine/article/0,9171,1718551,00.html.
152 *Resusci Annie:* "Evaluating Simulators for Medical Training: The Case of the Pelvic Exam Model," Carla Pugh, Mar. 2001, Stanford

University dissertation; and "Life and Times of Resusci Annie," United States Mine Rescue Association (Web site): http://www.usmra.com/guardian.

153 *"Sim One"*: "Medical Simulation Gets Real," Rebecca Voelker, *Journal of the American Medical Association,* Nov. 25, 2009, and *Essays on Medical Education*, Stephen Abrahamson, University Press of America, July 1996.

153 *"Gynny"*: "The lessons from patients," Rachel K. Sobel, *US News & World Report*, Oct. 12, 2003, and "Evaluating Simulators for Medical Training: The Case of the Pelvic Exam Model," Carla Pugh, Mar. 2001, Stanford University dissertation.

PART 3: GAMES AT WORK

156 Chris Rock standup routine: From HBO special *Kill the Messenger*, released on DVD on Jan. 20, 2009.

156 *"Work can be tough"*: Interview with Byron Reeves.

157 Jennifer scenarios: From *Total Engagement: Using Games and Virtual Worlds to Change the Way People Work and Businesses Compete*, Byron Reeves and J. Leighton Read (Cambridge, MA: Harvard Business School Press, 2009).

157 *manage the tens of thousands of avatars that IBMers have created:* Interview with Chuck Hamilton.

158 *"pointsification"*: "Can't play, won't play," Margaret Robinson, Hide & Seek company blog, Oct. 6, 2010: http://www.hideandseek.net/2010/10/06/cant-play-wont-play.

158 *"the badge measles"*: "Pawned: Gamification and Its Discontents," speech at Playful 2010, London: http://www.slideshare.net/dings/pawned-gamification-and-its-discontents.

160 *Chief engagement officer:* "Q&A: Gabe Zichermann, Author 'Game-Based Marketing,' on Gamification," Accenture company blog, April 13, 2011: http://www.accenture.com/us-en/Pages/insight-enabled-game-based-marketing-gamification.aspx.

Chapter 10: New World Order

162 *one in five customers (17 percent) surveyed:* "Social Media Raises the Stakes for Customer Service," American Express press release, May 2, 2012: http://about.americanexpress.com/news/pr/2012/gcsb.aspx.

162 *"horizontal growth"*: Interview with Richard Laermer.

163 *"It could be that hundreds of thousands or millions of people"*: Interview with Molly DeMaagd.

163 *90 percent of consumers that were surveyed found online reviews trustworthy,* etc.: "Game Changer: Cone Survey Finds 4 out of 5 Consumers Reverse Purchase Decisions Based on Negative Online Reviews," Cone, Inc., press release, Aug. 30, 2011: http://www.conecomm.com/contentmgr/showdetails.php/id/4008.

164 *Nielsen survey from 2012:* "Global Trust in Advertising and Brand," Nielsen press release, Apr. 10, 2012: http://www.nielsen.com/us/en/reports/2012/global-trust-in-advertising-and-brand-messages.html.

164 *Cuomo fined Lifestyle Lift, a cosmetic surgery chain, three hundred thousand dollars:* "Assurance of Discontinuance," Attorney General of the State of New York, In the matter of: Lifestyle Lift, June 5, 2009: http://i.usatoday.net/money/_pdfs/cosmetic/lifestyle-settlementpdf.pdf.

164 *Heather Armstrong and her brand-new thirteen-hundred-dollar Maytag washing machine:* "Queen of the Mommy Bloggers," Lisa Belkin, *New York Times*, Feb. 23, 2011: http://www.nytimes.com/2011/02/27/magazine/27armstrong-t.html?pagewanted=all&_r=0.

164 *"So that you may not have to suffer like we have":* Heather Armstrong tweet, Aug. 26, 2009: https://twitter.com/dooce/status/3562532010. *"Have I mentioned what a nightmare our experience was with Maytag?":* Heather Armstrong tweet, Aug. 26, 2009: https://twitter.com/dooce/status/3562572606.

165 *jewelry maker accused Urban Outfitters of ripping off her designs:* "Twitter erupts over accusations that Urban Outfitters copied designer's necklace line," Elizabeth Flock, *Washington Post*, May 27, 2011: http://articles.washingtonpost.com/2011-05-27/business/35232437_1_stevie-koerner-urban-outfitters-twitter-users.

165 *two employees filmed a prank in the kitchen of the restaurant:* "Video Prank at Domino's Taints Brand," Stephanie Clifford, *New York Times*, Apr. 15, 2009: http://www.nytimes.com/2009/04/16/business/media/16dominos.html.

165 *Kevin Smith, who was kicked off a flight:* "Kevin Smith Too Fat to Fly," by Yunji de Nies and Suzanne Yeo, ABC News, Feb. 14, 2010: http://abcnews.go.com/WN/kevin-smith-fat-fly/story?id=9837268#.UYcQUZXA20s.

165 *McDonald's required African Americans to pay additional service fees:* "McDonald's fighting quickly spreading rumor that there's a security surcharge for black customers," Nina Mandell, *New York Daily News*, June 13, 2011: http://www.nydailynews.com/news/national/mcdonald-fighting-quickly-spreading-rumor-security-surcharge-black-customers-article-1.131766#ixzz2STTrjz2O.

165 *"It's classic liberal hysteria about very nutritious, delicious, food":* "Olympic brand McDonald's suffers Twitter humiliation," Mark Sweeney, *The Guardian*, July 27, 2012: http://www.guardian.co.uk/media/2012/jul/27/olympic-brand-mcdonalds-twitter.

166 Joshua March and Conversocial material: Interview with Joshua March.

167 *In a survey conducted by New York University professor Liel Leibovitz:* "Consumer Study: 88% less likely to buy from companies who ignore complaints in social media," Conversocial press release, 2012.

167 giffgaff material: Interview with Mike Fairman, CEO of giffgaff.

168 Engine Yard material: Interview with Bill Platt, Engine Yard's vice president of worldwide customer service.

169 *"Oh, it's very interesting," his father replied:* Interview with HotorNot co-founder, James Hong.

170 LiveOps material: Interviews with Sanjay Mathur, LiveOps senior vice president of product management, and Kevin Ackroyd, CEO of Badgeville.

170 Patti Walbridge material: Interview with Patti Walbridge.

Chapter 11: Customer Feedback Loops

173 Philip Beauregard material: Interview with Philip Beauregard.

175 Matthew Grace material: Interview with Matthew Grace.

182 *Tom Weadock, took a shine:* Interview with Tom Weadock.

182 *"I might have been burnt down":* Interview with Ryan Clark.

Chapter 12: The Bug Tester

184 Ross Smith material: Interview with Ross Smith.

184 Games at Microsoft material: Interviews with Ross Smith, Robert Musson, Harry Emil, Jim Rodrigues, Alan Page, Dan Bean, Jennifer Michelstein, and Rakesh Tangirala.

185 Kurt Eichenwald and *Vanity Fair:* "Microsoft's Lost Decade," Kurt Eichenwald, *Vanity Fair*, Aug. 2012: http://www.vanityfair.com/business/2012/08/microsoft-lost-mojo-steve-ballmer.

187 *Eighty-five percent of hiring managers and human-resource executives polled by CareerBuilder.com:* "Career coach: The care and nurturing of 'millennials,'" by Joyce E. A. Russell, *Washington Post*, Aug. 2, 2010: http://www.washingtonpost.com/wp-dyn/content/article/2010/07/30/AR2010073005726.html.

187 *Workplace Solutions found that 68 percent of working Americans:* "Millennials Face Uphill Battle to Wow Co-Workers with Work Ethic: National Poll Shows Skeptical View of Young Workers' Engagement in the Workplace," Workplace Options press release, Nov. 28, 2011: http://www.workplaceoptions.com/news/press-releases/press-release.asp?id=E42B752BC8BB4DE293E8&title=%20Millennials%20Face%20Uphill%20Battle%20to%20Wow%20Co-Workers%20with%20Work%20Ethic.

187 *income instability, which he defined as a 50 percent swing in income: The Great Risk Shift: The Assault on American Jobs, Families, Health Care and Retirement And How You Can Fight Back*, Robert Hacker (New York: Oxford University Press, 2006).

188 *declares in a popular manifesto:* "We, the Web Kids," by Piotr Czerski, translated version posted to *Atlantic*, Feb. 21, 2012: http://www.theatlantic.com/technology/archive/2012/02/we-the-web-kids/253382.

188 *survey found that 60 percent of millennials expect to leave their current employers:* "Millennials: A Portrait of Generation Next," Pew Research

Center, Feb. 2010: http://pewsocialtrends.org/files/2010/10/millennials-confident-connected-open-to-change.pdf.

189 *"because who they are personally":* "The Beginning of the End of the 9-to-5 Workday?" Dan Schawbel, *Time*, Dec. 21, 2011: http://business.time.com/2011/12/21/the-beginning-of-the-end-of-the-9-to-5-workday/#ixzz2SX280TG7.

189 *By 2016, Gen Yers will comprise about 40 percent:* "Millennials: A Portrait of Generation Next," Pew Research Center, Feb. 2010: http://pewsocialtrends.org/files/2010/10/millennials-confident-connected-open-to-change.pdf.

189 *makes up 60 percent of the employee pool:* "The Beginning of the End of the 9-to-5 Workday?" Dan Schawbel, *Time*, Dec. 21, 2011: http://business.time.com/2011/12/21/the-beginning-of-the-end-of-the-9-to-5-workday/#ixzz2SX280TG7.

190 *discovered that two-thirds of those who left the company:* "What Gen Y Really Wants," Penelope Trunk, *Time*, July 5, 2007: http://www.time.com/time/magazine/article/0,9171,1640395,00.html#ixzz2SYUa7P00.

190 *Sun Microsystems embraced scheduling flexibility:* "Good place to work for its flexible work schedule but have to suffer for its annual layoff," Glassdoor post by supposed Sun employee: http://www.glassdoor.com/Reviews/Employee-Review-Sun-Microsystems-RVW13433.htm; and "5 Flextime-Friendly Companies," CareerBuilder.com, Dec. 18, 2009: http://www.careerbuilder.com/Article/CB-632-Job-Search-Five-Flextime-Friendly-Companies.

190 *Salesforce.com set aside 1 percent of its profits to pay employees to volunteer 1 percent of their work time:* "The Secret Weapon for Success: An Interview with Marc Benioff, Chairman and Chief Executive Officer, salesforce.com," Leaders Online, Apr. 2010: http://www.leadersmag.com/issues/2010.2_Apr/Making%20a%20Difference/Benioff.html.

190 *Estée Lauder provides training courses:* Interview with an Estée Lauder executive who requested anonymity.

190 *Zappos claimed it was suing the Walt Disney Company:* "Zappos Sues Walt Disney Company," Tony Hsieh, Zappos CEO and COO blog, Apr. 1, 2010: http://blogs.zappos.com/blogs/ceo-and-coo-blog/2010/04/01/zappos-com-sues-walt-disney-company.

190 *Google soothes its tightly knotted engineers with free massages:* "Benefits and Perks," Google Web site: http://www.google.com/intl/en/jobs/students/lifeatgoogle/benefitsperks.

190 *Twitter brags that it has "worked hard to create":* "Down with fun: The depressing vogue for having fun at work," *The Economist*, Sept. 16, 2010: http://www.economist.com/node/17035923.

190 *Red Bull installed a slide in its London office:* "Revisiting Red Bull's London Headquarters," Stephen Searer, Office Snapshots, January 24, 2013: http://officesnapshots.com/2013/01/24/red-bull-london-headquarters-office-design.

190 *the* Economist *to snark, "the cult of fun has spread like some disgusting haemorrhagic disease":* "Down with fun: The depressing vogue for having fun at work," *The Economist*, Sept. 16, 2010: http://www.economist.com/node/17035923.

191 *a slight uptick in trust in management was equivalent to a 36 percent pay raise:* "Well-Being and Trust in the Workplace," John Helliwell and Haifang Huang, working paper, National Bureau of Economic Research, 2008: http://www.nber.org/papers/w14589.pdf.

191 *age-old conflict between management theories: Theory X and Theory Y:* "Theory Y Meets Generation Y," Julian Birkinshaw and Stuart Crainer, *Business Strategy Review*, Winter 2008: http://www.managementlab.org/files/site/publications/labnotes/mlab-labnotes-010.pdf.

Conclusion

199 *big bang:* There are many primers, and NASA's is as good as any: http://science.nasa.gov/astrophysics/focus-areas/what-powered-the-big-bang.

200 *"substrate-independence":* "Are You Living in a Computer Simulation?" Nick Bostrom, *Philosophical Quarterly*, (2003) Vol. 53, No. 211, 243-255: http://www.simulation-argument.com/simulation.html.

201 *a thousand-dollar computer in 1980 had the brainpower of a bacterium:* "When will computer hardware match the human brain?" Hans Moravec, *Journal of Evolution and Technology*, 1998, vol. 1:http://www.transhumanist.com/volume1/moravec.htm.

201 *"to compute an entire human lifetime of 80 years":* "Whoa, Dude, Are We Inside a Computer Right Now?" Ben Makuch, *Vice*, Oct. 2102: http://www.vice.com/read/whoa-dude-are-we-inside-a-computer-right-now-0000329-v19n9.

201 *"If the simulators don't want us to find out":* "The Simulation Argument: Why the Probability that You Are Living in a Matrix Is Quite High," Nick Bostrom, *Times Higher Education Supplement*, May 16, 2003: http://www.simulation-argument.com/matrix.html.

INDEX